SKYWATCH EAST

A WEATHER GUIDE

SKYWATCH EAST

A WEATHER GUIDE

RICHARD A. KEEN

FULCRUM PUBLISHING
GOLDEN, COLORADO

Library of Congress Cataloging-in-Publication Data

Keen, Richard A.
    Skywatch east : a weather guide / by Richard A. Keen.
    p. cm.
    Includes bibliographical references and index.
    ISBN 1-55591-091-2 (pbk.)
    1. East (U.S.)—Climate. I. Title.
QC984.E28K44 1992
551.6973—dc20   91-58490
                                          CIP

Printed in Hong Kong

0 9 8 7 6 5 4 3 2 1

Fulcrum Publishing
350 Indiana Street, Suite 350
Golden, Colorado 80401

To Helen

CONTENTS

ACKNOWLEDGMENTS

It was a dark and stormy night . . .

So begins a rather mediocre novel that has nothing to do with weather, but in whose honor an award is presented to the author of the "worst book of the year." I'm not the least bit interested in receiving that award, but in a way, *Skywatch* also began with a dark and stormy night. More about that later.

Skywatch East: A Weather Guide is a sequel to my first book, *Skywatch: The Western Weather Guide.* The first book evolved from a suggestion by Betsy Armstrong, formerly an editor with Fulcrum. If it wasn't for her, I'd probably be doing something else for a living right now. President, perhaps?

Along the way, the folks at Fulcrum gave many useful suggestions that helped improve the final text, and especially valuable comments arose from Dave Ludlum's and Mike Mogil's reviews of the manuscript. Dozens of fellow weather buffs, including old friends and new acquaintances, also helped *Skywatch East* become what it is. Ron Holle, Joe Golden, Grant Goodge, and others of the National Oceanic and Atmospheric Administration were especially helpful. Jon Eischeid provided tons of numbers describing the East's climate. Other organizations whose people contributed in one way or another are the National Center for Atmospheric Research, National Weather Service, National Hurricane Center, U.S. Forest Service, Atmospheric Environment Service in Canada, Pennsylvania State University, Temple University, Lyndon State College, The Weather Channel, and quite a few public libraries.

There are also plenty of nonprofessional weather watchers outside the realm of colleges and government agencies who, following in the footsteps of the likes of Benjamin Franklin and Thomas Jefferson, watch the weather for the sheer delight of it. These folks also helped *Skywatch East* become what it is, particularly with photos and long chats on the phone (you should see my long distance bills!). Among these folks are Tim Marshall, Jay Brausch, Jack Corso, Vince Miller, Jim Vavrek, and others who enthusiastically supplied photos and facts, and my parents and brother, Larry, who keep me tuned in with the latest weather trivia from the Philadelphia area and Florida, respectively. Don't forget to check the credits beneath each of the photos: They're all heroes in my book!

I wrote *Skywatch East* at home, and some of my housemates unwittingly contributed to the effort. Sitting in front of a computer can be tedious at times, and Sarah, Daniel, Michael, Amanda, and Samantha provided frequent and sometimes welcome breaks in the long, silent hours of writing. Although her real interest in weather was limited to hiding under the bed when it thundered, my lap cat, Benjamin, who passed away early this year at age 20, helped edit the manuscript with swift movements of her paw. Finally, very special thanks go to my wife, Helen, for just being there.

Now, let's get back to that dark and stormy night. In the autumn of 1954, a wild lady named Hazel stormed through eastern Pennsylvania, ripping down roofs and ripping up trees and generally making a nuisance of herself. To at least one wide-eyed seven-year-old, however, she brought a sense of wonder and lasting fascination. That dark and stormy night thirty-seven years ago today marked the real beginning of *Skywatch East.*

Richard A. Keen
October 15, 1991

"Frankly, I don't like the look of the weather . . ."

INTRODUCTION

"There is a sumptuous variety about the New England weather that compels the stranger's admiration—and regret. The weather is always doing something there; always attending strictly to business; always getting up new designs and trying them on the people to see how they will go. But it gets through more business in spring than in any other season. In the spring I have counted one hundred and thirty-six different kinds of weather inside of four and twenty hours."

Mark Twain was talking, of course, about one of his favorite topics—the weather of his latter-day home, New England. He is also reputed to have quipped, "If you don't like the weather, just wait a minute," although Benjamin Franklin may have said it first. In either case, the comments hold true not just for New England, but for New Jersey, Nova Scotia, North Carolina, and any of the other states and provinces of eastern North America, from Florida to Newfoundland and Alabama to Ontario. Geographically, the region ranges from coastal lowlands along the Atlantic seaboard to the ridges and plateaus of the Appalachians and back to lowlands west of the mountains. For good measure, five of the world's fifteen largest lakes occupy the northwestern portion of what we call the East.

Although Twain's count of 136 different kinds of weather in a day may have been a slight exaggeration, the variety seen in the East is unexcelled by any other region of the globe. On the weather map, the East is a crossroads for the world's air masses. Tropical, arctic, ocean, and desert air all make their way into the East, and their meeting place along the Atlantic coast is one of the greatest storm tracks in the world. Nearly every town in the region has seen the likes of hurricanes, blizzards, tropical downpours, lightning, hail, ice storms, and tornadoes, and a few places even had dust storms! Virtually all the world's major weather types are represented here.

The East's vigorous climate claims some world records and many near-records. A gust of 231 mph atop New Hampshire's Mount Washington is the highest ever measured anywhere in the world, and in 1938 the strongest wind ever recorded over land during a hurricane (186 mph) whipped Blue Hill, Massachusetts, just outside of Boston. Places in Maryland, Pennsylvania, and West Virginia have been doused by extreme rainfall rates. And the 179-degree temperature range at Iroquois Falls, Ontario, is the world's greatest outside of a few valleys in Siberia.

The range of climates in the East is as impressive as the variety of weather. From Key West, Florida, which has never seen frost or snow, to the summit of Mount Washington, sometimes called "home of the world's worst weather," to the gale-swept shores of Labrador, the East's climates range from subtropical to subarctic. Not purely tropical or arctic, mind you, but getting there! Between the extremes, though, most of the East is delightfully temperate. Summers are a bit hot and humid, and the winters somewhat windy and cold, but the transition seasons of spring and fall are perhaps the most pleasant on the planet.

The East's location along the Atlantic storm track—one of the busiest in the world—is much more a benefit than a bane. The steady progression of coastal storms in the winter, and influx of humid, thunderstorm-breeding air in the summer, gives the East one of the world's most reliable supplies of water. Most years, the amount of rain and snow that falls in the East is within 20 percent of the average— a reliability unheard of most other places on the planet. In some northeastern states the variability is a mere 10 percent, the lowest in the world. You might think the storminess and steady rain means a dreary climate, but generally there are more sunny days than stormy ones. The storms that march up the coast may be strong, but so are the fair-weather high pressure systems between them.

What gives the East its 136 varieties of weather? It's a simple question with a complex answer, and that answer is what this book is all about. Descriptions of the fascinating variety of eastern weather—through words, pictures, and numbers—make great reading. But this book intends to go beyond that, I hope, and leave the reader with an understanding, or better yet, a *feeling*, for how the East's peculiar weather works. This is where the real satisfaction lies. It's like looking under the hood of a car and knowing why the distributor is there, or realizing how a human heart does its job.

Some reasons for the East's unique climate are obvious. The Gulf Stream, Appalachian Mountains, and Great Lakes all play their roles. But for a full explanation, we must go far beyond the local topography. Shifting currents in the equatorial oceans and the frozen wastes of the North and South poles are every bit as important to eastern weather as are the Gulf Stream and the Appalachians. The importance of all these factors, however, is dwarfed by the role played by ancient volcanoes that have since eroded into sand. They gave us air, and without air there would be nothing to write this book about. The story of these four-billion-year-old eruptions unfolds in the next chapter.

It may seem strange that the second photograph in this book is a landscape from the planet Venus, but there's a real lesson to be learned from our sister planet. Over the eons since those primordial volcanic eruptions, Earth slowly became the garden it is today, while Venus became a searing visage of hell. If nothing else, a look at the different fates of the two planets should help us appreciate how truly fortunate the Earth and its inhabitants are. Think about it the next time you see the surf

pounding the dunes at Cape Hatteras during a "nor'easter." It's a sight you'll see nowhere else on Earth or—barring some parallel solar system out of a "Star Trek" episode—in the entire Universe!

Weather is far too complex to be stuffed into a book. Like many things in life, the best way to learn about the weather is to observe it firsthand, in detail. So, this book ends with a chapter about watching the weather, with tips on observing the daily passage of foul and fair weather. My hope is that your learning experience just begins when you pick up this book.

Between the creation of the atmosphere and the construction of your own weather station, this book progresses in what seems to me an orderly and logical manner. The chapters are meant to read as independently of each other as possible. So if you have a hankering to read about hurricanes, you can do so without having to flip through the entire book.

Finally, a word about metric versus English units of measurement. I've always felt that the main purpose of a measurement system is to communicate information. Since the odds are that most readers of this book will be more familiar with the English system (or American system, as it's known in some remote valleys, although many Canadians still secretly use it), English units it is! So, snow and rain falls in inches, hailstones are weighed in pounds, wind blows in mph, and all temperatures are measured in degrees Fahrenheit. True, it's an old system of measurement and its arithmetic gets a bit tricky (quick: how many inches in a mile?), but as long as we both know how deep a foot of snow is, it works quite well.

WHY IS THERE WEATHER?

Why is there air? There is air to fill the basketball with!

—Bill Cosby

    Air is wonderful stuff. We breathe it, fly airplanes in it, burn things with it, and yes, fill basketballs with it. Most importantly (at least to meteorologists!), it gives us weather. Without air, there would be no weather; with it, weather is inevitable.

    It takes more than just air, though, for Earth to have the kind of weather we've become so used to. Five basic factors combine to create the alternation of sun and storm and of warm and cold that we call *weather*. The first factor, already mentioned, is atmosphere, the mass of air surrounding Earth. Second, Earth is sunlit. The third factor is Earth's rotation. The next factor—and one unique to Earth—is our planet's vast supply of liquid water. And finally, there is geography, the variety of surfaces, from oceans to continents to ice sheets, that cover Earth. In recent years we have been treated to close looks at other planets in our solar system, where the factors that control what might be called weather are incredibly different from ours. A survey of the conditions leading to Earth's weather will help us understand why it is the way it is, and comparisons with other planets will let us appreciate its uniqueness.

THE ATMOSPHERE

    Earth has about six million billion tons of air surrounding it. That's a lot of air; numbers like this make even the national debt seem small. But there are always ways to make small numbers look big and big numbers look small. To make the bulk of the atmosphere seem small, consider this: All those millions of billions of tons of air amount to a mere millionth of the weight of the entire Earth. Another way to look at it is to imagine a winter cold enough that the air itself freezes and falls to the ground as a layer of solid nitrogen and oxygen. This layer would be about 20 feet thick. That's a lot of frozen air to shovel your car out of. But on a planet 8,000 miles wide, 20 feet isn't really a whole lot, is it? Anyway, that's how much air there is; you decide whether it's a lot or a little.

    Where did the atmosphere come from? Four and a half billion years ago, when the planets formed out of the dust and gas surrounding the newborn sun, leftover gases collected around the infant planets. These gases were mostly hydrogen and helium, which is not surprising since they are the most abundant elements in the Universe. But hydrogen and helium are also the lightest of the elements, and Earth's gravity—strong as it may seem to us—was too feeble to keep them around for long. Farther from the sun, the gases were cooler and therefore more able to stick around the young planets. To this day, the distant planets Jupiter, Saturn, Uranus, and Neptune still have massive atmospheres of hydrogen and helium. Earth, however, like Mars, Venus, and Mercury, soon found itself without an atmosphere.

What Earth lost to space, it soon (geologically speaking) created from within. Heat in Earth's core sent columns of molten rock to the surface, erupting as volcanoes the likes of which we don't see very often anymore. Substances trapped in the rocks, such as water, carbon dioxide, methane, sulfur, and nitrogen, spewed into the vacuum surrounding Earth. Unlike hydrogen and helium, these heavier gases stayed close to the Earth's surface. Thus, our atmosphere was born.

By today's standards, this early atmosphere was a vile affair, consisting largely of carbon dioxide, steam, and clouds of sulfurous gases, and with no breathable oxygen. But a little chemistry and, later, biology, took care of the oxygen shortage. Most of the water fell as rain to form the oceans. For the first billion years or so, carbon dioxide mixed with water vapor to make rainfalls of carbonic acid. This acidic rain leached calcium from the surface rocks, and the ensuing chemical reactions formed calcium carbonate. Streams and rivers carried the calcium carbonate into oceans where it sank to the bottom, forming the thick limestone layers we see scattered around the globe.

It is interesting to compare Earth's history with that of Venus, which is 26 million miles closer to the sun. Although Venus is similar to Earth in size and (probably) composition of volcanic gases, its atmosphere is a hot and dense soup of mostly carbon dioxide. Apparently, intense sunlight on Venus prevented the planet from cooling quite enough for water vapor to condense into liquid. Without liquid water, no rains of carbonic acid could fall onto the rocks below. Venus' carbon dioxide remains in its atmosphere, while Earth's is locked in underground limestone, and all because of the relatively slight difference in distance from the sun. One may speculate on how narrowly Earth escaped Venus' hellish fate, or how narrowly Venus missed becoming the paradise that is Earth.

Half the diameter of Earth and one-tenth its bulk, the little planet Mars never had enough volcanoes to create much of an atmosphere. Like that of Venus, Mars' air is mostly carbon dioxide, but it is incredibly thin—only 1 percent as dense as the Earth's, and a mere ten-thousandth the density of Venus'. Nonetheless, thanks to trace amounts of water vapor and a rotation rate nearly identical to Earth's, Mars has more Earth-like weather than any other place we know of in the Universe. Automated weather stations sent to the red planet have detected fronts, cyclones, clouds, and even snow. But Mars is still a desert planet, and, as far as we know, lifeless.

Meanwhile, back on Earth, at the tender age of one billion years, plant life began releasing oxygen (through photosynthesis) into the atmosphere. Eventually, about half a billion years ago, there was enough oxygen to allow a layer of ozone (a molecule of three oxygen atoms) to form. Ozone constitutes only the tiniest fraction of the atmosphere—less than one molecule in a million. However, this minuscule amount is extremely important because it absorbs the sun's ultraviolet radiation, helping to protect us from sunburn and skin cancer. (This beneficial shield of ozone, 10 to 20 miles high, shouldn't be confused with the local concentrations of ozone pollution that form around today's cities.)

Protected from ultraviolet rays, early plant life increased dramatically. The greening of Earth led to a rapid increase in the amount of atmospheric oxygen, leading in turn to oxygen-breathing animals like dinosaurs, which needed lots of oxygen, and, at last, us. The modern-day atmosphere is comprised of 76 percent nitrogen, 23 percent oxygen, and 1 percent other gases.

SUNLIGHT

All this air would simply sit still without some source of energy to move it around. That source of energy is the sun. It may seem obvious to us that the sun is the main source of heat for the atmosphere, but there are planets where this isn't the case. On Jupiter, the largest of the planets and five times Earth's distance from the sun, sunbeams are so feeble and the planet's center so hot that the atmosphere is actually heated more from below than above. On Earth, though, most of our heat comes from the sun.

Not all places on Earth get the same amount of heat. In the tropics, when the noontime sun passes directly overhead, the ground gets the full effect of solar heating: a 1-foot-wide beam of sunlight heats up a square foot of ground. At higher latitudes outside the tropics, the noontime sun doesn't pass overhead, and its light strikes the ground at an oblique angle. Forty-five degrees from the equator, a foot-wide sunbeam has to heat 1 1/2 square feet of ground, and at 60 degrees latitude a sunbeam is spread over 2 square feet on the average; actual numbers vary depending on the season. Near the poles, 90 degrees from the equator, sunbeams hit the ground at such low angles that they are spread out over many square yards. Accordingly, the equator is heated more by the sun than are the poles.

As the sun heats Earth in this nonuniform manner, the planet warms up. If this heating went on forever, the planet would eventually melt. Since Earth as a whole is *not* heating up (or very, very slowly if it is), there must be some way for the planet to get rid of the solar heat as fast as it receives it. Earth does this by sending energy out to space in the form of infrared radiation. *Infrared* is a mixture of Latin and English meaning "below red," and refers to light waves whose frequency is less than that of red light. Although we cannot see infrared radiation, there are times when we can feel it—like the warmth we feel coming from a hot stove or from a radiator (hence the name!).

On the average, the entire planet must lose as much heat through radiation as it receives from the sun. As with sunlight, this loss of heat is not uniform around the globe. A hot object radiates heat faster than does a cold one. At a temperature of 80 degrees, for instance, the tropics radiate heat twice as fast as does the zero-degree Arctic. So not only do the tropics receive more heat than do the poles, they also lose it faster. However (and this is very important), gains and losses do not balance out locally, even though they do balance for the globe as a whole. In the tropics, there is a net gain of heat, as the incoming sunlight is greater than the loss through radiation. Conversely, the arctic regions see a net loss of heat. It is this difference in the *net* heating between the equator and the poles that drives Earth's weather.

Were the net heating of the tropics and the net cooling of the arctic regions to continue unhindered, Earth would end up with three equally obnoxious climate regions—an unbearably hot equatorial zone bounded on either side by two frightfully cold polar areas. The atmosphere, however, keeps this from happening. Remember that hot air is lighter than cold air, so as the air over the equator heats up, it rises. Conversely, the cooling of air over the Arctic causes it to sink. The rising equatorial air moves toward the poles, replacing the polar air that has sunk to the ground and is now crawling toward the equator. In this manner, the uneven heating of

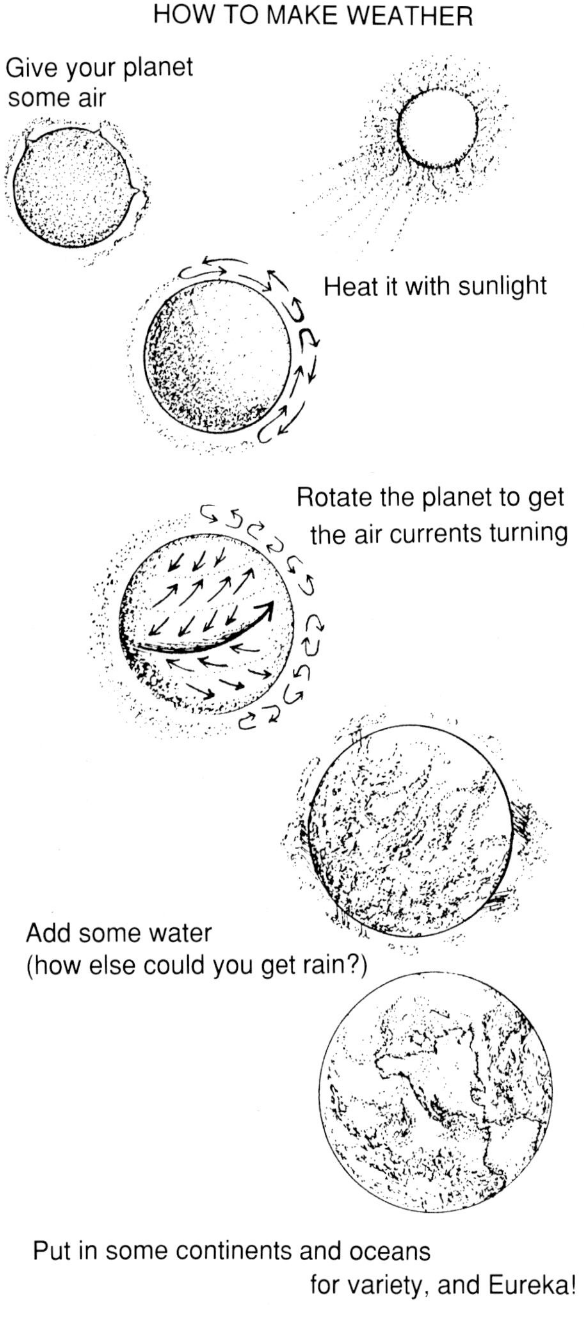

HOW TO MAKE WEATHER

Give your planet
some air

Heat it with sunlight

Rotate the planet to get
the air currents turning

Add some water
(how else could you get rain?)

Put in some continents and oceans
for variety, and Eureka!

Earth sets up atmospheric currents that modify what would otherwise be extreme temperature differences between the equator and the poles. To this day, meteorologists call this current of air the *Hadley circulation*, after the Englishman who thought of the idea in 1735.

A simple household analogy to this global current of air can be seen in a pot of boiling water on a stove. The stove supplies heat to the bottom of the pot, and the water loses heat by releasing steam at the top. Rising water at the pot's center carries the heat upward, and the returning, cooler (but still hot!) water sinks down near the edge of the pot.

This pattern of uneven heating and circulating currents of air changes during the course of a year due to the effect of the seasons. On the first day of summer, the noontime sun passes overhead at 23 degrees north latitude, while on the first day of winter, the sun's overhead passage is at 23 degrees south. The latitude of the greatest heating of the ground is correspondingly farther north during the summer months, and the resulting atmospheric currents in turn shift to the north. Meanwhile, the North Pole, which sees no sunlight at all from October through March, is bathed in twenty-four-hour sunshine during the summer. This decreases the difference in net heating between the tropics and the Arctic, thereby weakening the heat-driven currents. Thus, seasonal variations in the solar heating of Earth's surface lead to shifts in weather patterns, with the patterns being, in general, farther north and weaker during the summer.

AS THE EARTH TURNS

So now we have a simple heat-driven current that carries cold air to the equator and warm air aloft to the poles. That means that everywhere in between the North Pole and the equator, the winds (at ground level) must always blow from the north, right? Of course they don't, and the reason is that the wind flow is complicated by the well-known fact

NASA

EARTH— Combine the five ingredients in the proper proportions and the result is the weather of Earth.

that the Earth turns. The 7,918-mile-diameter Earth rotates once every twenty-four hours, carrying the people, houses, hills, trees, and air on the equator around and around in an eastward direction at a zippy 1,038 mph. Meanwhile, on the poles, where there are houses (sort of) and occasional people, these things are being carried along at a sluggish zero mph. They're turning around, but not going anywhere. Between the equator and the North Pole, Miami (25 degrees north) is moving east at 941 mph, and Montreal (45 degrees north) is going east at 734 mph. As the rising equatorial air moves toward the poles, its eastward motion of 1,038 mph becomes increasingly greater than the eastward

5

motion of the ground below. Unless something slows it down, the air will be moving 60 mph faster than the ground at 20 degrees latitude, and 140 mph faster at 30 degrees latitude. This rapid eastward flow of air is known as the *subtropical jet stream*, or just the *subtropical jet*. It is one of the strongest and most consistent winds of the world.

By the time air reaches the subtropical jet, its eastward motion is far greater than the poleward motion. However, equatorial air is still being pumped toward the subtropical jet, and begins to pile up. This excess air has nowhere to go but down (it can't go up into space!), so the sinking air piles up on the ground in a massive high pressure system called the *subtropical high*. On a simpler planet the subtropical high would ring the Earth, directly beneath the subtropical jet. On the real Earth, though, the subtropical high is broken into several high pressure systems, with the strongest ones over the oceans. The infamous *Bermuda High* of summer is one of these.

As with any high pressure system, air blows away from its center. The winds that blow from the subtropical highs back toward the equator are called *trade winds,* because their steadiness was a godsend to the sailing vessels that used them to ply their trade routes. The trade winds from the subtropical highs in both hemispheres meet near the equator, where they join the rising air current to complete the Hadley circulation.

George Hadley's 250-year-old theory actually works in the real atmosphere, except for one thing. Instead of going from the equator to the poles and back again, his circulation pattern extends no farther than 30 degrees on either side of the equator—barely a third of the way to the poles. Farther from the equator, the winds aloft still blow to the east, but with nowhere near the regularity of the subtropical jet, and there's no steady trade winds to help the sailors. This belt of winds is known as the *prevailing westerlies,* from the meteorologist's (and mariner's) habit of referring to winds by the direction they blow *from*.

Meanwhile, up around the poles the simple circulation pattern tries to re-establish itself as radiatively cooled air piles up near the ground and heads south (in the Northern Hemisphere), like a chilled version of the trade winds. This, too, is broken up by Earth's rotation. In between, in that region known to meteorologists as the mid-latitudes, the poleward transport of warm air and the equatorward flow of cold air is accomplished by a real mishmash of swirling eddies of many sizes and shapes, all embedded in the general west-to-east flow of the prevailing westerlies. We know these eddies as cyclones and fronts, and they will be the subject of the next chapter.

WATER

Think of it—a world without clouds, where never a drop of rain or a flake of snow ever fell from the sky. Never a cooling fog or a dewy summer dawn, and no frost on the windows. Pretty dull, eh? That is what weather would be like if there were no water vapor in the air. Remember the composition of the atmosphere, with its 99 percent nitrogen and oxygen and 1 percent other gases? Only a fraction of that remaining 1 percent is water vapor. And yet, slight as it is, that small concentration of water in the air is responsible for much of what we call weather. In fact, nearly all of the visible phenomena that make the weather so interesting are comprised of water in one form or another.

The importance of water in the atmosphere goes far beyond its role in making weather visually appealing. Water's place in the history of the Earth is assured, having kept our planet from becoming a Venus-like carbon dioxide pressure cooker. Even now, water is an essential ingredient of our weather. In its vapor state, water contains vast amounts of energy, which, when released, can literally unleash a storm. The energy in water vapor is called *latent heat*. *Latent* means "present, but not visible or felt," and while latent heat cannot be felt as what we

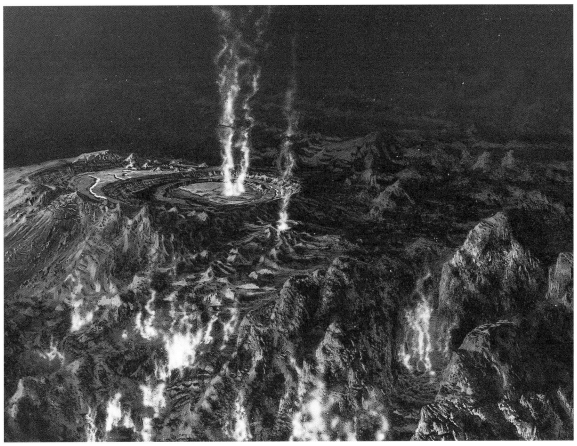

VENUS—This view of the surface of Venus, drawn by NASA artists, is a scene straight out of Dante's Inferno. *In size, Venus is Earth's twin sister, and its early days were probably much like Earth's. Along the way, however, Venus evolved into a parched hell, with a thick 850° atmosphere. Life as we know it is completely impossible on Venus.*

normally sense as heat (called *sensible heat*), it is very much present in moist air. Latent heat gets into water when it evaporates from the sea surface or wet ground. You know the cooling sensation of water evaporating from your skin—a cooling caused by water taking away your body heat. Where does this heat energy go? It goes into the water molecules and

keeps them away from others of their kind, allowing the molecules to remain a vapor. When the vapor does condense back into liquid water, the latent heat is released into the atmosphere as sensible heat, where it causes rising currents of air.

Earlier, we talked about the heating of Earth by sunlight. Since 71 percent of Earth's surface is covered by water, most sunlight falls onto oceans. Earth's oceans weigh 1.6 billion billion tons, or 270 times more than the atmosphere. Most sunlight that strikes the oceans goes into heating that huge bulk of water, and very little goes into directly heating the atmosphere above. Rather, the atmosphere receives solar energy in the form of latent heat, as winds help to evaporate water from the sea surface. The amazing thing about latent heat is that it can be carried thousands of miles from its source before being let loose. Thus, energy absorbed from the sun by water vapor over the Caribbean may eventually fuel a snowstorm over Greenland. The mobility of latent heat allows the heat-driven motions of the atmosphere to concentrate over certain parts of the world, leading to some of the particular weather patterns that circle Earth.

GEOGRAPHY

Even if Earth were as smooth as a billiard ball, with no oceans, continents, or mountain ranges, it would still have many of the familiar features of our weather, such as storms, fronts, jet streams, and the like. But there would be no climate differences between east and west. Cape Hatteras, Oklahoma City, and Los Angeles, being at nearly the same latitude, would have the same climate. This, of course, is not the case, and the reason is geography.

We have seen how the heating of Earth's surface by sunlight is the ultimate energy source that drives the weather. The way the sun heats the atmosphere is, however, profoundly affected by the nature of the underlying surface, be it lowland, highland, or ocean. Furthermore, heat can be moved thousands of miles by ocean currents, such as the Gulf Stream, before entering the atmosphere as latent heat, and yet more thousands of miles by the

atmosphere itself before being released as sensible heat. And mountains, by their sheer obstructive mass, can divert, destroy, or help form storms and shift jet streams.

The effects of geography on weather are as varied and detailed as geography itself. The role of geography in specific weather phenomena will be pointed out in later chapters. You will hear a lot about the effects of the Gulf Stream and the Appalachian Mountains on our weather. However, even such distant features as the Rocky Mountains, Pacific Ocean, and Arctic ice sheets directly influence the weather of the East. Remote influences on our weather go even farther—to the continents and oceans of the tropics. Strangely, while the oceans absorb most of the solar energy received by the tropics, the bulk of this energy ends up being released over land. Water vapor evaporated from the three tropical oceans—Indian, Pacific, and Atlantic—is carried by trade winds to the three main land masses of the tropics—Africa, South America, and the islands and peninsulas of southeast Asia. Over these land masses, latent heat is released in huge clusters of thunderstorms, resulting in rising currents of air that lead to powerful but localized Hadley circulation patterns.

The Hadley circulations over the three tropical land masses are stronger than over the oceans and consequently generate subtropical jet streams that are faster and farther north. These speedy subtropical jets—with winds averaging 150 mph—usually cross the Middle East, Japan, and the southeastern United States. Elsewhere, the subtropical jet is weaker and closer to the equator. The winds of the subtropical jet often supply energy to mid-latitude storms, so we can begin to see how thunderstorms over Indonesia and South America can shape the weather of the East.

MARS—More familiar to earthlings, perhaps, is this view of a Martian landscape, taken by NASA's Viking lander in 1976. The scene could be Death Valley or the Sahara Desert, but it's not—it's Mars. The weather on Mars might seem familiar, too, with clouds, frost, snow, fronts, and dust devils. However, Mars' thin atmosphere is less than one percent as dense as Earth's, and even in the Martian tropics, nighttime temperatures regularly reach 125 degrees below zero. With no liquid water, Mars is an eternal desert that is, so far as we know, lifeless.

FRONTS, JETS, CYCLONES

In the previous chapter, we saw how the great winds of the world—the subtropical jets and the prevailing westerlies—are powered by sunlight falling on a rotating Earth. Important as these currents of air are, they are not what we normally perceive as weather. We think of weather as something smaller and more changeable, and as something we can see from (or in) our backyards. Here in the mid-latitudes—including the East—it is the day-to-day passage of fronts and cyclones, of high and low pressure systems, that really makes up the weather. While these weather systems are not on as grand a scale as their globe-circling counterparts, they are caused by the same forces and are just as essential a part of the atmosphere.

To geographers, the mid-latitudes are the zones (one in each hemisphere) between 23 and 66 degrees latitude that separate the tropics from the Arctic and Antarctic. Meteorologists define the mid-latitudes as the regions dominated by the prevailing westerlies. Their location on the globe changes from day to day and season to season but, roughly, the mid-latitudes extend from 30 to 60 degrees latitude. (Most of the year, the Florida peninsula is in the subtropics, not the mid-latitudes.) More important, the mid-latitudes are where fronts and cyclones perform the vital task of carrying surplus heat northward from the tropics and returning cold air to the south. In the process, the opposing air masses clash and eventually mix, giving us our ever-changing weather.

THE MAKINGS OF A STORM

What happens when warm air meets cold air? First of all, there is a boundary between the two types of air, called a *front*. Yes, this is a term taken straight out of the military books, by Norwegian meteorologists who came up with the concept shortly after World War I. Indeed, to this day fronts are shown on weather maps in a fashion identical to battle lines on military maps. Usually more than one front separates the tropical and arctic air masses. One front may divide tropical air from somewhat cooler air to the north, while another front divides that cooler air and some downright nippy air north of that, and yet another divides the nippy air and the bitterly cold arctic air near the North Pole. To understand these meteorological battles, we will first consider just a single front.

Fronts are three-dimensional. There's cold air to the north, warm air to the south, and a

10

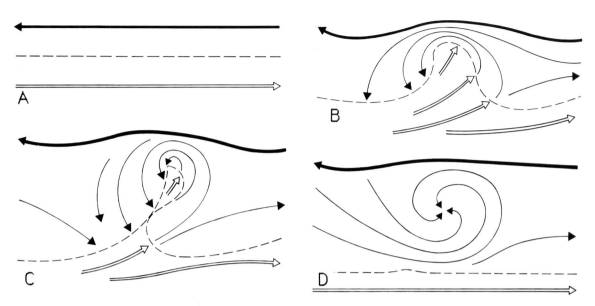

LIFE OF A STORM—a. The storm begins along the boundary between cold air to the north and warm air to the south. b. A ripple forms along the front, with cold air moving southward and warm air northward. c. The storm intensifies as the cold and warm air masses swirl around the center. Eventually, the faster-moving cold front catches up to the warm front, creating an occluded front. d. The fronts disappear when the air masses mix and blend together; all that remains is a dissipating swirl embedded in the original cold air mass.

boundary between the opposing air masses that often runs east-west. Air masses have depth, so fronts also extend upward into the atmosphere. The upper section of the front usually looks quite different from the part near the ground. Meteorologists like to slice the atmosphere into five or six layers, each at a different height, to get a more complete idea of its workings. Let it suffice here to slice it into two layers, an upper level at 30,000 feet or so, and a lower level near the ground.

Pressure—that number you read off a barometer—is simply "the weight of the overlying air." That's why the pressure goes down when you (and your barometer) go up. There's less air overhead at higher elevations. Furthermore, at the same pressure (and, roughly speaking, the same eleva-

tion), cold air is denser than warm air, meaning that the same amount of air is packed into a smaller volume. If you go up, say, 1,000 feet, you'll rise past more air if it's cold. Thus, in cold air, the pressure drops faster with increasing altitude. Conversely, in warm air, the pressure drops more slowly. The end result is that high above a front (say, at 30,000 feet), the pressure will be lower on the cold side of the front and higher on the warm side. Sometimes this is complicated by pressure differences across the front at ground level. If the surface pressure is higher on the cold side of the front, the pressure at 30,000 feet will be correspondingly higher on the cold side. Most of the time, though, this effect isn't great enough to change the final result: Cold air has lower pressure at higher altitudes.

Pressure differences are important, since air tends to move from high pressure to low pressure. Open the valve on an inflated tire, where the pressure is higher inside than outside, and you'll see what I mean. At 30,000 feet, for instance, air tries to blow from the warm side to the cold side of the front. But remember, the Earth is still turning. The warm air at, say, 40 degrees north and moving eastward with the Earth at 796 mph, heads north to 50 degrees latitude, where the ground below is moving at only 668 mph. So, the air ends up moving to the east at 128 mph. Strong westerly winds (blowing *from* the west) are usually found along fronts at the upper levels of the atmosphere, and are called *jet streams*, or just *jets*.

Unlike the subtropical jet, these frontal jets come and go as their fronts develop, move, and dissipate. Frontal jets can sometimes form near enough to the subtropical jet to be able to pick up some of the subtropical jet's wind speed. The frequently powerful subtropical jet over the southeastern United States often gives developing storms along the Atlantic coast an extra kick. The combined energies of the frontal jet streams and the subtropical jet lead to upper-level winds over eastern North America that are, on the average, stronger than anywhere else in the Northern Hemisphere (except eastern Asia, where the situation is similar).

With cold air to the north and warm air to the south, a front extends in an east-west direction with

COLD FRONT—*Everybody is familiar with cold fronts as those blue lines that adorn weather maps. Once in a while, cold fronts can also be seen in real life. Here a line of cumulus clouds marks the leading edge of an arctic air mass advancing (from the right) into the Florida Keys.*

Richard A. Keen

a westerly jet blowing along its upper edge. This situation doesn't last long, since eventually the cold air starts moving southward, and the warm air northward. This *must* happen for the arctic and tropical air masses to mix. At this point the east-west front begins to twist. The southward bulge ahead of the advancing cold air is called a *cold front,* and, not surprisingly, the northward bulge leading the warm air is called a *warm front.* These are the beginnings of a storm.

Let's get back to the turning Earth. We've seen, in several instances, northbound winds being turned to the east by the rotation of the Earth. Conversely, southbound winds are deflected west. In either event, the air flow is swerving to its *right.* No matter which way the air is moving, it always tends to curve right in the Northern Hemisphere (we see the opposite effect south of the equator). This is called the *Coriolis effect,* after Gaspard Coriolis, the French engineer who, in 1843, proved it mathematically.

There are some important sidelights to the Coriolis effect. Initially, a low pressure center sucks in air from all sides, leading to inward currents converging on the center. By bending each of these currents to its right, the Coriolis effect sends the air flowing *around* the low pressure center in a counter-clockwise direction (in the Northern Hemisphere). As always, the opposite holds true for high pressure. Now, think about it. The counterclockwise winds blowing around a low pressure center are also worked on by the Coriolis effect, which tries to make the winds start moving *away* from the low pressure center. Meanwhile, the low pressure tries to suck the air back in. The end result is a sort of balance, with the air going around and around in a counterclockwise direction, but never heading into or away from the low pressure center. In reality, this balance never exactly occurs, and some air does leak into or away from the *low,* as meteorologists are fond of calling low pressure areas. However, the near-balance keeps the low from either collapsing in on

itself or flying apart and allows the storm to keep on spinning as long as it does (a week or so).

We return now to the bulging fronts. Take the case of the cold bulge occurring to the west of the warm bulge. The cold air heads south and tries to turn west while the northbound warm air tries to head east. The two flows are trying to move away from each other. With air moving away in two directions, a partial vacuum develops in the middle. In other words, a low forms. The low pressure then counteracts the diverging warm and cold air flows, starts to pull them back toward the center, and we end up with a low center with cold air pouring down its western side and warm air streaming up its eastern side. This is called a *cyclone,* from the Greek word, *kykloun,* meaning "to go around."

West of the cold bulge there may be another warm bulge. Between the bulges, the turning effects will be the opposite of that leading to a cyclone, and the result is known as an *anticyclone.* This is a region of high pressure, so it is called a *high.* In the Northern Hemisphere, winds blow clockwise around a high. The eastern edge of the high, where winds are from the north, is colder than the western side.

Meanwhile, back at 30,000 feet, the jet is twisting with the bulging fronts. The jet dips south with the cold front and blows north with the warm front, and the line depicting the jet on a weather map may take on the sinuous appearance of a snake. The northward bends of the jet overlying the warm air are called *ridges.* The southward-bending *troughs* are above the cold air, so pressure in the trough is lower than in the ridge. Near the surface, the cyclone remains located in the middle of the whole mess, with the ridge to its east and the trough to its west. A peculiar thing happens—the center of low pressure aloft is not above the surface cyclone, but to the west of it.

As the storm continues to develop, the cold air plunges even farther south. The trough often becomes so sharp that it breaks off from the rest of

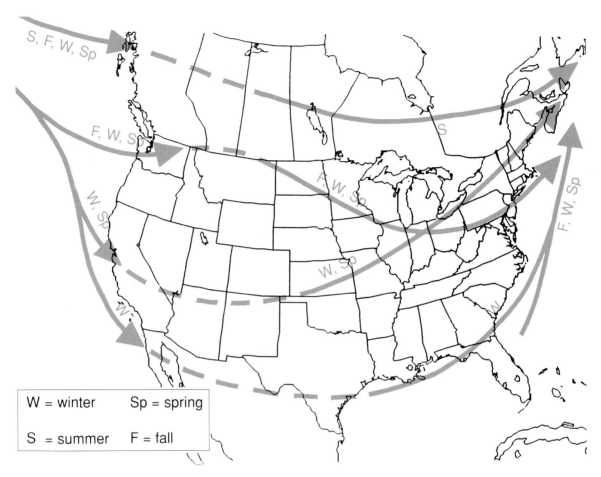

THE MAJOR STORM TRACKS OF NORTH AMERICA—Solid lines show the main storm tracks and dashed lines show the frequent paths of storms that break up over the Rockies and regenerate over the plains or along the Gulf of Mexico. The seasons when the tracks are most active are marked.

the jet stream, forming an *upper level low*. Sometimes the "upper low" (an interesting combination of terms!) separates from the low-level storm, and the two go on their separate ways. This happens frequently over the north Atlantic, the "graveyard of storms," where the *lower low* withers away somewhere between Iceland and Greenland while the upper low moves on toward Europe.

WEATHER PATTERNS OF THE EAST

Although jets may wiggle, their winds still blow, for the most part, from the west. Everything associated with a jet, including cyclones, fronts, and even the wiggles, is carried eastward with the jet's winds. We may therefore think of jet streams as *storm tracks,* the paths taken by cyclones as they live out their lives. This is one reason jet streams are such important features on weather maps—their average positions give a good idea of where the main storm tracks are. Over North America, "average" jet streams from the Arctic, Pacific, and subtropics all converge over the northeastern states and southeastern Canada, making the eastern seaboard one of the stormiest places in the world. In the course of a year, places like New England and the Maritime Provinces see more low pressure systems pass by than just about any other spot on Earth. These storms ride in on the jets from all sorts of places, and many more storms form right in our own back (or front) yards. Many storms from the Pacific survive their passage across the Rockies and continue into the East. Many cyclones plunge southward from the arctic regions of northwestern Canada. The most important storms to affect the East, though, form right along the coast and march up the seaboard.

There are several reasons why the East is so stormy. Consider what causes storms. Sharply contrasting air masses are a must for healthy cyclones, and having a strong subtropical jet nearby doesn't hurt. In winter, both conditions are met to a tee over the eastern coasts of North America and Asia, where chilly air over the continents clashes with balmy air above the warm offshore currents. North America has two such prime locations for cyclone formations: the Gulf of Mexico and the Atlantic Coast from Florida to Cape Hatteras. Currents from the Caribbean keep the Gulf of Mexico warm all year, and the famous Gulf Stream draws mild water from the tropical Atlantic and sends it up the coast. North of Cape Hatteras the Gulf Stream heads out to sea and toward Europe, and its northern edge passes several hundred miles southeast of Cape Cod and Nova Scotia.

Even in midwinter, the waters of the Gulf of Mexico and the Gulf Stream remain in the 65- to 75-degree range. A good cold air mass over the southeastern states can send temperatures there well below freezing, leading to a 30-, 40- or 50-degree

contrast between the offshore water (and the air above it) and the land. If other conditions are just right, particularly if a strong upper-level disturbance passes overhead to get the coastal front turning and twisting, the development of a cyclone can be explosive. Storm researchers have named storms that grow from minor disturbances to major cyclones in twenty-four hours or less *bombs*, and have found that the northern edge of the Gulf Stream, from Hatteras to Newfoundland, is one of the world's favorite places for "bombs" to blow up. "Bombs" are relatively rare, with only a half dozen

BLIZZARD FROM SPACE—Some Atlantic coast "bombs" become strong enough to develop a hurricane-like "eye." This cyclone buried Washington, D.C., under 18.7 inches of snow on February 18–19, 1979.

NOAA

Richard A. Keen

CIRRUS CLOUDS—The first sign of an approaching storm is usually the appearance of feathery cirrus clouds in the southwestern sky. Composed mostly of ice crystals 5 to 8 miles up, cirrus clouds form as warm air rises over a warm front on the eastern side of the storm center.

or so a year, but they can be memorable. Many of the East's greatest snowstorms have been "bombs."

The name *bomb* can also refer to the effects of these storms on weather forecasts. These rapidly growing storms frequently fool forecasters, leading to predictions that also "bomb." In recent years there have been several large-scale experiments aimed at improving forecasts of "bombs" (and of lesser coastal storms). The largest of these were the Genesis of Atlantic Lows Experiment, or GALE, and the Canadian Atlantic Storms Project, both run during the winter of 1986. As part of these experiments, automated weather stations and lightning detectors were set up all along the east coast (concentrating on the Carolinas, Nova Scotia, and Newfoundland), weather-reporting buoys were placed offshore, and planes were instrumented to fly through developing storms (similar to the *Hurricane Hunter* flights). As you'd expect from new research, there were some surprises. Perhaps the biggest surprise was the importance of thunderstorms in the development of coastal storms. It had been thought that since these were mid-latitude cyclones, most of their energy came from the contrasting warm and cold air masses. However, it was found that the strongest cyclones contained a lot of thunderstorms, and that the strong updrafts and downdrafts in the thunderstorms gave the cyclones an extra kick.

16

Richard A. Keen

MAN-MADE CIRRUS—Whether we want to or not, humans affect the weather. Contrails—short for condensation trails—made of moisture and soot spewed from high-flying jet engines streak the sky above Barnegat Light, New Jersey.

The Gulf Stream isn't the only reason East Coast cyclones are so hard to predict. If storms simply moved in from far away, all you'd have to do is look where they've been to guess where they're going. However, most storms that track into the East have a little barrier to cross—the Appalachian Mountains. While not as formidable as the Rockies or the Himalayas, this 2,000-mile long chain of 3,000- to 6,000-foot-high mountains is quite capable of slowing down, weakening, or even destroying passing storm systems.

Think of the storm as a rotating swirl of air extending from sea level to 6 miles up. To cross the barrier, 6 vertical miles of storm must squeeze into just 5 miles. Like a stepped-on plum, the cyclone responds to this squeeze by spreading horizontally. This horizontal spreading slows down the cyclone's rotation, just as a twirling figure skater who extends her arms will spin slower. This squashing weakens most storms, and already anemic storms might break up entirely.

Sometimes the storm regains its strength as it passes east of the Appalachian crest. It's the exact opposite process; as it moves back over lower ground, the storm stretches vertically, tightens inward horizontally, and spins faster once again. Frequently, though, the lower low is halted by the mountains, leaving the upper low to move on

17

relatively unaffected. If the upper low encounters a strong frontal boundary along the coast, it may regenerate into a new and powerful cyclone just offshore. These *secondary lows*, as they're known in the business, are the curse and challenge of forecasters up and down the coast. No one really knows where the new storm will develop until it actually starts to happen, and a difference of 50 miles or less can easily mean the difference between rain or snow, or even nothing, for twenty million people.

These are the storm tracks of winter. Cyclones from the Canadian prairies and subarctic, the Midwest, and even the Pacific Ocean converge on the eastern shores of North America, sometimes finding new strength after crossing the Appalachians. Meanwhile, new storms develop along the Gulf Coast and grow as they move up the coast. The arrival of spring on the calendar brings very little immediate change. March is the windiest month of the year in many places, and April is a close second, partly because the cyclones in those months are every bit as strong and numerous as their wintertime counterparts.

Eventually and inevitably, the warming of the Northern Hemisphere, as it spends more time facing the sun, leads to weaker and fewer cyclones. There are two reasons—a global and a local one—for this. Globally, the warming of the North Pole after the sun rises on March 21 dramatically decreases its temperature contrast with the tropics. The reduced contrast reduces the need for cyclones to move excess heat from the tropics northward. Locally, the temperature contrasts that individual cyclones feed on also decline as the continents (and the air above them) heat up faster than the oceans. Of course, land and sea at the same latitude receive just about the same amount of heat from the sun. However, waves and currents mix warm water from the surface with cooler water from the depths, while the heating of the land is confined to the topsoil. With the same amount of heat spread over more matter, the *temperature* of the ocean and over-

lying air rises less than the temperature of the topsoil and its overlying air. So, as both the ocean and land warm at different rates, the contrast between them fades.

The first storms to go as spring turns to summer are the Gulf Coast storms. By April the southern states have become as warm as the Gulf of Mexico, and the weakening of the polar air masses at their source makes cold fronts a rarity. The Hatteras-type storms fizzle out in May and June, as the mid-Atlantic region becomes nearly as warm as the Gulf Stream. Even in midsummer, though, there's always the chance for a cyclone to develop along the east coast, because there's always the temperature contrast between the Gulf Stream and the cooler coastal water north of Cape Hatteras. And, since the Arctic never gets quite as warm as the tropics (there's ice on the Arctic Ocean all year around), there's still reason for cool air masses to make their way south.

At the height of summer, in July, August, and into September, the arctic air masses are so weak they have trouble clearing customs and crossing into the United States. The main storm tracks are in Canada—one along the southern border, and another along the edge of the ice in the high Arctic. The Bermuda High, one of the subtropical high pressure systems you read about in a previous chapter, covers the southeastern states for weeks on end, leaving southerners to gasp and pray for the first front of fall. The Bermuda High extends into the northeastern states, too, but occasional cool fronts break the heat once a week or so. Canadians manage to avoid the Bermuda High for most of the summer.

For most of the year, most of the region we call the East—the eastern parts of the United States and Canada—remain in the zone of the prevailing westerlies. Fronts and cyclones are fewer and weaker in the summer, but they still come from the west. There is one exception, however—the Florida peninsula in summer. From the end of June until well into September, the core of the Bermuda High is north of the 30th parallel. Recalling that winds blow away from a high in a clockwise direction, you'll see that winds south of the Bermuda High come from an easterly direction. This places Florida in the belt of the trade winds for most of the summer, and that gives the peninsula a completely different weather pattern than that seen by most of us in the prevailing westerlies.

The trade winds that breeze into Florida blow all the way across the tropical Atlantic. Several times a summer clouds of dust blow all the way from Africa's Sahara Desert to put a silver sheen in Florida's normally blue skies. The trade winds also bring such things as easterly waves, tropical depressions, and hurricanes into Florida. The most common of these—the *easterly wave*—deserves a few words. In essence, an easterly wave is a bend or kink in the trade winds, much like the troughs that appear in jet streams. However, those troughs appear on the north sides of the subtropical highs, while easterly waves traverse the south sides of the subtropical highs (in the Northern Hemisphere). So, in a way, easterly waves are like upside-down troughs. Unlike troughs, though, there isn't much of a temperature contrast from one side of an easterly wave to the other, but there is a lot of humid tropical air. The passage of an easterly wave can bring torrential rains, and if the wave intensifies and gets a bit too big for its boots, it might grow into a tropical storm or hurricane. But more about that in a later chapter.

September sees the sun set over the high Arctic, and the cold air masses begin to intensify. Farther south, the fading sunshine cools the continents and oceans alike, but the heat stored during the summer in the upper layers of the ocean keeps it—and the air above it—warmer than the land. Hatteras-type coastal storms may become frequent once again in October, and by November the South has cooled enough for Gulf Coast storms to start up.

Urban Archives, Temple University

COASTAL STORM—The Great Atlantic Coastal Storm of March 1962 battered 1,000 miles of shoreline and washed this New Jersey home out to sea.

With most of the Arctic in continuous darkness, and with the oceans still holding on to much of the summer's stored heat, the temperature contrasts reach a maximum in late November and remain large through February—the season of the "bomb."

STORMY WEATHER

The passage of cyclones and anticyclones brings a never-ending variety of weather. Like snowflakes, no two storms are identical. And as cyclones progress through their life cycles, the type of weather

Richard A. Keen

STRATUS CLOUDS—The name stratus *means "layered" in Latin, and vast sheets of these layered clouds may blanket areas in the cold air to the north of a passing cyclone. Frequent stratus clouds, such as these along the coast of Labrador, help make northeastern Canada one of the cloudiest regions in North America.*

they bring also changes. However, most cyclones have some common features that are worth describing. The most important and simple guide to understanding the weather of high- and low-pressure areas is to remember that rising air brings clouds, rain, and snow, while sinking air brings clear skies. Three principles of physics make this so: (1) atmospheric pressure decreases with increasing altitude, (2) air expands and cools when it rises into the realm of lower pressure, and (3) cool air is less able to hold water vapor. So the vapor condenses back into droplets of liquid water (or crystals of solid water), forming clouds. With enough moisture in the air, the droplets and crystals coalesce into raindrops and snowflakes.

The twisting fronts around a cyclone determine where the air currents rise and where they fall. Since most lows move east (or northeast for coastal storms), the northward moving warm front is ahead of the low center—the "warm before the storm"—and the southbound cold front follows the passage of the low. Since warm air is lighter, it tends to overrun the cold air. This usually brings thickening and lowering clouds followed by steady precipitation in the form of rain or snow. As it plunges south and east, the heavier cold air cuts under the lighter warm air. The undercutting cold front shoves the warm air upward, often in a fairly narrow line, setting off brief but heavier precipitation in showers, squalls, and thunderstorms.

20

Paul Neiman

AT THE END OF THE STORM—Westerly or northwesterly winds following the passage of a cyclone or cold front often bring in a layer of stratocumulus clouds. These summertime stratocumulus clouds over Ithaca, New York, also brought a rainbow; in winter the same clouds may bear snow squalls and flurries.

The exact sequence of weather depends on lots of things, like the age and intensity of the storm, shape of the storm (some have multiple centers!), temperature of the air masses, and the storm's movement. However, the most important single factor is whether the storm center passes to your north or south. That determines whether or not you get into the *warm sector* of the storm, that slice of warm, moist air behind the warm front and ahead of the cold front. The warm sector is generally south and east of the storm center. If the storm center passes to your south, you stay in the cold air, and both temperature and precipitation remain fairly steady. In the winter, the precipitation is likely to be snow or cold rain. The winds with these *northeasters*

usually start out from the southeast, shift to east, northeast, north, and finally from the northwest as the storm clears out. When the storm passes north of you, its winds go from southeast to south, southwest, west, and finally northwest. The precipitation may start out as steady rain or snow changing to rain, but becomes more showery or stops completely as the warm front passes. The sun might break out, and even in midwinter the temperature can rise into the 60s or 70s. Passage of the cold front brings heavier rain showers, sometimes thunderstorms and plummeting temperatures, followed by clearing skies.

The cyclone passes, and its potpourri of precipitation has come and gone. It is now the

21

anticyclone's turn to take charge of the weather. This high brings clearing and cooling and blustery northwest winds, and the day after the storm passes is usually a chilly one. The winds diminish as the center of the high passes over, and at night calm winds and clear skies allow the temperature to fall even more. The second night after the storm is typically the coldest—farmers and gardeners take note! As the high continues east, southerly winds usher in warming. Then high-level clouds appear on the horizon, foretelling the approach of the next cyclone.

At many places in the mid-latitudes, cyclones pass at three- or four-day intervals. This rule of thumb usually works pretty well in the East. Sometimes, though, the storm track from the Pacific splits when it comes inland, with alternating cyclones taking a different route: One goes north into Canada, the other goes south toward the Gulf of Mexico. The coastal storms along the Gulf and Atlantic are then spaced a week apart, with the in-between cyclones crossing the Great Lakes and southern Canada. Sometimes a front will stall along the coast or the Appalachians, with cyclones tracking along the front at two- or three-day intervals. Sometimes there's a persistent run of lows coming out of arctic Canada. Then there are the occasional *blocking weather patterns*, so named by the action of large, slow-moving highs or lows (or a combination of both) in blocking the regular west-to-east flow. These sluggish weather systems can bring days of lingering inclement weather followed, fortunately, by an equally long spell of fine weather.

One reason weather never gets boring is that these storm patterns can change at any time. Sometimes one particular storm track will lock in for weeks or even months, only to suddenly break into a completely different pattern. The result can be cold, snowy winters that suddenly thaw out, mild winters that end with a freak cold wave, or winters that never seem able to make up their minds. The exciting part about this for weather watchers is that they never know which it's going to be!

MEMORABLE CYCLONES AND ANTICYCLONES

November 9, 1913—The Freshwater Fury, one of the worst gales of November in Great Lakes history, sent eight ore freighters and two hundred sailors to the bottom. Cleveland was buried by its heaviest snowstorm on record—22 inches—driven by high winds.

April 12, 1934—A springtime cyclone crossing New York state lashed the summit of Mount Washington, New Hampshire, with 231-mile-per-hour gusts—the highest wind speed ever measured on Earth. The southeast winds were probably enhanced somewhat by funneling by mountain ridges.

September 24, 1950—Northwesterly winds behind a cold front carried a dense smoke cloud from burning forests in northwestern Canada across eastern Michigan, northeastern Ohio, and eastern Pennsylvania, darkening the skies along the way. At mid-afternoon birds and chickens went to roost and outdoor lights had to be turned on.

November 24–26, 1950—Mild Atlantic air and the bitterest November cold wave ever seen in the Great Plains combined in a cyclone that tracked along the Appalachians into Canada. Gusts as high as 110 mph (at Concord, New Hampshire), flooding rains east of the mountains, and heavy snow west of the ridges (57 inches at Pickens, West Virginia), caused damage that in many places exceeded the Great New England Hurricane of 1938.

January 8–12, 1962—The most extensive anticyclone of the century swept southeast from Alaska, setting record high barometer readings from Alaska to Mississippi. On January 10, the North American weather map featured a single high stretching from the Yukon to Florida, with all of the "lower forty-eight" states beneath this massive, coast-to-coast anticyclone.

March 5–9, 1962—Outside of a few hurricanes, this enormous, slow-moving, late-winter cyclone was probably the most damaging Atlantic coastal storm in history. A 1,000-mile fetch of gale-force winds over the ocean east of Delaware sent waves as high as 30 feet crashing ashore from Florida to Massachusetts. Boardwalks and hundreds of beachside homes were destroyed, and new inlets were carved along the New Jersey coastline. Two hundred miles inland, the storm dropped 42 inches of snow on Virginia's mountains.

January 3–11, 1970—A massive high pressure system from Siberia crossed into Alaska, where it set record high barometer readings, before plunging south into the Caribbean. The associated cold front crossed Panama into the Pacific before dissipating within 300 miles of the equator. This cold wave, along with others later in the month, made it New England's coldest January in one hundred years (since 1780 in some places!).

April 2, 1973—Southeast winds ahead of a low over Rhode Island blasted the 4,040-foot-high

OCEAN CITY—The name of this New Jersey shore resort took on a new meaning during the four-day storm of March 1962. At the height of the storm, the island city was reduced to a mere shoal, with water from the Atlantic (top) pouring unimpeded into Great Egg Harbor (below).

Urban Archives, Temple University

A GATHERING STORM—A thickening sheet of translucent altostratus clouds usually means rain or snow within a few hours.

summit of Cannon Mountain, New Hampshire. The pointer on the wind dial pegged the top of the scale—200 mph—three times.

February 2, 1976—A coastal "bomb," the Groundhog's Day Storm, exploded over Delaware and plowed north into Labrador. Along the coast, heavy rains in the warm sector brought high waters that instantly froze as temperatures plunged from the 50s to near zero in a few hours. Glazed roads, high winds (up to 104 mph at Cutler, Maine), and blizzard conditions caused numerous traffic accidents, downed trees, and power lines, and ripped ships from their moorings from Virginia to Maine. At one time the atmospheric pressure difference between the storm and a high over the Yukon was a whopping 3 inches of mercury, or 100 millibars, about 10 percent of normal sea-level pressure.

January 20, 1977—An intense cyclone dropped the barometer to 27.76 inches, or 940 millibars, at Saint Anthony, on the northern tip of the Island of Newfoundland. Outside of a few hurricanes, it was the lowest barometer reading ever recorded in the East. The cold air outbreak responsible for the cyclone brought snow to South Florida.

February 23, 1977—Following a dry winter, a windy cyclone lifted tons of dust from Colorado, Texas, and New Mexico (where gusts reached 117 mph), and sent it east behind a fast-moving cold front. Two days later the cloud of Great Plains topsoil was still dense enough to reduce visibility and hamper air traffic in the Southeast. The storm was reminiscent of several that occurred during the "dust bowl" years, 1930–1939.

January 26–27, 1978—An inland "bomb" exploded over the Ohio Valley, bringing blizzard conditions from the Dakotas to Pennsylvania, 40 inches of snow to Indiana, freezing rain to New York and Quebec, tornadoes to the southeastern states, and damaging high winds as far as 700 miles from its center. Ten inches of snow and 100-mile-per-hour gusts made it Ohio's worst blizzard of the century.

February 14, 1982—Another "bomb" went off near Newfoundland, kicking up 50-foot waves over the Grand Banks. The heavy seas and hurricane-force winds capsized an oil drilling rig 200 miles east of Saint John's, drowning eighty-four workers, and sank a Soviet freighter, with a loss of thirty-three more lives.

January 20–22, 1983—A cyclone born in the Gulf of Mexico spread sleet, snow, and freezing rain from Mississippi to Quebec, knocking out power to half a million homes (most in the Deep South). As with several other storms that winter, the upper-level disturbance that triggered the cyclone could be traced back to an enormous area of thunderstorms south of Hawaii—part of the El Niño that upset much of the world's climate.

All streams run to the sea, but the sea is not full; to the place where the streams flow, there they flow again.

—Ecclesiastes 1:7

The climate of the East is, in at least one way, one of the most favorable in the world. You might think the summers are too hot and muggy, the winters too cold and damp, and that hurricanes and lightning are too frightening. However, the area has been blessed with one of the world's most reliable supplies of water. Most years the amount of rain and snow that falls on most places is within 20 percent of the average—a reliability unheard of in most other parts of the world. In some northeastern states the variability is less than 10 percent, the lowest in the world.

The moisture that falls on the East comes in many forms, some liquid and some frozen. Rain, sleet, hail, snow—all those inclemencies that mail carriers must go through—are all lumped together under the common name *precipitation*. Precipitation is the depth of rain and melted snow, hail, and other frozen stuff that would be standing on the ground after a storm if none ran off, soaked into the ground, or evapo-

rated. The measurement of precipitation reflects this concept. Korean agriculturalists put out buckets to measure rain in the fifteenth century; and two thousand years earlier the Indians (of India) used bowls for the same purpose. Ever since, no matter how sophisticated they may look, most measuring devices for precipitation are still essentially buckets. Some of these devices use heating elements or automobile antifreeze to melt snowfall and some have digital readouts. But all are still cans or buckets that show the water depth at the end of a storm. Add these measurements over the course of a year and you get the annual precipitation for your locale. Do this for several years and you can get the average annual precipitation. This number—average annual precipitation—is one of a few single numbers that best describes the climate of a location.

The wettest weather station in the East is at Rosman, in the hills of southwestern North Carolina, with an average annual rainfall of 82 inches.[1] The driest spot in the East is somewhat a matter of definition. Generally speaking, the farther west you go in the United States, and the farther north in Canada, the drier it is. Within the states east of the Mississippi and the southern parts of eastern Canada, the driest places

MEAN ANNUAL PRECIPITATION IN THE EAST (in inches)

average 27 to 28 inches of precipitation a year. Among the places in that category are Mount Morris, New York; Green Bay, Wisconsin; Mackinaw and Bay City, Michigan; and Killaloe, Ontario.

As best as it can be figured, the average annual precipitation for the twenty-six states east of the Mississippi is a bit over 44 inches, while the seventeen states within 200 miles of the Atlantic coast average nearly 46 inches. The rest of the "lower forty-eight" states average only half as much, about 23 inches, making the East the wettest third of the country. The same is true for Canada, with the populous sections of southern Ontario and Quebec, and the Maritime Provinces, receiving around 40 inches a year. This

amount of precipitation is enormous. Forty-four inches a year comes out to 1.3 million gallons of water per acre. In over 1 million square miles of the eastern United States and southeastern Canada, the annual soaking amounts to 700 cubic miles of water, or over 3 million million tons of water. That's six times the volume of Lake Erie. The amounts are awesome. Where does it all come from?

There is always some water vapor in the atmosphere. The amount of vapor varies considerably from season to season and even day to day, but typically the total volume of moisture over the states and provinces east of the Mississippi averages to about 15 cubic miles of liquid equivalent (about half that amount in the winter and twice as much in summer). This is enough to cover the region with an inch of liquid water. However, again on the average, an inch of precipitation falls on the East every eight days. This means there must be a continuous replenishment of atmospheric moisture over the East.

We know that the moisture evaporates from the surfaces of the world's oceans because, ultimately, that is where it all returns. The cycle of evaporation from the oceans, transport by winds to land areas, precipitation, runoff into rivers, and return to the ocean is known as the *hydrologic cycle*. In reality, the hydrologic cycle is complicated. Water can be stored for long intervals in lakes, soil, trees, underground water supplies, and even in snowpack and glaciers before being released back to the oceans. Even the atmospheric transport of moisture may be circuitous—water can precipitate and evaporate several times before reaching its "final" destination.

North America is surrounded on all sides by oceans. Most of the continent lies in the zone of the prevailing westerlies, making the world's largest ocean, the Pacific, a possible source of moisture. However, most Pacific moisture falls on the coast and mountain ranges of the western states and provinces. East of the Rockies, the dry climate of the Great Plains tells us that the westerlies need to tap new sources of moisture before reaching the East. If the prevailing westerlies *always* blew straight from the west, there would be no new moisture sources, and the East would be a desert. Fortunately, cyclones embedded in the westerlies turn the wind in all directions, allowing those seas and oceans to our south and east—the Gulf of Mexico, the Caribbean, and the Atlantic (and especially the subtropical Atlantic south of Cape Hatteras)—to be put to good use.

Year round, the temperatures of these subtropical seas range from 70 to 85 degrees. At these temperatures, water evaporates at a pretty good clip. The 700,000 square miles of the Gulf of Mexico loses about an inch and a half of its surface water per week, or 70 inches a year, to the air above. That amounts to 700 cubic miles of water a year. If this figure sounds familiar, it should—that's how much water falls on the eastern United States and Canada per year! There's a little bit of coincidence here, since some of the Gulf's moisture blows away to other parts of the world, and some of the moisture that rains on the East comes from other parts of the ocean. Wherever it comes from, there is an enormous amount of water vapor that blows ashore to become rain for the East.

HIGH WATER MARKS—A century of floods on the Susquehanna River are chronicled on this building at Millersburg Ferry, Pennsylvania.

SUMMER RAINS

Over most of the East, the regularity of precipitation from season to season is as remarkable as it is from year to year. For a typical eastern city, the wettest month of the year, on the average, is no more than twice as wet as the driest month. In other words, unlike much of the world, there are no pronounced wet and dry seasons. The only real exception is (of course) southern Florida, which, like most subtropical climates around the world, has a summer rainy season and winter dry season.

Nowhere, though, is the precipitation exactly evenly distributed throughout the year. There's always one season that's a bit wetter than the rest, and which one it is depends on where you are. It's useful to look at different kinds of storms that affect different places during their wettest seasons. That's because these particular storms are the ones most likely to produce floods when they get out of hand, and the ones most likely to bring drought when they don't happen enough.

For most of the East, summer brings the most—and heaviest—rains of the year. July and

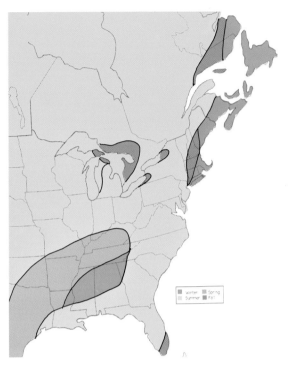

RAIN (OR SNOW) SEASONS ACROSS THE EAST—This map shows which of the four seasons receives the most precipitation for different areas.

August are the wettest months for a vast area from the Gulf Coast and Florida, northward up the seaboard and Appalachians into New York, Ontario, and Quebec. These are the months the Bermuda High has its greatest influence over the East, sending steamy tropical air inland on southeast and south winds. Thunderstorms break out almost daily over the southeastern states, but the heaviest rains come from occasional tropical storm systems, including hurricanes, that sweep in from the ocean. Farther north, thunderstorms are less frequent, but the humid air is more likely to run into a cold front or get drawn into a passing cyclone. When it does, the rains can be torrential.

WINTER STORMS

You probably never noticed this before, but the 55-mile drive from New York City to Bridgeport, Connecticut, takes you from the land of summer rains into the zone with a wintertime precipitation peak. Admittedly, the seasonal differences aren't very important in either place, with all months of the year confined to the 3- to 4-inch precipitation range. The winter peak gets more significant farther north in New England and extends into the Canadian Maritimes. Most places actually show a double precipitation peak—the main one during November and December, with a secondary peak in March.

The storms that bring the heaviest rains are the coastal cyclones that develop near Cape Hatteras and intensify as they track to the north and northeast along the northern edge of the Gulf Stream. This is a favorite area for "bombs" to blow up, and when they do, their target is often the rocky shores of New England, Nova Scotia, and Newfoundland. Even in midwinter, the air that gets drawn into these rapidly strengthening cyclones can be quite warm and humid. Sometimes these coastal locations briefly see temperatures in the 60s as the warm sector of the cyclone passes. The combination of nearly tropical air and the strong upward air currents in the cyclone can produce wintertime rains that would do justice to a hurricane.

APRIL SHOWERS

For the vast area between the Mississippi River and the Appalachians, from the Gulf Coast to the Great Lakes, springtime brings the heaviest rains. The season begins in March, with the last of the Gulf Coast lows drawing moisture from the warming Gulf of Mexico and dumping it as far north as Kentucky. The worst floods along the Ohio and Mississippi Rivers happen at this time of year, when heavy rains falling on melting snowpack send a double dose of runoff into the river. In April and

May cyclones from the west take over, drawing the moist Gulf air farther north and converting it into thundershowers and general all-day rains. These storms can often bring more than just April showers; April is peak tornado season in this area. The Great Lakes area receives its heaviest rains in June as the storm track and Gulf moisture continue moving north.

AUTUMN: HURRICANES AND BLIZZARDS

Several different parts of the East receive their heaviest precipitation in the autumn months of September through November and into early December (which may seem more like winter, but it's officially autumn until the twenty-first). One is the southeast coast of Florida, where the wettest month of year is September. September is the height of the hurricane season, and it's the occasional hurricane combined with the much more frequent, but less intense, tropical disturbances that bring the downpours.

The other places with an autumn precipitation peak are some locales east of each of the Great Lakes. Here the peak occurs during November and December. Lakes of this size can deliver large amounts of water vapor into the atmosphere, particularly when the lake is warmer than the air blowing across it. This occurs in late autumn and early winter, when the first outbreaks of arctic air reach a lake still retaining the warmth of summer. On the coldest days moisture can be seen entering the atmosphere as twirling streamers of mist above the lake surface. Take a cup of hot coffee outside on a winter day and you'll see this in miniature. Usually, this moisture doesn't rise very high into the atmosphere; but when the lake is warm enough and the air cold enough, low clouds and *lake effect snow* may develop over the downwind side of the lake.

At times, the lake can be 40 or more degrees warmer than the air. Intense warming of the lower atmosphere by the lake can set off strong updrafts,

triggering snow squalls sometimes accompanied by thunder and lightning. Snowfall rates of 5 to 10 inches an hour have been measured in these squalls—the winter equivalent of a heavy summer thunderstorm. A day of squalls from Lake Ontario buried Highmarket, New York, under 70 inches of snow in 1988, and a week-long storm in 1966 dumped 102 inches on nearby Oswego. Lake effect snows are usually highly localized, and only 15 miles from the center of the Highmarket storm, snowfall was less than 6 inches. However, within the band of heavy snowfall, nearly a billion tons of snow dropped on a four-county area—enough to build a snowman 3 miles high!

Lake effect snowstorms become less important as the winter wears on, with the lakes steadily cooling off and starting to freeze over. Because it's

BACKYARD BLIZZARD—Steam from a power plant in West Virginia fed a man-made snow storm that dropped up to an inch of snow. The temperature at the time was 10 degrees.

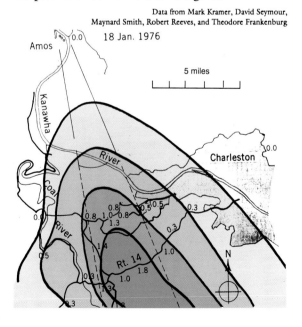

Data from Mark Kramer, David Seymour, Maynard Smith, Robert Reeves, and Theodore Frankenburg

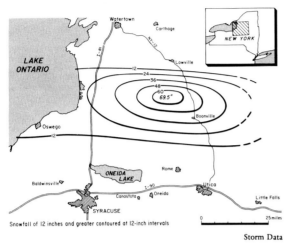

Snowfall of 12 inches and greater contoured at 12-inch intervals

0   25 miles

Storm Data

LAKE EFFECT SNOW—Up to 69.5 inches of snow fell around Tug Hill, New York, during an intense but localized lake-effect snow storm on January 4–5, 1988.

the shallowest of the five, the southernmost Great Lake—Erie—is usually the first (and only) one to ice over completely. When it does, the lake effect snow season comes to a close in the snowbelt between Buffalo and Erie (the city). Lakes Superior, Huron, and Michigan are usually half covered by ice at the end of winter, and rarely freeze up completely. Lake Ontario has frozen over only three times since 1860, and remains 85 percent ice-free during a normal winter, so the snow belt of upstate New York continues to get dumped on all winter.

The smaller the lake, the smaller its lake effect is. How small can a lake be and still make a snowstorm? Lakes the size of New York's Finger Lakes and Lake Champlain are capable of producing a few flurries along their shores before cooling down and freezing up. Much smaller than that, though, lakes and ponds freeze over fairly quickly when the air gets really cold, and never have much of a chance to create a snowstorm. But when a lake is used to cool the burners in factories and power plants, its water stays warm all winter long. Occasionally—when the atmospheric conditions are just right—miniature snowstorms coat the ground downwind from factory-heated lakes and even large cooling towers.

These "backyard blizzards" are not particularly rare, but often they're not recognized as such when the source of the moisture is far enough away to be out of sight and mind. One well-observed storm left up to an inch of light, fluffy snow along a 20-mile long swath downwind from a power plant near Charleston, West Virginia, on a 10-degree morning in January 1976. As far as snowmen go, there was enough snow to make one 800 feet high. That's a *big* snowman, but in terms of the hydrologic cycle, it was nothing—only a few millionths of 1 percent of the East's total precipitation that year. However, these little storms do illustrate the hydrologic cycle on a scale that we can grasp.

DROUGHT AND DELUGE

Droughts are relative, and even the northeastern states, with the world's most reliable rainfall, can suffer from water shortages and crop failures. During the Great Northeastern Drought of 1963–66, rainfall in many places averaged 15 inches a year below their usual 40 to 45 inches. In many parts of the world, a 30 percent shortage of rainfall is barely noticeable, but in a region whose inhabitants are adapted to a consistent water supply, the shortage sent Philadelphia and New York into a legal war over water rights to the Delaware River.

A logical explanation for droughts would be that less water evaporates from the nearby oceans, or that the moisture that does evaporate blows somewhere else. In either case, less moisture drifts inland, and the air over the East would simply be drier. This theory sounds very reasonable, but it just ain't so. Look at humidity statistics for wet years versus dry years, and there's hardly any difference—maybe 1 or 2 percent, but nothing like the 30 percent difference in rainfall.

More (or less) moisture in the air does not necessarily mean you'll get more (or less) rain. The most humid air in the world is found along the desert shores of the Persian Gulf. To get rain, you need storms. Storms are the machines that turn vapor into rain. If, for some reason, there are fewer storms on your storm track, or they're avoiding you, you'll have a drought. That's what happened in the Great Northeastern Drought. The cold pool of water that normally hugs the coast from Virginia to Newfoundland was larger (and cooler) than normal, pushing the Gulf Stream farther out to sea. This kept those Hatteras "bombs" farther out to sea as well, leaving the coast high and dry. During the summer, the cold near-shore water kept thunderstorm activity down as well, further aggravating the situation.

The story is essentially the same elsewhere. A shortage of Gulf Coast cyclones in early 1986 led to the severest drought on record in Georgia, Tennessee, and the Carolinas. Be they thunderstorms and hurricanes over Florida or springtime cold fronts in the Ohio Valley, it's changes in storm tracks that make the difference between drought and deluge in the normally benign climate of the East.

RECORD RAINFALLS

Over the years, most of the East has recorded the steadiest and most reliable rainfall rates in the world. That doesn't necessarily mean the rains are *always* steady, however, and on occasion the rainfall rates can be downright excessive. Following are some extreme rainfall rates for a variety of places in the East—some are even world records!

1 min.	1.23 inches, Unionville, Md., July 4, 1956
40 min.	9.25 inches, Guinea, Va., August 24, 1906
1 hr.	10 inches, Catskill, N.Y., July 26, 1819
2 hrs., 10 min.	19 inches, Rockport, W.Va., July 18, 1889 (world record)
3 hrs.	16 inches, Concord, Pa., August 5, 1843
4 hrs., 30 min.	30.8 inches, Smethport, Pa., July 18, 1942 (world record)
8 hrs.	27 inches, Massies Mill, Va., August 19–20, 1969
9 hrs.	24 inches, Ewan, N.J., August 31–September 1, 1940
15 hrs.	34.5 inches, Smethport, Pa., July 17–18, 1942
24 hrs.	38.7 inches, Yankeetown, Fla., September 5–6, 1950
41 days	48.9 inches, Maysville, N.C., August 11–September 20, 1955
1 year	129.6 inches, Rosman, N.C., 1964
1 year	130.14 inches, Mt. Washington, N.H., 1969[2]

By contrast, the *driest* years ever recorded in the eastern United States and southeastern Canada were 1919—7.76 inches of precipitation recorded in Oshawa, Ontario—and 1930—9.5 inches in Upper Tract, West Virginia. Aficionados of extremes should note that Guinea, Virginia, received nearly as much rain in 40 minutes as Upper Tract, West Virginia— only 107 miles away—did in an entire year!

ICE STORM—Freezing rain leaves a beautiful but destructive coating of clear ice on a pine bough.

SNOW AND RAIN

But it never rained rain. It never snowed snow. And it never blew just wind. It rained things like soup and juice. It snowed mashed potatoes and green peas. And sometimes the wind blew in storms of hamburgers.

—Judi Barrett, *Cloudy with a Chance of Meatballs*[3]

In the past three chapters we have seen how the sun makes the wind blow and how the wind brings enormous amounts of water from the world's oceans into North America. That leaves us with 10 or 20 cubic miles of water sitting in the atmosphere east of the Mississippi on an average day. However, this water is in the air and, instead of being a refreshing liquid that animals and plants can enjoy, it's all vapor. That brings us to the question of how to get all this water out of the sky and onto (and into) the ground.

CONDENSATION

Water vapor is a gas and will never fall to the ground. To return to earth it needs to turn into liquid water or solid ice through a process called *condensation*. Did you ever notice how your laundry on the line dries faster when it's warm outside?

Warm air has less trouble evaporating water because it can hold more water vapor than cold air can. If air containing water vapor gets chilled, it eventually reaches a point where it can no longer hold its supply of vapor. The excess vapor condenses into tiny drops of liquid water. If the air is cold enough, the vapor may form ice crystals through a process called *sublimation*. Later we'll see that vapor can condense into liquid water even at temperatures well below the freezing point, although the drops may later freeze.

One way to describe the amount of vapor in the air is to measure the temperature at which condensation occurs. This temperature is called the *dew point*, and the higher the dew point, the more moisture the air contains. Roughly, the amount of vapor in, say, a cubic foot of air doubles for every 20-degree increase of the dew point. A 70-degree dew point means four times the moisture as a 30-degree dew point.

There's an old army saying that "the only things that fall from the sky are rain and paratroopers." Of course, meteorologically speaking, that just isn't true. It's not just rain and snow, either, or even peas and hamburgers. Water can condense into an astounding variety of shapes and sizes before it falls

NOAA/AES

AVERAGE ANNUAL SNOWFALL IN THE EAST (in inches)

from the sky. The form of precipitation that reaches the ground tells you a lot about what's happening miles overhead.

CLOUDS

Most of the time, there must be clouds before there's precipitation. Amazingly, if the atmosphere were completely "pure" and contained only gaseous molecules like oxygen and water vapor, we would never see a cloud. Even though air may cool below its dew point, water vapor still needs something to condense *on*. Water can't just condense in thin air. Fortunately, the air isn't pure; it is chock-full of minuscule particles of dust, pollen, sea salt, smoke, and even tiny drops of turpentine blown off of trees. The amount of these *condensation nuclei* varies greatly from place to place, but usually there's between a thousand and a million of them in every cubic *inch* of air. Of course, there are more above cities than over rural areas and more over land than over sea. However, water vapor molecules rarely have to go very far to find a place to condense.

There are two main ways to cool air down to the dew point. The first is to lift the air; as it goes higher, the pressure around it lowers, and the air expands and cools. At a given altitude the temperature will fall to the dew point, and condensation occurs. This altitude is the *condensation level*; above this level sits a cloud. Often, this lifting of air takes place in cyclones, as described earlier. Sometimes, particularly in the summer, solar heating of the ground can send warm "bubbles" of air up to the condensation level. Yet another way to lift air is to simply blow it up a mountainside.

The second way to chill air is to set it out at night and let its heat radiate into space. At first, most of the radiation leaves the ground, not the air, and the air gets cold by contacting the cold ground. When stones and blades of grass on the ground cool below the dew point, dew or frost condenses; when the air gets to the dew point, a cloud—fog—forms near the ground. Blanketed by a layer of fog, the ground no longer radiates its heat directly to space. Now the radiational cooling occurs at the top of the fog bank, and the fog thickens and deepens. This is how valley fog forms. A variation on this theme is to run the air over a cold surface, be it ground or ocean. Maine's famous coastal fog develops this way.

You don't necessarily have to cool air to its dew point to get condensation. Raising the dew point to the air's temperature is another way to accomplish the same thing. To do this you need a ready supply of liquid water to evaporate. Up in the sky, evaporating raindrops can provide moisture for ragged *scud clouds* to form beneath the main cloud

SOGGY SNOW—Up to 50 inches of heavy, wet snow downed trees and power lines across southeastern Pennsylvania on the first day of spring, March 20, 1958, leaving millions of residents (including the author) without electricity for up to five days.

deck; on the ground, wet soil and open water surfaces are great moisture sources for fog. *Steam fog* forms when moisture evaporating from the wet ground after sunrise condenses in the still cool morning air or when rain evaporates from hot streets and roofs after a thundershower. Over the ocean (or lakes, ponds, and even creeks), cold weather *sea smoke* marks the condensation of vapor rising from the water surface.

The drops of water that condense to make clouds are incredibly small. They average much less than a thousandth of an inch in diameter, and it would take ten thousand of them to cover the head of a pin. Drops this small would take a week to fall

to the ground, except that they would never make it. Once outside the cloud, they evaporate in seconds. These lazily floating droplets are the answer to that nagging childhood question: How do clouds stay up? But don't be fooled. There are a *lot* of these droplets in a cloud, and even the smallest puffy cloud on a summer afternoon can easily outweigh an automobile.

RAIN

We know that rain falls and clouds don't, so raindrops must be heavier than cloud droplets. It takes about a million cloud droplets to make one average raindrop. Initially, a cloud droplet grows by

35

Bruce Berryman

RADIATIONAL FOG—After nighttime cooling, a humid air mass creates a blanket of fog. The cooling results as heat radiates through clear skies into space, hence the name for fog formed this way. Within a few hours the fog will "burn off," or evaporate, under the increasing heat of the rising sun.

condensing more water vapor onto its tiny spherical surface. Eventually it gets large enough to start falling through the cloud. On its downward journey, our growing drop bumps into and absorbs some of the many droplets still hanging in the cloud. This growth process is called *coalescence.* When the drop gets as big as a sixteenth of an inch across, it's a genuine raindrop and down it goes.

Coalescence works well in thick clouds with a good supply of very moist air, so the droplets have plenty of opportunities to bump into each other. This happens in the tropics, including Florida in the summer. Coalescence doesn't work very well, however, in the cooler air over most of North America.

If clouds are thinner and there's not as much water vapor around, drops don't grow to full size. These immature drops fall as *drizzle,* a common form of precipitation from thin clouds and fog banks along the coast and in weak storm systems. If the air doesn't have the moisture to form even a drizzle, the cloud releases no precipitation.

SNOW

While coalescence seems like a perfectly reasonable way to make rain, the truth is that in most places outside the tropics, most rain is really melted snow (or hail, in the summer). This is partly because in mid-latitudes any cloud big enough to make

Mike Mogil

ADVECTION FOG—Fog also forms when warm, moist air moves (or advects) over a colder land or ocean surface. This kind of fog may persist for hours—or days—until a drier air mass arrives.

precipitation is probably tall enough to have its top portion well below freezing. Another factor is the way snowflakes grow faster than raindrops.

Raindrops may begin their lives as snowflakes, but there's yet another twist: Snowflakes start out as water droplets! When water vapor condenses out of the atmosphere, it nearly always does so as droplets of *liquid* water. When the air is colder than 40 below zero, vapor may condense into minute ice crystals, but this is relatively rare. When the air temperature is between 32 above and 40 below, condensation results in peculiar creations: droplets of *supercooled water* whose temperature is below freezing.

You've probably heard stories about ponds in the north woods that have cooled below 32 degrees but haven't frozen over. An unfortunate duck alights in the water, and the pond immediately freezes around the poor critter's feet. There's reason to believe that ducks never suffer this ignominy, but the duck's tale does illustrate a point: Supercooled water freezes immediately when disturbed. In the air, the disturbances come as little particles called *freezing nuclei*. Just as condensation nuclei start the condensation of vapor into droplets, freezing nuclei start the freezing of droplets into crystals.

Most freezing nuclei are the same kind of dust and smoke particles that work so well as con-

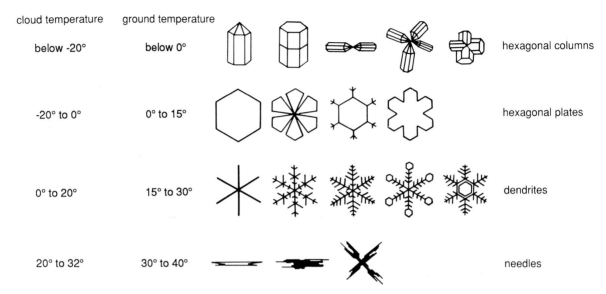

cloud temperature	ground temperature					
below -20°	below 0°					hexagonal columns
-20° to 0°	0° to 15°					hexagonal plates
0° to 20°	15° to 30°					dendrites
20° to 32°	30° to 40°					needles

from Nakaya

TYPES OF SNOW CRYSTALS

densation nuclei, although it may be that different shapes and sizes of nuclei do better at freezing. Even meteor dust—the ashes of "shooting stars"—might do the job. Then there are the artificial nuclei, such as silver iodide crystals, that cloud-seeders intentionally put into the air to trigger the freezing. Duck feet do not work well.

Once a droplet freezes into a crystal, it turns into a wolf among sheep. Ice particles act as both condensation and freezing nuclei, grabbing moisture out of the air more efficiently than water droplets could. Growing ice crystals even steal moisture from nearby droplets and become snowflakes within ten to twenty minutes.

Snowflakes are famous for their infinite variety of six-pointed shapes, and it's probably true that no two flakes are exactly alike. Each snowflake is made up of thousands of billions of billions (otherwise known as sextillions) of molecules of water that can be arranged in quadrillions of septillions of centillions of ways. The number of flakes that fall

annually on Earth is in the sextillions—about the same as the number of molecules in a snowflake, but far, far fewer than the number of possible different flakes. So it's very likely that in the entire lifetime of our planet, there will never be a snowflake that's identical to any other past, present, or future flake.

All these centillions of possible snowflakes can be lumped into several categories. The category a snowflake will fall into is pretty much decided by the temperature at which the flake forms. Those flakes that grow from the skimpy water supply at 20 degrees below zero or colder form *hexagonal columns* that look like pieces of a six-sided pencil. Around zero to 10 below the crystals take the shape of flat, six-sided wafers called *hexagonal plates*. With the more plentiful supply of water vapor at zero to 20 above, the crystals can grow into the large but delicate six-pointed stars that typify our idea of snowflakes. These crystals are called *dendrites*, from the old Greek word meaning "branched like a tree."

38

The warmest crystals, those that grow between 20 degrees and freezing, grow into splinter-shape bits of ice known as *needles.*

In moderate snowstorms, the individual crystals can make it to the ground without hitting and sticking to other crystals. With a magnifying glass you can see an incredible variety of crystal shapes. They show up well on dark surfaces, such as wooden railings or winter coats. When snowfall increases, however, crystals stick together. These aggregates can get quite large at times, sometimes growing to several inches across.

For skiers, the best snow is the light powder, which means the aggregate flakes contain lots of air and little water. The biggest crystals—dendrites—make the fluffiest flakes. The biggest dendrites form when air temperature is about 5 above. Since most snowflakes in a snowstorm are formed several thousand feet up, the ground-level temperature where these flakes fall is 20 to 25 degrees. What this means is that the fluffiest, lightest snow falls when the temperature at ground level is in the low 20s. On the average, 13 inches of this snow melts down to an inch of water.

When the ground level temperature is closer to freezing, snow comes down as bunches of needle crystals, looking somewhat like a handful of pine needles. These more densely packed crystals make a heavier layer of snow on the ground; 10 inches of this snow makes only about an inch of water. Interestingly, when the ground-level temperature is below 10 degrees, the snowfall also gets denser. The little hexagonal plates and columns don't stick to each other very easily, and the layer they make on the ground doesn't hold very much air. However, it never gets too cold to snow—reports of snow with temperatures of 20 to 40 below are fairly common in the Arctic. Extremely cold air doesn't contain much moisture, but what there is can be made into ice crystals. There just isn't very much of the stuff.

DIAMOND DUST

When it's *really* cold, zero or below, cloud droplets don't last too long before they freeze. This means extremely cold clouds are made largely of ice crystals, most of which are hexagonal columns and plates. When fog forms at extremely low temperatures, it, too, freezes quickly into crystals. This *ice fog* is common during Canadian winters, and is occasionally seen farther south during severe cold waves. Often the air will be full of fairly large hexagonal plate crystals falling slowly from a clear sky—there are so few water droplets that any fog or cloud is invisible. The twinkling and glistening of these crystals in the sunlight has earned the spectacle the name *diamond dust.* The meteorological name is more mundane—*ice crystals.* Diamond dust is fairly rare in temperate latitudes, but high atop the 1- or 2-mile-thick ice sheets of Greenland and Antarctica most of the snow that falls is really ice crystals descending from clear skies.

Diamond dust crystals fall with their flat sides parallel to the ground. This cloud of minuscule mirrors, each facing straight down, leads to one of the weirdest nighttime lighting effects the weather can produce. All along the horizon, above each and

WINDOW ICE—A frozen water drop (center) acted as a nucleus for these feathery ice crystals that grew on a window pane as the outside temperature fell below zero.

Richard A. Keen

Richard A. Keen

SNOW? NO, IT'S HAIL!—One inch of pea-size hailstones mixed with autumn leaves covers a street after an unusual October hailstorm roared through the Philadelphia area in 1977. Most of the hail fell in just three minutes. The lavender sky is lit by frequent lightning in this nighttime photograph.

every distant street lamp and approaching head-light, are long and narrow rays, shifting beams pointing straight up like searchlights—light reflect-ing off millions of crystals between you and the light source.

SNOW GRAINS

Sometimes, when a cloud is warm enough (but still below freezing), supercooled droplets can coalesce to the size of drizzle before they freeze. If the cloud deck is fairly thin, perhaps less than a thousand feet from top to bottom, the frozen droplets leave the bottom of the cloud before they grow much more. The white, sand-size bits of snow that fall to the ground are called *snow grains*. Few roads have been closed due to falls of snow grains, which rarely amount to much more than a light dusting.

Jay Brausch

DIAMOND DUST—These "searchlight beams" are really the reflections of street lamps off millions of tiny, flat ice crystals suspended in the air. These crystals often form in clear air when the temperature is below zero.

GRAUPEL

Yet another form snow can take is *snow pellets,* also known as *soft hail* and, more commonly, by the German name *graupel.* These roundish or cone-shaped, BB- to marble-sized snowballs usually descend in quick showers and bounce once or twice. Heavy graupel showers sometimes come with thunder and lightning. These snow pellets grow as turbulent air currents inside the cloud carry them through swarms of water droplets, which freeze onto their crystal structure. Since they pick up whole droplets, snow pellets are heavier, grainier, and lack the delicate features of snowflakes.

GLAZE ICE

On a sultry summer afternoon, it just doesn't seem believable that the rain shower steaming from the sidewalks started out as a snowstorm. But the

41

higher up you go, the colder it is, and eventually the temperature falls below freezing. This freezing level changes from day to day, but even in the heat of the summer—indeed, even in the tropics—it never gets higher than 19,000 feet above sea level. Summer showers often tower to twice that height, so the top halves of their clouds actually harbor raging snowstorms. At a rate of 3 to 5 degrees every 1,000 feet, the snowflakes warm as they fall, and when they drop below the freezing level, they melt into raindrops. Most of the time raindrops stay melted and soak into the ground or run off into streams. However, a nasty thing happens if there is a layer of cold air near the ground: The rain freezes on everything in sight. Trees, wires, grass, and even roads can be coated with a sheet of glossy ice called *glaze,* or, appropriately, *freezing rain.*

The beauty of these "ice storms" can't be denied; even the most mundane of objects, from trees to television antennas, assume the elegance of fine crystal. Unfortunately, the reality is that glaze often reduces the value of whatever it touches. Heavy accumulations bring down wires and branches, and driving and walking can become treacherous. Glaze ice is usually a fraction of an inch thick, but 3-inch-deep coatings have been seen on wires and trees. At that rate, a 100-foot length of wire would be burdened with 1,300 pounds of ice, and the branches of a typical spruce would be loaded with several tons.

Freezing rain often happens when a lingering arctic air mass gets overrun by warm air ahead of an approaching storm, creating an inversion. The temperature near the ground may be 10 degrees below the freezing point, but several hundred or thousand feet aloft there's a warm layer of above-freezing air. Above that it cools off in the usual manner. Arctic air that settles into the valleys of the Appalachians is not easily dislodged by coastal storms, which themselves bring no shortage of melted snowflakes. The Appalachians can also shove southwesterly winds from the Gulf of Mexico up and over cold air masses entrenched along the eastern seaboard. Some valley locations in the Pocono, Catskill and Berkshire mountains of Pennsylvania, New York, and Massachusetts, respectively, get glazed a dozen times a year on the average.

Ice storms are rare in the deep South where it just doesn't get cold enough, and right along the coast where the neighboring ocean quickly warms the air above freezing before the rain begins. *Rime ice,* a close relative of glaze, is more common on mountaintops and ridges. Supercooled fog, rather than rain, freezes directly onto whatever gets in its way, leaving a white coating of ice. Usually rime forms quarter-inch-long spikes that grow especially well on twigs and pine needles. In heavy rime storms, though, the thick coating looks like the stuff that used to fill freezers before the days of frost-free refrigerators.

SLEET

If the low layer of cold air is deep enough, raindrops might freeze solid on their way down. At other times, rain drops are blown back up to the colder levels of a storm, where they freeze and fall back to earth. In either case, these clear pellets of frozen rain are known as *sleet,* which bounces when it hits the ground. Although usually less than a sixteenth of an inch in diameter, sleet pellets are round and slippery, and it doesn't take much of the stuff to foul up traffic. Sleet is most common—twelve or more times a year—in New England. To the north in Canada, the "warm" layer aloft is often below freezing, so the snow never melts, and south of New England, the cold layer near the ground is often not cold enough to freeze the rain drops.

Sleet pellets, being small and solid, fall faster than snowflakes. They are more likely to reach the ground without melting when the temperature is above freezing. That is why places that rarely ever see snowflakes (like the Bahamas) do get to see sleet once in a while.

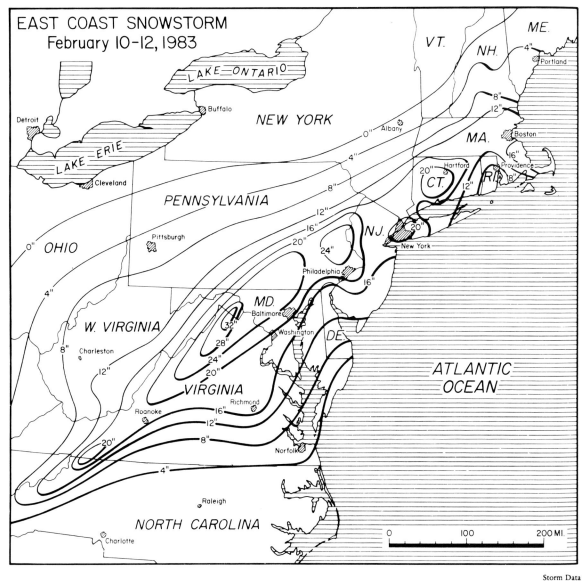

EAST COAST SNOWSTORM
February 10-12, 1983

THE BIG SNOW OF '83—*The massive snowstorm of February 10–12, 1983, left 1 to 2 feet of snow in a huge swath from North Carolina to New Hampshire. In the Blue Ridge Mountains, Glen Gary, West Virginia, received 35 inches. Although the snowfall amounts were exceptional, the pattern of snowfall was fairly typical of coastal "Hatteras-type" storms.*

Richard A. Keen

RIME UP CLOSE—The delicate nature of rime spikes, each composed of hundreds of frozen water droplets, is shown in this close-up photograph.

MIXED PRECIPITATION

Meteorologists formally call it *mixed precipitation;* informally, they (and everyone else) call it "slop." It's what you get when the weather can't make up its mind—snow mixing with rain, changing to freezing rain, then to sleet, and back to snow (or rain!). The indecisive weather is usually caused by changes in the thickness and temperature of that warm layer of air. A few degrees warmer, or a few hundred feet thicker, and the layer can change sleet to freezing rain or just plain rain; a few degrees colder, and the snowflakes might make it all the way to the ground. For places like Washington, Philadelphia, and New York, slight changes in wind direction can make the difference between cold air arriving overland and milder air coming off the sea, and in some storms the winds can shift from northeast to southeast several times before it's all over.

It may sound completely unpredictable, but most of the time there's some rhyme and reason to the changing precipitation, because mixed precipitation is most common with approaching warm fronts. When the above freezing layer first appears a few thousand feet up, the cold layer near the ground is still deep enough to freeze the melting snow into sleet. As the warm, melting layer thickens and the cold layer gets shallower, the melted snow doesn't freeze until it hits the ground and becomes glaze. Finally, the freezing layer near the ground blows away entirely, and it's all rain. So, the commonest sequence of mixed precipitation is snow, sleet, glaze, and rain.

HAIL

The last member of our precipitation potpourri is one of the nastiest—hail. It's also one of the rarest—most places in the East see hail only once or twice a year, on the average. Rare it may be, but hail still does millions of dollars of damage to crops every year, and storms have driven unlucky farmers out of business in less than ten minutes. People have been killed by hail, although, fortunately, these cases are rare. Cattle have less opportunity to find shelter when hail strikes, and their casualties over the years have been much higher. Damaged roofs, broken windshields, and dented automobiles all bear testimony to the destructiveness of hail.

Hail is yet another form of refrozen raindrops. It begins just like sleet, with rain blown back up into colder parts of the cloud. With hail, though, the upward winds are much stronger. A frozen drop may spend enough time high in the cloud to gather a frosty layer of ice; when it falls back down it picks up water droplets. The growing pellet may then be blown back up a second time, freezing its coating of water droplets. High in the cloud, the stone picks up another layer of icy condensation. This up-and-down cycle can happen ten or more times before the hailstone becomes too heavy for the winds to keep it up.

Next time it hails, cut one of the stones in half with a warm knife. You might see concentric rings of white and clear ice. These are alternating layers of accumulated frost and frozen droplets. The number of layers tells you how many loops the stone made through the storm cloud.

Hailstones can range in diameter from an eighth of an inch up to 4 inches or more. It takes a mighty powerful updraft to send the biggest stones back up for more ice. Stones weighing nearly 2 pounds and measuring half a foot across have been reported in Kansas, Nebraska, and Iowa, while a 3-pounder once fell in Russia. In the East, hail the size of baseballs has bombarded Maryland, Virginia, South Carolina, and other places. The impact of a large stone can be lethal, with baseball-size hailstones hitting the ground at 90 mph—the speed of a major league fastball. Notice what catchers wear to protect themselves from such forceful flying objects! Fortunately, giant hailstones are rare—but not unknown—in the East.

HOW MUCH SNOW?

Snow lovers and snow haters alike will have no trouble finding their favorite climate somewhere in

RIME—A night of fog at subfreezing temperatures can leave thick deposits of rime on trees, tractors, and anything else that juts above the ground. This Vermont scene was coated by a freezing fog that rolled in from nearby Lake Champlain on a zero-degree night.

Richard A. Keen

the East. At the snowy end of the scale, Boonville, New York, in the snowbelt between Lake Ontario and the Adirondacks, receives an average of 207 inches per year. In the same neck of the woods, the hamlet of Hooker was buried by 462 inches of snow during the winter of 1976–1977. There are similar snowbelts downwind (east) of each of the Great Lakes, with seasonal averages of 100 inches or more in parts of Ontario, Michigan, Ohio, Pennsylvania, and New York. Most of the higher spots in New England also average over 100 inches a year, and in New Hampshire, the weather station atop 6,262-foot Mount Washington measures 251 inches in an average year (564.9 inches in the winter of 1968–1969). There's also a snowbelt in the 100-inch category along the higher ridges of West Virginia.

A hundred inches a year is a lot by American standards, but it's par for the course in Canada. Most of Quebec and the Maritimes receive well over 100 inches a year, with seasonal totals approaching 200 inches in eastern Quebec and Newfoundland. The snowiest winter ever recorded in eastern Canada was at Cartwright, just inland from the rocky coast of Labrador, with 339 inches during the winter of 1942–1943.

On the other extreme, the southern parts of Mississippi, Alabama, Georgia, and South Carolina average less than an inch of snow a year, and most years see but a trace or two of the stuff. Measurable snow (a tenth of an inch or more) has fallen several times in the recorded history of northern Florida, and once or twice as far south as Tampa. Fort Myers saw a few flurries in 1899, and south of Miami, snow showers dusted Homestead in 1977. However, the spotty flakes missed the weather station at the Miami airport, so "officially" the Magic City has never seen snow. Nor has Key West, the southernmost point on the U.S. mainland (sort of), ever had snow. The least snowy spot in Canada is also its southernmost point, Pelee Island in Lake Erie, with a mere 32 inches a year.

ICE FROM THE SKY

It's amazing how much trouble something as ordinary as ice can create when it comes out of the sky. For example . . .

May 8, 1784—Baseball-size hailstones raked a narrow, 2-mile wide swath along the Wateree River, South Carolina, killing "several negroes, a great number of sheep, lambs, geese . . ." according to the *South Carolina Gazette*. It was the East's worst hailstorm ever in terms of loss of human life.

March 11–14, 1888—The Blizzard of '88 dumped a foot or more of wind-driven snow from Washington, D.C., to New England. Connecticut was hardest hit, with 50 inches at Middletown and winds reaching 70 mph. Deaths from the storm exceeded four hundred.

April 27, 1890—"A dense black cloud-mass, tinged with purple and green, was . . . rapidly approaching. There was a sound like the roll of musketry, and the storm burst suddenly upon the city with an almost deafening roar as the hail stones rained down upon the tin roofs and crashed into windows. . . . For 15 minutes the city was in a state of complete panic, and then the storm passed away almost as quickly as it had come." This was the Baltimore Weather Bureau's description of a storm that pounded the city with hail 2 to 3 inches in diameter, with some stones reported as "as large as a man's fist."

February 11–14, 1899—The Blizzard of '99 blasted the Mid-Atlantic states with subzero cold (15 below in Washington, D.C.) and massive snowfalls (36 inches at Cape May, New Jersey). Snowflakes fell as far south as Fort Myers, Florida.

April 3, 1915—Easter eggs were hard to find in Philadelphia. They were all buried under 19 inches of snow that fell in twelve hours the day before.

December 29–30, 1942—Freezing rain coated trees with ice as thick as 6 inches in New York and Pennsylvania.

February 17, 1943—Forty inches of snow buried the village of Colinet in southeastern Newfoundland—eastern Canada's heaviest one-day snowfall ever. Farther north, the winter total of 339 inches at Cartwright, Labrador, was eastern Canada's snowiest winter ever.

December 26–27, 1947—The Big Apple's biggest snow—26 inches.

January 28–February 4, 1951—"Probably the most destructive ice storm in the United States," according to a U.S. Weather Bureau report, damaged buildings, trees, and wires from Texas to New England. Hundreds were hurt in falls on slippery sidewalks.

January 8–11, 1953—Up to 4 inches of freezing rain in Pennsylvania, New Jersey, and New York knocked out electricity and telephone service for days, but made for excellent sidewalk ice skating.

February 13–17, 1958—One of the most well-traveled snowstorms in history set depth records from Louisiana and Florida to New Hampshire and Quebec. Thirty inches fell from Pennsylvania to Vermont.

March 19–21, 1958—A soggy spring storm socked southeastern Pennsylvania with up to 50 inches of snow, stranding hundreds along the Pennsylvania turnpike and knocking out power to two million homes. Meanwhile, places only 30 miles away received mostly rain.

January 17, 1959—A "snowburst" from Lake Ontario buried Bennett's Bridge, New York, with 51 inches of snow in just sixteen hours.

October 29, 1963—As Hurricane Ginny came ashore over Nova Scotia with 100-mile-per-hour winds, she dropped 18 inches of snow (yes, snow from a hurricane!) in northern Maine.

February 24–28, 1969—A meandering low southeast of Cape Cod left 97.8 inches of snow at the Mount Washington weather station—a record five-day fall. Boston had 26 inches.

December 26–28, 1969—The Connecticut

River valley of New Hampshire and Vermont got glazed with up to 2 inches of ice, some of which remained for six weeks. Farther north, the same storm dumped 28 inches of snow on Montreal.

February 9–10, 1973—A winter low tracking across Florida buried the lowlands of Alabama, Georgia, and South Carolina with 1 to 2 feet of snow, setting records in many places. Meanwhile, 600 miles to the north, Philadelphia had no measurable snow for the entire winter—also a record.

January 28, 1977—The savage Buffalo Blizzard began when a sharp cold front roared off Lake Erie into Buffalo, New York. Temperatures and visibility both dropped to zero within minutes and remained there until the next day, stranding thousands of motorists and even snowplow operators. Snowfall totaled just one foot, but gusts to 69 mph whipped it into drifts 25 feet high. Blizzard conditions continued for four days. Twenty-nine people died in the storm, including nine who were in snow-buried automobiles. Two weeks earlier another cold front dusted snow around the Miami area.

February 6–7, 1978—Boston's biggest snow ever—27 inches—shut down the town for five days. A slow-moving low just south of Long Island brought heavy snow from Washington, D.C., to Maine. On Cape Cod, where it rained, winds peaked at 100 mph. Although it was clearly a winter storm, the intense cyclone had a clear, hurricane-like "eye" on satellite pictures.

January 13, 1982—An Air Florida 737 jetliner crashed into the Potomac River shortly after taking off from Washington, D.C., National Airport in a snowstorm. A heavy accumulation of ice and snow on the wings—and the crew's failure to have it removed—was blamed for the disaster.

February 10–12, 1983—A blizzard punctuated with thunder and lightning buried the Mid-Atlantic states with up to 31 inches of snow. It was the deepest storm on record at several cities, including Philadelphia, Allentown, and Hartford.

Richard A. Keen

HAIL—A hailstone's appearance tells a lot about how it forms. The growing stones pick up clear ice in the warmer, lower parts of the storm cloud, where they collect liquid water that later freezes. The white centers of the stones are rime ice gathered near the top of the cloud. Some stones have several layers of clear and white ice, telling of two or more up-and-down trips through the storm.

April 2–5, 1987—Up to 60 inches of snow buried Great Smoky Mountains National Park on the Tennessee–North Carolina border, crushing scores of small buildings. Farther north, flooding from the same storm washed out a bridge on the New York State Thruway, sending ten motorists to their deaths.

December 23–24, 1989—Freezing rain, sleet, and light snow gave parts of northern Florida their first white Christmas ever. The storm also brought down trees and power lines and closed airports and highways as far south as Ocala and Daytona Beach, stranding thousands of travelers. The cold wave that brought the ice sent the temperature to 5 below zero on the beach at Jacksonville, North Carolina, and sixty-one people froze to death from Florida to Pennsylvania. Seventy-five of Florida's 1,200 remaining manatees also died when their watery habitats became too cold for their tropical metabolisms.

THUNDERSTORMS

Tall, dark columns of thunderclouds seem to boil up through flatter layers and climb into the upper atmosphere. . . . Electric flashes of lightning brilliantly illuminate from within the thunderclouds that generate them. The huge clouds seem to light up instantly and magnificently like enormous bulbs, and a single lightning bolt often seems to trigger a chain reaction of flashes from cloud to cloud so that the lightning appears to be walking its way for hundreds of miles across the darkened earth.

—Joseph P. Allen, *Entering Space*[4]

Whether from the perspective of an astronaut orbiting on board the *Columbia* or from the viewpoints of the rest of us stranded here on Earth, few phenomena of nature are more impressive than lightning. Lightning and its inseparable offspring, thunder, are the necessary attendants of thunderstorms, and combined they give us some of our deadliest and most thrilling weather.

Depending on where you live, thunderstorms range from rare to unavoidable. The middle of the Florida peninsula is struck by 130 thunderstorms over the period of 100 or more days a year, making it the thunderstorm capital of the United States. There's even a roadside marker about thunder-

storms on Highway 192 east of Disney World. At the other end of the coast, windows in Eastport, Maine, rattle less than twenty times a year. In Canada the frequency of thunderstorms ranges from forty or more in southern Ontario to five or less in Newfoundland and Labrador.

Eastern thunderstorms are, in general, not as severe as their larger midwestern cousins. That is not to say, though, that severe weather has never visited the East. Tornadoes, hail, gusty winds, and downpours have struck every eastern state and province, and at times with terrible losses of human life and property.

CLOUDS AND CONVECTION

Clouds need water if for no other reason than just to be seen. Clouds are the liquid droplets of water condensed from the vapor contained in rising currents of air. However, thunderstorms need water for more than droplets—it's the latent heat they're really after. When water vapor condenses in those rising air currents, its latent heat is released, warming the air surrounding the new cloud droplet. Like a bubble in a pool, this warmer—and lighter—air rises more swiftly, leading to even more rapid condensation. Meanwhile, increasing amounts of fresh air drawn into the base of the cloud keep the condensation going. This process of rising, condensation, heating, and faster rising currents is called *convection*. Without it, there would be no thunderstorms.

Even the meanest thunderstorm needs something to get it going. Nothing happens until the air starts rising. For many thunderstorms, the updrafts begin with air heated by the sunlit ground below. Some storms, though, start with the air currents in different sections of cyclones, especially where the cold front wedges under the moist air and shoves it upward.

There's plenty of water in the air, and no shortage of sunlight and fronts to get those currents going. Nonetheless, thunderstorms are relatively infrequent. Even those places that get thundered on one hundred days a year *don't* get thundered on the other 265 days. The average storm lasts an hour or

two, which means only two hundred hours—or eight days—out of the one hundred are actually thundering. So, even in the thunderstorm capital of Florida, it's actually thundering only about 2 percent of the time during an average year. Most people spend more of their lives in the shower than they do hearing thunder.

Clearly, atmospheric conditions have to be just right for thunderstorms to develop. The necessary condition is called *instability,* the opposite of *stability.* To physicists, a stable object (or situation) is one that returns to its original position after being moved (or changed). A bowling ball sitting in a ditch is stable—give it a shove, and it will settle back into the ditch. A bowling ball balanced on a roof is unstable—give it a kick and off it goes.

Like a bowling ball, the atmosphere can be stable or unstable. Cold air in a valley—an inversion—is stable, since the air becomes warmer with

LIFE CYCLE OF A THUNDERSTORM—During its lifetime, which may last one or several hours, a thunderstorm goes through three stages: the towering cumulus stage, with updrafts building the cloud; the mature stage, with updrafts feeding moisture into the cloud, to fall as rain in downdrafts; and a dissipating stage, in which the supply of fresh moisture is cut off and the water in the storm is "raining out."

NCAR/National Science Foundation

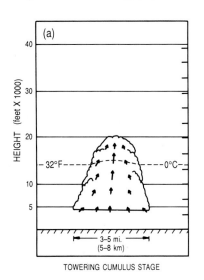
TOWERING CUMULUS STAGE

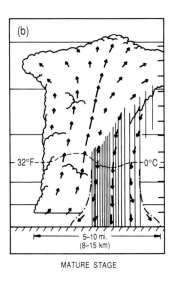
MATURE STAGE

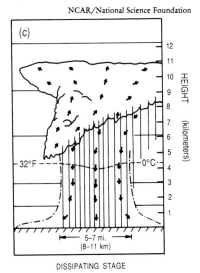
DISSIPATING STAGE

height. Lift the cold air off the ground, say, 100 feet, and it is surrounded by warmer, lighter air. Let go, and the cold air returns to the valley floor. With stable air, those little rising currents won't get very far.

With unstable air, the temperature drops off fairly rapidly with height—about 25 degrees per mile. If ground-level air is lifted, it expands and cools as the pressure gets lower. However, despite the cooling, the lifted batch of unstable air remains warmer than the air around it, and keeps going up. Instability is even stronger if there's water vapor in the air to release its latent heat. If you give an upward kick to part of an unstable air layer, that part will continue to soar upward in a relatively warm stream.

There are several ways to make unstable air, all of which involve either warming the lower atmosphere or cooling the air aloft. Sunlight is great at heating the ground and the air just above it. Almost any sunny day the air becomes unstable to some extent, although not always enough for thunderstorms to develop. The exact opposite happens at night when cloud tops and haze layers radiate their heat out to space, sometimes cooling the upper atmosphere (3 to 6 miles up) more than the lower levels. This occurs most frequently over tropical oceans and nearby shorelines—nighttime lightning is a common sight off the coasts of Florida.

Yet another way to cool the upper atmosphere is to bring cold air in from somewhere else. Many winter and early spring storms result from cold air aloft blowing in ahead of a cold front. Once again, the reverse—warmer air streaming in at ground level—is also possible. We're all familiar with how the winds die down at night. What we don't see from below, though, is that the atmosphere compensates for this by increasing the wind speed just above the ground, several hundred to several thousand feet up. Some of the midnight lightning storms over the Ohio Valley and Mid-Atlantic states are brought on by low-level southerly breezes that pick up during the evening.

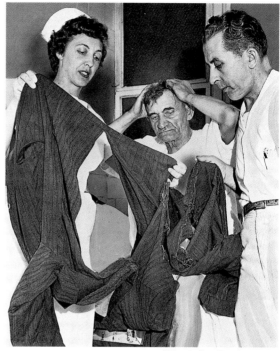

DIRECT HIT—Lightning literally blew the pants off this Philadelphia man (center), who was embarrassed but otherwise unhurt.

One final variation on these unstable themes is to run cold air over a warm ocean. The underlying water moistens as well as heats the lower atmosphere, doubling the destabilizing effect. This appears to be the cause of some phenomenal lightning storms spotted over the Gulf Stream during several winter storm experiments. Of course, any combination of the above is possible, making the causes of instability an easy multiple choice question but a sometimes tricky forecasting problem.

You can't have rising currents of air everywhere, or the lower atmosphere would soon run out of air. That's why thunderstorms are so scattered. The clear spaces between thunderstorms, which are

Ronald Holle

CUMULUS CLOUDS—Many thunderstorms begin when a cottony cumulus cloud takes on added vigor and rises above the rest.

TOWERING CUMULUS—The characteristic "cauliflower" appearance indicates a rapidly growing cloud.

Ronald Holle

CUMULONIMBUS—This massive cumulus cloud is starting to develop an icy "anvil" and has grown large enough to produce rain, earning it the name "cumulonimbus."

MATURE CUMULONIMBUS CLOUD—A full-blown thunderstorm, topped by a spreading "anvil" cloud of ice crystals, fills the sky over Sturbridge, Massachusetts.

SHELF CLOUD—As seen from the ground, the only visible evidence of a growing thunderstorm overhead may be solid-looking, flat-bottomed clouds extending beneath the main cloud deck. These "shelf clouds" result from powerful, concentrated updrafts feeding moisture into the storm.

Grant Goodge

DOWNPOUR—*The localized nature of thunderstorm rains is evident as a storm douses one section of Asheville, North Carolina, while sparing the rest of the city.*

LIGHTNING—*Cloud-to-ground lightning strikes the highest point in New York City, the World Trade Center. Unlike most lightning strikes, this one branches upward toward the cloud.*

Grace Davies

MAMMATUS CLOUDS—*These pouch-like formations hanging from the side of a cumulonimbus are called mammatus clouds from their remote resemblance to the breasts of female mammals. The cloud formations are caused by downdrafts of cool, moist air, and are most often seen after the storm has passed.*

much wider than the storms themselves, are where the air is sinking back to the ground. Ultimately, the net effect of these up and down currents is to send the warm air near the ground skyward, and the cool air aloft down toward the ground. This makes the air more stable. Thunderstorms are one way unstable air "rights itself" and becomes stable once again. Meanwhile, stable air has little reason to change. The very nature of instability, in the atmosphere or anywhere, makes it a relatively unusual condition. Thunderstorms, the offspring of instability, are rare as a result. How often do you see a bowling ball balanced on a roof?

LIFE OF A CUMULONIMBUS

Like humans, thunderstorm clouds change their size and shape as they grow, reach their prime, and then get ready to check out. The first clouds to form are white, cottony puffs called *cumulus*, a Latin word meaning "pile" or "heap." Who among us has never seen the fleeting forms of sheep, giraffes, and dragons in these heaps of water droplets? As they turn more vapor into droplets, cumulus clouds grow into billowing cauliflower shapes called *towering cumulus*.

Three or four miles up (lower in the winter) lies the freezing level. Above this line, the air is colder than 32 degrees, and clouds that go higher may freeze. It usually takes a while for an ascending droplet to find a freezing nucleus, so for several thousand feet above the freezing level, the cloud is made of subfreezing, but still liquid, water droplets—supercooled water. The cloud may reach 30,000 feet before its droplets start to freeze.

With a frozen top, the cumulus cloud becomes a different animal. The cloud top loses its solid, cauliflower appearance, and takes on the stringy, fuzzy appearance characteristic of ice clouds. High winds aloft may blow the ice crystals away from the main cloud; the flat, spreading tops of ice are often called *anvil clouds*.

The changing appearance is a sign that something more meaningful is happening in the cloud. In the moist interior of the cloud, the ice crystals grow rapidly into snowflakes, which fall and melt into rain. *Nimbus* is the Latin word for "rain," and our cloud has matured into a *cumulonimbus*, meaning, loosely, "a raining heap!"

While cumulus and towering cumulus clouds are growing, air currents all head upward. But as ice crystals form, some of this air starts coming back down, bringing with it snow and rain. As the downdrafts reach the ground, they spread out, bringing us the first gusts of cool air that so often are followed by sudden rains. On the ground, the storm has begun.

If a raindrop loses its downdraft, it may blow back up above the freezing level to become hail. The up and downdrafts can approach a hundred miles an hour in a mature cumulonimbus cloud. Loaded with hail, these vertical winds give pilots good reason to avoid thunderstorms. Even on the ground, the hail may arrive on hurricane-force winds, giving the earthbound equally good reason to get out of the storm.

At some point, the supply of fresh, warm, moist air runs out, and the thunderstorms begin to fade. Inside the cloud, the updrafts weaken, shrink, and finally cease, leaving sinking currents of rain- and snow-filled air. The cloud's edges begin to evaporate, and it takes on a ragged appearance. Above, the ice-crystal anvil cloud may separate and blow off with the high-level winds, while below, light rain falls out of a disappearing cloud. The entire cycle of growth, maturity, and decay may take one to three hours, and by the fourth hour there may be no visible remnants of a once mighty storm!

Not all storms run out of steam quite so quickly. If the thunderstorm is on the leading edge of a cold front plowing through a moist air mass, or if there's a steady flow of moisture toward a slow-moving storm, the action can go on for the better part of a day. The key to all these long-lived thunderstorms is organization—updrafts feed fresh vapor into one part of the storm and downdrafts send the spent air somewhere else. With, in effect, no mixing of the fuel intake and the exhaust, the storm efficiently converts moisture into rain and latent-heat-driven, winds.

Sometimes thunderstorms line up like half-backs and march forward into the moist air, scooping up fresh water vapor as they go. The approach of one of these *squall lines* can be an imposing spectacle, with a wall of dark, thundering clouds stretching from horizon to horizon. Squall lines often develop along a cold front, but, like a miniature cold front, the cold air from the downdrafts blows out ahead of the storm, starting new updrafts. New towering cumulus clouds develop on the leading edge and merge with the storm, or a new thunderstorm develops out in front.

PATH OF A THUNDERSTORM—The National Lightning Detection Network, headquartered at the State University of New York in Albany, uses dozens of electronic lightning sensors to locate nearly every lightning strike in the eastern United States. The sensors are essentially directional radio antennas that pick up ground waves from the lightning; a few seconds later, a computer displays the location of the lightning as a colored cross. On this particular day, March 7, 1991, a series of thunderstorms ahead of a cold front tracked from northern Alabama into the Atlantic off of Cape Hatteras.

Richard A. Keen

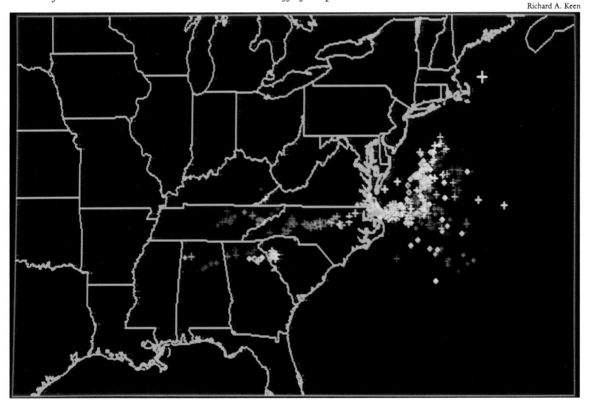

Eventually the squall line separates from the parent front and continues advancing on its own, as long as the moisture supply and other conditions allow.

POPCORN PATTERNS

In the old school of meteorology (say, thirty or forty years ago), there were two basic kinds of thunderstorms: the "scattered afternoon and evening thundershowers" that appear in weather forecasts on muggy summer days, and the more organized ones that develop along cold fronts and squall lines. It's relatively easy to see how cold fronts give moist air masses the initial upward kick they need to get convection going—as mentioned before, just visualize a wedge of cold, heavier air sliding along the ground, physically shoving the warmer air up. It's the scattered storms that raise the difficult questions of where, when, and why they form.

Historically, the scattered type of storms have been called *air mass thunderstorms.* They develop and die, seemingly at random, within a mass of warm, humid air, and the main conditions necessary for their formation are that the air mass be moist enough and unstable enough, and that there be enough sunshine to get a few updrafts going. From space, the cauliflower tops of these storms have been likened to popcorn. Earthbound meteorologists have also noted a resemblance to popcorn in the way air mass thunderstorms *act,* popping up here, then there, with no apparent rhyme or reason. Forecasting the time and place a thunderstorm will develop can often be as tricky (if not impossible) as predicting which kernel of corn will pop next.

One of the principles of science is that few things in nature—not even thunderstorms—are truly random (and therefore unpredictable). Research ventures such as the Thunderstorm Projects in Ohio and Florida in the late 1940s and the Florida Area Cumulus Experiment in the 1970s, along with thousands of years of combined experience of weather forecasters around the world, have uncovered some

of the behavior patterns of these capricious popcorn thunderstorms. Like most meteorological experiments, these projects used closely spaced ground-based weather stations to measure the bottoms of the storms, airplanes to probe their upper reaches, and weather balloons to investigate the regions in between. Perhaps the most revealing, and potentially most useful, device used in thunderstorm research is a recent innovation called Doppler radar.

Radar was developed around the beginning of the Second World War by American and British engineers. The name *radar* stands for *radio detection and ranging*, and in its original application, works by sending out a radio beam and, a thousandth or so of a second later, receiving the echo reflected off a distant ship or airplane. Knowing the brief time elapsed between the signal sent and the echo returned, and that the speed of radio waves is 186,000 miles per second, the distance of the object is readily calculated. Add in the direction of the antenna at that moment, and the object's location is pinpointed. By the end of the war it was found that by using higher radio frequencies (shorter wavelengths), smaller objects such as raindrops and cloud droplets could also be located, and weather radar was born.

Ordinary weather radar measures three things: distance, direction, and strength of the return echo. In general, the stronger the echo, the bigger the raindrops, and the heavier the rainfall. Extremely strong radar signals often mean hail. As the antenna scans the horizon, the continuous readouts of echo strength versus distance add up to produce a map of rainfall patterns within the 100- to 200-mile range of the system. Weather radar is great for locating thunderstorms, but it really isn't very useful for predicting where and when new storms will develop. After all, any storm producing enough rain to be detected by radar has already been around for a while.

Along with distance, direction, and echo strength, Doppler radar throws in another measurement: the *motion* of the raindrops. The motion is detected from slight changes in the frequency of the radio waves bounced back to the antenna—higher frequencies mean the drops are moving toward the radar, and vice versa. By the way, Christian Doppler was an Austrian physicist who described the similar frequency (pitch) changes in sound waves coming from moving objects (like trains). Doppler radar actually measures only the speed along the line-of-sight, that is, toward or away from the antenna, but even so, it tells a lot about the winds within a thunderstorm. With more sensitive electronics, Doppler radar can be made to pick up nearly anything floating in the air, like dust and insects, along with cloud droplets, rain, and hail. (A less sensitive version, used by police, won't pick up anything smaller than an automobile.) Since there's *always* stuff in the air, this refinement means that there doesn't need to be rain or hail for the radar to measure the motion of the air. This gives Doppler radar its greatest use, that of measuring wind patterns inside and outside, and before, during, and after, thunderstorms.

So, then, what causes thunderstorms? The simple idea that solar heating starts most thunderstorms is only partially correct—it is the most common cause of instability. However, something has to launch the initial updraft that becomes a thunderstorm. It turns out that the trigger that determines when and where thunderstorms develop lies within the motions of the atmosphere, and that the same basic motions trigger all storms, be they scattered or squall lines.

The mechanism is quite simple, actually. If a wind from the north meets a wind from the south, air starts to pile up—unless, of course, the excess air goes somewhere else. It can't go down, because the ground's there. Some of it might sneak out to the east or west. Most likely, though, it will go *up*. That, in a nutshell, is how updrafts start. Sometimes winds from all directions converge on a point, but more often it's two currents of air meeting along the line that separates them. The line can be straight, angled, or curved.

POPCORN PATTERNS FROM ABOVE— Thunderstorms build several miles inland, along the leading edge of the sea breeze, while skies above the cool waters of Lake Okeechobee remain clear, in this view of the Florida peninsula from space.

Meteorologists call these lines *convergence lines*, and they're places where thunderstorms are born.

Convergence lines take many forms. It can be one air mass plowing into another, or two air masses butting together like rams. It can be two nearly parallel streams of air merging like traffic at a freeway entrance, or a faster mass of air overtaking a slower one. All you really need is for the wind on one side of the line to blow a bit faster, or slower, or in a different direction than the wind on the other side.

A "BOLT FROM THE BLUE"—Positive lightning flashes across a clear sky, from the positively charged top of the thundercloud to the ground several miles from the storm.

The origins of convergence lines are as varied as their forms. The most obvious example is a cold front, along which winds from the north or west meet winds from the south. Afternoon sea breezes, caused by cool air from the ocean blowing onshore, act very much like little cold fronts when they encounter the hot air over land. Many of Florida's numerous thunderstorms develop along a line several miles inland, right on the leading edge of a sea breeze. There are also *lake breezes* from inland bodies of water, like Lakes Okeechobee (Florida) and Erie, that set off thunderstorms (although over the lakes themselves, there are 20 percent fewer thunderstorms due to the cooler air). At night, *land breezes*—cool air from the continent blowing out to sea—do the same job, especially over the subtropical waters south of Cape Hatteras. Thunderstorms themselves may create little cold fronts as their downdrafts reach the ground and spread out, sometimes triggering new storms. Squall lines form this way, as do occasional enormous clusters of storms that can produce as much rain as a hurricane. Like seedlings sprouting in a fallen tree trunk, it's yet another example in nature of new life springing from the decaying remains of the old.

Whatever their cause, convergence lines can be seen on satellite pictures as strings of cumulus

Richard A. Keen

FAMILY PORTRAIT—Three stages in the life cycles of thunderstorms are evident in this view from a research aircraft above Florida's Big Cypress Swamp. Cumulus clouds dot the lower part of the picture, a towering cumulus has sprouted at right, and in the distance a mature cumulonimbus sports an anvil.

clouds, and they stick out like sore thumbs on Doppler radar. You'll hear a lot about Doppler radar in the next few years, as the National Weather Service begins installing them around the country, replacing the old-style weather radar. Already some television weather forecasters show Doppler radar displays on their evening weather broadcasts, although in a three-minute time slot they have a hard time explaining how it works and what it shows. The idea of seeing only winds blowing toward or away from the radar takes some getting used to, but once you do, you can see thunderstorms, cold fronts, and even tornadoes, sometimes before they form!

KING LEAR'S QUESTION

First let me talk with this philosopher. What is the cause of thunder?

—Lear to Edward,
in Shakespeare's *King Lear*

The Norse had an answer—the mischievous Loki forged bolts and gave them to Thor, who pitched them earthward. When Thor rode his chariot, thunder rumbled across the heavens. However, thunderstorms are about as uncommon in Norway as they are in Maine or Labrador, so perhaps we shouldn't really

65

consider the Vikings the experts. Their explanation was as good as any, though, until Benjamin Franklin performed his legendary lightning experiment in 1752.

We all recall how Franklin flew his kite into an approaching thunderstorm. Contrary to popular belief, though, his kite was *not* struck by lightning; if it had been, Franklin's signature would have never appeared on the Declaration of Independence. The developing storm was generating a lot of static electricity, though, and sent fibers on the kite cord standing on end. Suspecting the presence of electricity, Franklin touched a metal key tied to the end of the cord. His suspicions were brilliantly confirmed.

Two centuries after Franklin's experiment, the source of all this electricity is still a mystery. The National Oceanic and Atmospheric Administration (NOAA), our nation's largest weather research outfit, noted that "no completely acceptable theory explaining the complex processes of thunderstorm electrification has yet been advanced. But it is believed that electrical charge is important to formation of raindrops and ice crystals, and that electrification closely follows precipitation."

In other words, electricity appears to be produced by the freezing of supercooled water droplets. For some reason, when some drops freeze, the ice crystals take on a positive charge, and the remaining droplets become negative. Not only does the ice-crystal anvil formation atop a cumulonimbus portend rain, it also means lightning and thunder. That's why cumulonimbus clouds are more popularly known as thunderclouds.

At this point of freezing, the electrical charges in the cloud separate, with the positive charges gathering near the icy cloud top and the negative charges gathering in the lower parts. Under normal conditions, the ground is also negatively charged. Now, however, the concentration of electrons in the lower cloud repels the negative ground charge (like charges repel; opposites attract), leaving a positively charged ground for several miles around the cloud base.

As the charges gather, voltages build up to as high as 100 million volts within the cloud and between cloud and ground. Air is a terrible conductor, meaning that it is fairly effective at holding electrical charges apart. In clouds, air can separate voltages at the rate of 3,000 volts per foot, or 15 million volts per mile. However, enough is enough, and when a thundercloud's 100 million volts show up, something has to give.

Sparks fly when the cloud voltage reaches the breaking point, but their flight is not a direct one. One hundred feet at a time, a *leader stroke* makes its way downward from the base of the cloud. Too faint to be seen, the leader ionizes the air along its path, meaning that this air can now conduct electricity. It pauses for a few millionths of a second, then jumps another 100 feet. After a hundredth of a second, the leader stroke arrives within a few hundred feet of the ground. At this point, similar leader strokes stream upward from hilltops, trees, antennas, golfers, and the like to join the downward leader. This meeting completes an electrical circuit between the cloud and the ground.

With the cloud and ground connected with a conducting "wire" of air, the electrical charges go into action. A *return stroke* shoots up the leader path at one-sixth the speed of light. Sometimes, return strokes will follow each of the branching leader channels up from the ground, to join several hundred feet up into a single massive stroke. The intense electrical currents, concentrated in a path a few inches across, heats the air almost instantaneously to tens of thousands of degrees—several times as hot as the surface of the sun! We see this glowing channel of hot air as the familiar and spectacular flash of lightning.

The return stroke doesn't last long; in less than .00005 seconds, it's over. If there's still some electrical charge left in the cloud, another leader stroke may head down the path of ionized air left over from the first stroke. When it reaches the ground, another powerful return stroke heads back up the channel. Every .05 seconds or so, this cycle will repeat itself until the cloud is discharged. There's often enough electricity to make two or three separate strokes. Sometimes there's ten or more, giving some lightning a flickering appearance. Properly speaking, these repeated strokes are called *flashes* of lightning. The popular term "bolt" is not precisely defined and is considered colloquial by meteorologists.

This sudden heating literally explodes the air all along the length of the flash, and we hear the detonation as thunder. Thunder can usually be heard 8 or 10 miles away from the lightning that produced it, but there are some reports of the sound being heard 20, 30, and even 70 miles away. You can measure the distance of lightning by counting the seconds until you hear the thunder. The boom of thunder travels at the speed of sound, one-fifth of a mile per second, so by dividing the elapsed time by five you'll get the distance in miles. Next time your ears are rattled by a thunderbolt, just remember that less than one percent of the lightning's energy goes into making noise.

Lightning that zaps from cloud to ground is called, with the usual scientific honesty, a *cloud-to-ground flash*. Lightning also jumps between differently charged regions within a cloud, such as from the lower regions to the icy top. This *inside cloud lightning* is actually about ten times as frequent as the cloud-to-ground variety. Lightning connecting differently charged parts of *different* clouds is called, as you might expect, *cloud-to-cloud*. You don't necessarily need a cloud to have an electrical charge, so there's yet another kind of lightning—*cloud-to-air*—where the electricity leaps out of a cloud into thin air. There is a popular conception that *heat lightning* is a special form of lightning, but it really isn't—those diffuse flashes in the sky are no more than the reflection by clouds and air of ordinary lightning too distant to be seen directly.

Kevin Alexander

CLOUD-TO-GROUND LIGHTNING—
Lightning rakes the Boston skyline.

These four types of lightning are well known to meteorologists, and each even has its own abbreviated code name for transcribing onto weather reports. Recently, yet another kind of lightning has been documented, and it may be the nastiest kind of all. Recall that cloud-to-ground flashes go from a negatively charged cloud base to the positively charged ground directly underneath. However, several miles away from the storm, the ground is *negatively* charged. This sets the stage for cloud-to-ground lightning to jump from the positively charged cloud top to the negative ground. Since they discharge the positive region of the cloud, these flashes are often called *positive flashes*.

67

NOAA

THUNDERSTORM FREQUENCY—Number of days per year with thunderstorms.

Positive lightning flashes are not just your usual negative flashes going the opposite direction. For one, the distances they traverse can be enormous. From a 40,000-foot cloud top to the ground 5 or more miles from the storm, a single flash may extend 10 or even 20 miles—five times the length of a typical negative flash. Fortunately, only one strike in thirty is one of these high-energy positive flashes. Positive flashes are often among the last thrown off by an about-to-die storm. They seem to prefer wintertime thunderstorms—perhaps because the positively charged icy parts of the cloud are closer to the ground.

There is a treacherous quality to these posi-tive flashes. Coming from a storm miles away, they may appear to strike out of a clear sky. I once saw one of these flashes come from a storm that was passing several miles to the south. The lightning left the storm, passed across blue sky directly overhead, and connected to a ridge off to the north. There are doubtlessly some unfortunate souls who take the proper precautions during a thunderstorm, only to be struck by a "bolt from the blue" as the storm moved on and the sun was shining.

There's an old adage that "lightning never strikes the same place twice." I can assure you that this is not so, having once been in a truck that was struck three times in five minutes, and on another occasion watched a utility pole endure three strikes in twenty seconds. In neither case was there any damage! These six strikes illustrate how much lightning there actually is. A lightning detection system covering the United States has been picking up forty million cloud-to-ground strikes per year, or about thirteen every square mile. In Florida's "lightning alley" the rate exceeds thirty per square mile, with similar rates found over the Gulf Stream 200 miles east of Myrtle Beach, South Carolina. New York City's Empire State Building is often struck ten or more times in a single storm, a fact meteorologists have taken advantage of by equipping the building with devices to measure the varying electrical currents in a lightning strike. With that much lightning to go around, some is bound to find a target that's been struck before. If there's any truth to the adage, it's because some targets just aren't there after the first strike.

It's easy to describe the power of lightning with some very large numbers. The *instantaneous* peak rate of energy usage may exceed a trillion watts, equivalent to the *average* consumption rate of the entire United States. But lightning strokes are in-credibly brief, ranging from millionths to thou-sandths of a second long, and the *total* electrical energy expended by an average lightning flash is several hundred kilowatt hours. It depends on where

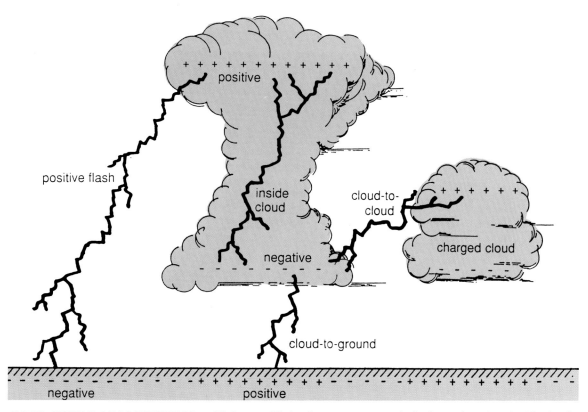

FOUR KINDS OF LIGHTNING—All forms of lightning connect oppositely charged regions inside clouds or on the ground.

you get your electricity, but from where I get mine, an average flash would cost about fifty dollars

It is a bit more meaningful to measure the power of lightning in terms of what it does to its targets. Perhaps the most impressive and lasting monuments to lightning are glassy masses of melted and solidified sand called *fulgerites*. Fulgerites, which may be several inches across and 20 to 40 feet long, often mark the path of electricity as it skims along the ground. Their total weight can run up to several hundred pounds. Sand melts at 3,100 degrees; now consider the energy it takes to heat 200 pounds of

sand to that temperature, all in a fraction of a second!

It is no wonder that lightning is one of the world's deadliest weather phenomena. Over the past thirty years, lightning has killed an average of one hundred Americans every year, nearly as many as tornadoes and hurricanes combined, and injured 250 more. One of every ten lightning casualties is in Florida, due to the combination of frequent thunderstorms and year-round outdoor activities. Meanwhile, only one Vermonter is struck each year, on the average.

69

A total of 10,535 Americans were struck by lightning between 1959 and 1988. That's the population of a small city, like Ocean City, New Jersey. However, when you take into account the population of the United States (250 million) and our average life span (seventy-five years or so), your odds of being struck by lightning sometime in your life are one in 9,492 (approximately). To those who like numbers, this fact puts meaning behind the proverbial "about as likely as getting hit by lightning." The statistics—and proverbs—may mean something completely different to Roy Sullivan, a park ranger in Virginia. Between 1942 and 1977, he was struck seven times, with varying degrees of injury.

Many of those killed and injured by lightning were engaged in outdoor activities, such as boating, golfing, and baseball. Hikers on peaks and ridges are particularly vulnerable; atop a mountain, a climber may be the most tempting lightning target. However, even some indoor activities can be dangerous during a thunderstorm—people talking on the telephone have died in mid-conversation when a nearby strike came "over the wires." Lightning is beautiful and spectacular, but it also deserves a great deal of respect.

LIGHTNING'S GREATEST HITS

June 10, 1752—Benjamin Franklin found out what lightning is made of: electricity.

July 5, 1900—Newark Bay turned to flame when lightning lit the Standard Oil refinery at Bayonne, New Jersey. Oil spilling into the bay fueled the fire for three days.

July 10, 1926—"The most damaging lightning strike on record" struck an ammunition magazine at the U.S. Naval Depot at Lake Denmark, New Jersey, igniting a fireball that leveled a square mile. Damage totaled seventy million dollars, 16 people died, and debris fell 22 miles away.

July 1, 1933—More oil went up in smoke as lightning struck the Texas Oil Company at Elizabeth, New Jersey.

December 8, 1963—Lightning from a winter storm struck a Philadelphia-bound jetliner near Elkton, Maryland, apparently igniting fuel vapors in an empty wing tank. The wing blew off, and all eighty-one people aboard died in the crash.

December 24, 1966—Six hours of thunder and lightning started several minor house fires in southeastern Pennsylvania. There's nothing particularly unusual about lightning-lit fires, but these Christmas Eve thunderstorms accompanied a near-blizzard that buried the same area under 20 inches of snow.

November 14, 1969—Just forty-three seconds into its flight to the moon, *Apollo 12* literally lost its bearings when a lightning strike knocked out its electronic guidance system. Mission control briefly considered aborting the flight, but decided on a "go." The crew continued on to the second successful moon landing.

July 13, 1977—An evening lightning strike on a major power line plunged New York City into a darkness that lasted until dawn. Damage due directly to the lightning strike was minor, but the night of looting that followed cost nearly a billion dollars.

October 2, 1981—Lightning blasted out a crater in a city street in Prospect, Connecticut, then apparently continued along a water main into nearby buildings, damaging plumbing.

March 26, 1987—Once again, lightning struck a space-bound rocket and disabled its guidance system. An unmanned *Atlas* rocket and its exhaust plume acted as an enormous lightning rod, triggering a lightning discharge from a developing storm. The uncontrollable rocket had to be blown up by ground control.

VIOLENCE IN THE SKIES

Fierce fiery warriors fight upon the clouds,
in ranks and squadrons and right form of war.

> —Calpurnia to Caesar,
> in Shakespeare's *Julius Caesar*

Caesar's wife saw thunderstorms as omens of his impending death. We see thunderstorms as welcome bringers of rain and relief from summer heat. That relief is not always benign, and the ominous dark clouds of an approaching thunderstorm may still presage destruction and even death.

HAIL AND HIGH WATER

Thunder and lightning aren't the only mischief thunderstorms can make. Thunderstorms can also be prodigious rainmakers, and when too much rain falls too fast in too small a place, the result is a flash flood. Lightning is quick and tornadoes are awesome, but no weather-related disaster kills more North Americans than flash floods.

The first requirement for a thunderstorm to make a flood is the obvious one—that it produce an exceptional amount of rain. However, this is not enough. Most thunderstorms move along at a

sprightly 10 to 40 miles an hour, which means the storms last half an hour or so at any one place. Flash flood storms, on the other hand, stand still for hours. Tremendous amounts of rain can dump on one valley, while the next valley—within earshot and hearing thunder throughout—gets a sprinkle.

Why do a select few thunderstorms stand still while most of their peers move? The motion of thunderstorms is not a simple process. To some extent, it is controlled by the upper-level winds, which continually nudge along the top portions of thunderclouds. Thunderstorms may also move because they're growing faster on one side than on the other, and the cloud mass shifts in that direction. Squall lines do much the same thing—cold downdrafts spreading out at the base of the storm give moist air an upward shove, and new cumulus towers build on the leading edge of the thundercloud. The growing cumulus towers tap fresh supplies of water vapor, keeping the thunderstorm alive.

It may seem contradictory to have a stationary thunderstorm produce lots of rain, since cold air collecting at the base of the storm should cut off its moisture supply. But, what if a squall line tries to move, say, eastward into the face of an east wind? If the speeds match, the squall line stands still and easterly winds feed fresh, moist air into the squall's hungry jaws.

Thunderstorms are more likely to stay put if there's a mountain nearby, since sloping terrain encourages a storm's growth by forcing moist wind upward. That's why many of the East's heaviest rainstorms are in the mountains. The problem is compounded by the channeling of the runoff down narrow valleys—right where most of the population in these mountainous areas live. Of course, you don't need a mountain to make a flash flood. In flat places like Florida and New Jersey, a stationary front can do the job just as well. However, the rain water is likely to remain more spread out, and less life-threatening, when it falls on the flatlands.

Not all of the water falls as rain. Two chapters ago we saw how strong updrafts can blow raindrops back into the frozen parts of the cloud. These frozen drops grow into hail. There's not much more to say about hail here, except that the stronger the updraft, the bigger the hailstones can grow. Strong updrafts also feed water vapor into the cloud at a faster rate, stepping up the production of raindrops. So, hail and high water very often go together.

GUST FRONTS

At its peak of vigor, a healthy thunderstorm has both updrafts and downdrafts. Each has its role: Upward currents lift moist air to the condensation level, and downward currents carry the load of rain and hail earthward. The core of the downdraft may be

DOWNBURST DANGER TO AIRCRAFT—Air currents spread as a strong downdraft reaches the ground causing rapidly changing winds that can prove fatal to unwary aviators.

NCAR/NSF

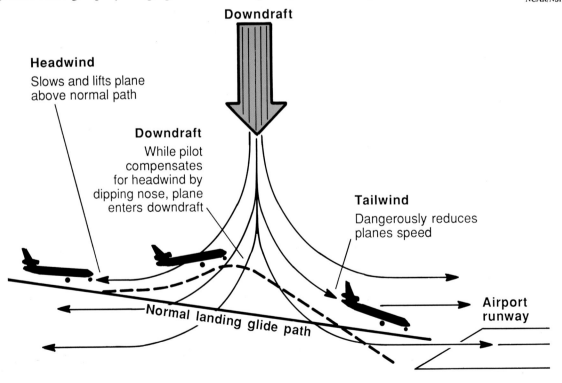

Downdraft

Headwind
Slows and lifts plane above normal path

Downdraft
While pilot compensates for headwind by dipping nose, plane enters downdraft

Tailwind
Dangerously reduces planes speed

Normal landing glide path

Airport runway

James Vavrek

GUST FRONT—The overhead passage of a smooth shelf cloud (left), followed by a turbulent-looking cloud base (right), marks the arrival of a gust front, accompanied by sudden, gusty winds and falling temperatures.

several miles wide, but as it approaches the ground it has no choice but to spread out horizontally. The leading edge of the expanding outflow of cold air is known as a *gust front*, which may spread over an area 10 or 20 miles wide.

Gust fronts are often more than breezes; they've flattened trees and buildings, sunk boats, and sent cars off the road with their 100-mile-per-hour winds. They have broken up human works, from picnics to airplanes. Sometimes they spawn small whirlwinds strong enough to be called tornadoes.

The passage of a gust front is marked by a sudden rush of wind and a drop in the temperature, often by 10 or 20 degrees in as many minutes. If the ground is dry and dusty, the gust front may actually become visible as a 1,000-foot-high, dust-laden wall

73

of air. Dusty gust fronts are known as *haboobs*, a word which, all jokes aside, comes from the Sudan, where such things are commonplace. They're not real common in the East. In moister climates, ragged bands of low clouds may form along the gust front. Sometimes these low cloud bands form in layers, and sometimes they rotate like a log rolling on the ground; their respective names are *shelf* and *roll clouds*.

To meteorologists, any difference of wind speed or direction between two places is called a *wind shear*. Usually it's nothing to worry about, but in recent years the sharp wind shears along gust fronts have crashed a mounting number of airplanes, in some cases killing one hundred or more people. Such tragedies have led to several research projects, such as JAWS (Joint Airport Weather Study) and CLAWS (Classify and Locate Airport Wind Shear), aimed at improved detection of these deadly winds.

DOWNBURSTS

Using such sophisticated equipment as Doppler radar, which can measure wind speeds throughout the interior of a storm, along with more basic techniques such as observers in the field with binoculars and cameras, researchers have discovered a diminutive downdraft that may cause the most dangerous wind shears. The narrow streams of air are less than a mile across and may only span 100 yards or so. As the stream hits the ground, its 50-mile-per-hour downdrafts may turn into spreading winds of 100 mph or more, sort of like water from a faucet splattering into the sink. The sudden, nearly explosive, winds that result have earned these intense downdrafts the name *downbursts*.

Strong downbursts have felled trees in radial patterns, with all the lumber pointing away from the center; sometimes the damage area is only a few hundred feet across! Lawn chairs have been sent flying, while outside the downburst, picnickers watch in disbelief. Sometimes downbursts are visible as expanding rings of dust picked up by the winds.

Look fast, though—the typical downburst lasts but two or three minutes.

The brief but high winds of a downburst can down trees and houses, but their greatest havoc is wreaked upon aircraft. Airplanes are kept in flight by the lift of the air flowing over their wings; the faster the airspeed over the wings, the greater the lift. *Airspeed* is the speed across the wings, and is the combination of the plane's ground speed plus the speed of a headwind (or minus the speed of a tailwind). Every plane has a specific airspeed, called the *stall speed*, below which there's not enough lift to keep the plane flying.

Airplanes are most susceptible to downbursts right after takeoff or just before landing. At these times airplanes are closest to the ground, where the strongest downburst winds occur. It is also when planes are flying the slowest and may be barely above the stall speed. Encountering a downburst, a jetliner may see a 30-mile-per-hour headwind change to a 30-mile-per-hour tailwind in ten seconds. If the sudden loss of lift occurs at too low an altitude, the plane has no chance to recover. In 1975, a jetliner with 124 people aboard was downed by a downburst while trying to land at Kennedy International in New York City; there were only twelve survivors. Downbursts have contributed to two takeoff disasters, one in New Orleans in 1982 and one in Dallas three years later. There have been numerous other incidents of jetliner crashes and near-crashes in the East (including a near-miss involving *Air Force One* and President Ronald Reagan in 1983), but, fortunately, without any deaths.

Downdrafts in thunderstorms are usually accompanied by brief heavy rain. Pilots know this and avoid flying through rain showers. Usually doesn't mean always, however, and some of the strongest bursts have happened on hot, dry, and rainless days. These dry downbursts are often visible only by the dust they raise. Although they're dry when they reach the ground, these downbursts begin as rain showers,

Storm Data

TORNADO OUTBREAK—The paths of forty-three tornadoes that ravaged Ontario, New York, Pennsylvania, and Ohio during the massive outbreak of May 31, 1985, are shown on this map, numbered in order of touchdown. The notations F1, F2, etc., next to each of the paths indicates the strength of the tornado on the Fujita scale, described in appendix 3 at the end of this book.

but the rain never reaches the ground. As the rain-laden downdraft drops below the cloud, raindrops start evaporating. Cooled by the evaporation, the downdraft air becomes heavier and falls faster—the

exact opposite of condensation in convective updrafts.

Most people have probably seen downbursts in the making in the form of thin, dark streamers of rain dropping from a cloud. If the shaft of rain disappears before reaching the ground, it's called *virga,* and beneath it there's probably a stiff downdraft. If the cloud doesn't make a lot of rain, the downburst may fall as a bubble of cool air; when it hits the ground and splats like a water balloon, its winds might last only seconds.

Downbursts are small, brief, and scattered. Some fall from thunderstorms, but others come out of the most inoffensive-looking cumulus clouds. This makes them difficult to detect while they're happening and virtually impossible to predict even minutes in advance. Fortunately, there are downburst detection devices currently under development that should make landing and taking off a bit safer in the not-too-distant future.

There is one practical step you frequent flyers can take to reduce your odds of being ruined by a downburst. Downbursts nearly always descend from cumulus and cumulonimbus clouds, and are most likely at the same times thunderstorms are most likely—afternoon and evening. The moral is: Fly early!

TORNADOES
Big whirls have little whirls that feed on their velocity and little whirls have lesser whirls. . . .

—L. F. Richardson, meteorologist

Richardson's Rhyme, as this little ditty is called, is well known in the weather business, because it so succinctly sums up (as only poetry can!) how the atmosphere works. The message is particularly true for *tornadoes.* Spun from rotating thunderstorms embedded in the turning winds of cyclones, tornadoes themselves may spin off lesser whirls a few feet across.

The concentrated motion—and power—in tornadoes make them a very special form of weather. Nowhere else does the atmosphere show its stuff in a more visual and dramatic style. Folks who would otherwise never look up at a cloud will take note of a tornado. When they strike, it's news. But's let's

make it clear right here: Few people will ever see a tornado, and fewer still will be injured by one.

Like downbursts, tornadoes have powerful winds. However, in tornadoes, most of the air is going up! Tornadoes are picky, too, and happen only when there's a very special set of weather conditions. First, the air has to be moist enough to feed a growing thunderstorm. Next, the atmosphere has to be highly unstable to get some extremely strong updrafts going. It also helps to have a strong jet stream aloft—most tornado-producing thunderstorms are movers. Finally, the tornado needs to get its spin from somewhere, so the lowest layers of air must already be turning. If the jet stream is blowing in a different direction than the winds lower down, the shifting currents can give some extra spin to the growing thunderstorm.

Meteorologically speaking, the favorite haunts for tornadoes are the warm sectors of strong cyclones, where all the above ingredients are found to one degree or another. Hurricanes have no shortage of moisture, instability, and rotation, and have been known to unleash tornadoes—thirty-four along the Atlantic seaboard during Hurricane David in 1979, and as many as 115 in one Texas storm. Even isolated thunderstorms can whip up a tornado, if the air currents are just right enough to get a little spin going.

When a thunderstorm develops in these unusual conditions, the powerful updrafts draw in the slowly rotating air. This concentrates the spinning motion, like water swirling faster as it approaches a drain. As the updraft strengthens, the spinning speeds up, until the updraft becomes a narrow, rotating column—a tornado.

In exceptional cases, the whole thunderstorm cell may start rotating, becoming a parent cloud that may spawn tornadoes every few minutes for an hour or more. These awesome *supercell thunderstorms* ravage the Midwest many times every year. Supercells are less frequent east of the Appala-

76

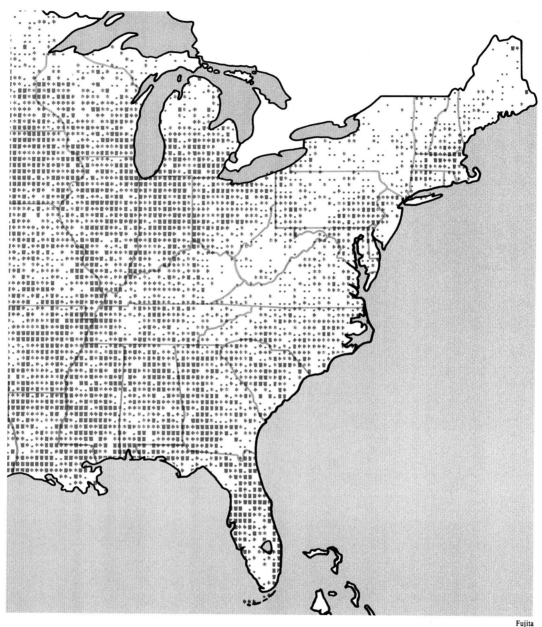

TORNADOES IN THE EAST—This map, produced by Theodore Fujita of the University of Chicago, locates every tornado known to have touched down in the eastern United States over a sixty-six-year period. Note that tornadoes tend to avoid the Appalachian Mountains and prefer open, flat terrain, like the Ohio Valley, the coastal plains from Mississippi to North Carolina, and Florida. There are even small "tornado alleys" in eastern Pennsylvania and eastern Massachusetts.

chians, but several times a year they're seen somewhere along the Atlantic seaboard—often with tornadoes. Once or twice a decade, a springtime cyclone heading east from the Rockies spawns supercells and tornadoes by the dozen on its march to the sea. The ensuing atmospheric reign of terror may spread devastation across several states and leave hundreds dead and thousands injured.

Tornadoes come in many sizes, shapes, and strengths. The largest can be a mile or more across with 300-mile-per-hour winds, and may scour the land along a 50- to 250-mile path before dissipating. Fortunately, these mile-wide monsters are rare in the East, but they are not unknown. One plowed through Worcester, Massachusetts, in 1953. In 1984, an unbelievable (but true!) 2.5-mile-wide funnel passed near Laurinburg, North Carolina. At the other extreme,

tiny twisters may touch down for a few seconds, damaging a single tree or part of a roof before disappearing. I saw one leave a neat and narrow 30-foot wide path in a cornfield, and another with winds barely strong enough to pick up cardboard boxes (although it sent newspapers spiralling thousands of feet up into the base of the thunderstorm!). The typical tornado, based on nationwide statistics, has winds of 150 mph swirling around a 700-foot-wide funnel, and moves at 40 mph over a 5-mile-long path during its five- or ten-minute lifetime. Like the 1.9-child family, though, this "typical" tornado is actually the rarest of them all.

The appearance of a tornado can vary as much as its size, ranging from fat cylinders to thin, coiling ropes. The famous funnel cloud comes from the condensation of water vapor inside the rotating

TORNADOES THAT GLOW IN THE DARK—These twin tornado funnels ripped through Toledo, Ohio, during the Palm Sunday tornado outbreak in 1965. In this nighttime photograph, the dimly glowing tornadoes were apparently illuminated by electrical discharges within the funnels.

James R. Weyer

Paul L. Hexter, Jr.

DOUBLE TROUBLE—Two huge funnel clouds over Chesapeake Bay threaten Calvert County, Maryland, on September 3, 1961. A much smaller funnel appears at the lower left (arrow). None of the funnels reached the ground.

Joseph H. Golden

FAIR-WEATHER WATERSPOUT—A long, stringy waterspout stretches thousands of feet from a cumulus cloud to the warm waters near the Florida Keys. Although the skies are obviously cloudy and rain is falling in the background, these "fair weather" waterspouts are so named because it doesn't take much of a cloud to make one.

Bernard Ginaitt

TORNADIC WATERSPOUT—This enormous waterspout churned the chilly waters of Narragansett Bay near Warwick, Rhode Island, on July 3, 1986. Unlike the fair-weather variety, this waterspout was a true tornado that happened to touch down over water. It stayed about a mile from shore during its ten-minute lifetime, and did no damage.

column, where the pressure and temperature are lower. When the funnel cloud fails to touch the ground, the odds are that the rotating tube of air doesn't go all the way down either, or if it does, its winds are very weak. Powerful tornadoes often look like ice cream cones, and in extreme storms the base of the thundercloud itself may appear to simply dip to the ground. Miniature, snake-like whirlwinds, a few feet across and lasting only seconds, might be seen along the fringes of the main funnel. Often the funnel is surrounded by rain, and not visible at all. The classic *Wizard of Oz* elephant trunk funnels are photogenic and popular in weather books, but they're not all that common, especially in the East.

The unique weather conditions of central North America make our continent the most tornado-prone in the world. Three-fourths of the world's twisters touch down in the United States, making the tornado as American as the hot dog and apple pie. Canada hosts another 5 percent of the global total (including five or ten that crossed the border from the States), leaving only one tornado in five for the rest of the world. Of the eight hundred tornadoes that touch down in the United States and Canada during an average year, about 120 of them hit the seaboard states from Florida to Maine. For comparison, the entire continent of Australia reports an annual average of fourteen tornadoes, Japan has eleven twisters per year, and Italy, New Zealand, and Great Britain each see twenty-five or so in an average year.

Some locales in North America are more susceptible to tornadoes than others. The world's greatest "tornado alley" stretches across the prairies from Texas to Iowa, with eastward extensions into Ohio and extreme southern Ontario, and across the Gulf states to Georgia. The heart of tornado alley lies in central Oklahoma, where there are more tornadoes per acre than any other place on Earth.

The whole expanse of tornado alley is characterized by flat, open terrain where storms can concentrate their spin undisturbed by mountains. The area is also frequented by moist, unstable air masses from the Gulf of Mexico and by strong cyclones tracking east from the Rocky Mountains. In short, all the ingredients are there, like nowhere else on Earth.

To a lesser extent, the same conditions prevail along the Atlantic coastal plain. The open spaces aren't quite as wide, and the air is usually not quite as unstable as in the Midwest, so the tornadoes are less frequent and tend to be weaker. Localized tornado alleys along the eastern seaboard appear over the central Carolinas, southeastern Pennsylvania, and southern New England. The Florida peninsula is another busy place. The Sunshine State is second only to Oklahoma in sheer numbers of tornadoes, but most of these are of the short-lived and weak variety associated with isolated thundershowers. If you eliminate these weak little twisters, Florida drops out of tornado alley almost entirely.

Tornadoes can happen any time of year, although April and May are the peak months nationwide. Early in the year, most of the action is along the Gulf Coast, but as spring marches north, so do the tracks of cyclones and tornadoes. The tornado belt reaches the northern plains states, southern prairie provinces, and New England by July, and after August heads back south for the winter.

The smaller and briefer a weather phenomenon is, the harder it is to predict. The problem is multiplied with tornadoes because of their lethal nature.

In his book *Tornadoes*, John Finley gave the following assessment of the tornado forecasts issued by the U.S. Army Signal Corps: "Tornado prediction is no longer a mere possibility, but in many respects may be considered an accomplished fact. By this I do not mean absolute perfection, but reasonable success." These words were written in 1887, but despite vast advances in our understanding of tornadoes and their causes, they could have been written yesterday.

Over the century since Finley issued his first warnings, forecasters have improved their skills at recognizing the proper conditions—moisture, instability, and so on—in which tornadoes are likely to break out. When these conditions occur, the National Weather Service issues a Tornado Watch stating that tornadoes are possible in an area 100 or so miles across sometime during the next few hours. Until recently, however, they couldn't issue a Tornado Warning, meaning a twister *will* strike a certain place at a certain time (in other words, duck!), until someone had actually seen the funnel cloud or the tornado had already touched down. In the 1990s, the latest in meteorological technology, Doppler radar, will become operational across the United States. By virtue of its ability to sense wind motions in the atmosphere, and in particular little swirls that may become tornadoes, Doppler radar may provide up to twenty minutes advance notice of developing twisters. Twenty minutes is not a whole lot of time, considering it takes five or ten minutes just to get the warning out to the public, where it will do some good. However, the remaining ten minutes is still sufficient time to get a school full of children into the basement or hallways.

WATERSPOUTS

Waterspouts are often described as tornadoes over water. True, both are rotating tubes of updraft air extending from the ground (or body of water) into the clouds, and both usually have visible funnel clouds of condensed moisture inside the tube (waterspouts are *not* solid columns of water!). It's also true that many waterspouts originate as tornadoes that move offshore, or become tornadoes when they reach land, or stay over water but are otherwise identical to their land-lubbing cousins. These have been dubbed, in the usual straightforward manner, *tornadic waterspouts.*

Tornadic waterspouts have been spotted just about wherever there's water. They've churned the waters of the Gulf of Mexico, Lake Erie, Chesapeake and Narragansett bays and even the Hudson and Ohio rivers. Recent studies of Atlantic storms hint at the possibility of tornadoes, and possibly lots of them, in wintertime supercell thunderstorms over the Gulf Stream, 200 miles off the Carolina Capes. Of course, actual sightings are sketchy at best from the high seas, but you mariners may wish to keep a lookout.

The large majority of waterspouts, though, are not tornadic. These "fair weather" waterspouts are smaller and weaker than typical tornadoes, and form under different conditions. The air over the ocean is often more humid than over land, but since the sea surface doesn't heat up as quickly during the day as does the land, it doesn't get quite as unstable. Therefore, outside of unusual places like the Gulf Stream in winter, supercell thunderstorms are probably not very common over the ocean. As a matter of fact, most waterspouts don't even form under thunderstorms—very often the cloud above never gets to be more than a billowy towering cumulus. Because the sea is so smooth, it may not take much of a swirl in the atmosphere to form a waterspout, but because the original swirl is so weak, so is the result.

Waterspouts are quite rare over the chilly coastal waters north of Cape Hatteras. They're a lot more common farther south, where the water is warmer and the air moister. Down in the Florida Keys they're almost a weekly occurrence, especially in the summer. It may be that the winds blowing around and between the islands generate the whirls in the atmosphere that become waterspouts, and it's likely that waterspouts are more common near islands than they are over open water.

THE BIG BOOMERS

May 4, 1761—A huge tornado became a 1,000-foot-wide waterspout when it crossed the Ashley River at Charleston, South Carolina, where it sank five British warships. The spout reportedly exposed the muddy river bottom.

Joseph H. Golden

SPIRAL WATERSPOUT—The spiral pattern of wind-ruffled water clearly shows the motion of air into the lower parts of this giant fair-weather waterspout.

February 19, 1884—Sixty or more tornadoes in the warm sector of a low over Illinois struck nine states from Mississippi to Virginia. As many as eight hundred people, most in rural areas, died in the onslaught. The disaster led to the first experimental tornado warnings issued by the Army Signal Service (forerunner to the National Weather Service).

August 19, 1896—The famous Vineyard Sound Waterspout churned the water between Martha's Vineyard and the Massachusetts mainland for eighteen minutes, long enough to allow precise measurements of its size—3,600 feet high to the cloud base, 240 feet wide at the bottom, 144 feet in the middle, and 840 feet at the top. Ocean spray was raised to 420 feet. The spectacle was the highlight of the summer for many vacationers.

April 4, 1902—A 40-foot-wide waterspout off Cape Hatteras struck the SS *Hestia*. According to the captain, a "deafening roar was quickly followed by strong gusts of wind and a sudden shock as the spout struck amidships and passed over the deck toward the stern." Tarps and planks were thrown into the air and a deck rope did "an Indian snake dance," but besides "a temporary feeling of apprehension," no harm was done.

April 5–6, 1936—Two of the most lethal individual tornadoes in history struck less than twelve hours apart. The first left 216 dead in Tupelo, Mississippi, on the evening of the 5th, while the second killed 203 in Gainesville, Georgia, the next morning.

June 17, 1946—Ignoring customs, a Michigan tornado crossed from Detroit into Windsor, Ontario, where it killed fifteen residents (making it one of eastern Canada's deadliest tornadoes). Ten days later another tornado crossed the border the other way—from Windsor to Detroit!

June 7–9, 1953—During its three-day rampage across the country, a cold front triggered forty-five or more tornadoes from Nebraska to New Hampshire. On the eighth, 116 people died in a tornado in Flint, Michigan, and the next day a mile-wide funnel devastated Worcester, Massachusetts, killing ninety.

January 30, 1954—Not all tornadoes occur in "tornado alley" during "tornado season." One of the most out-of-place, out-of-season twisters ever reported touched down at White Point Beach, Nova Scotia, in the middle of winter.

April 11, 1965—Palm Sunday was anything but peaceful as thirty-seven tornadoes, including several double funnels, wrecked towns from Iowa to Ohio. In eleven hours, 257 people died and over 3,000 were hurt.

April 4, 1966—Two "coast-to-coast" tornadoes cut parallel paths across the Florida peninsula, from Tampa Bay to Cape Canaveral. The twisters moved at 60 mph along their 140-mile-long tracks.

July 4, 1969—A severe squall line broke up Fourth of July activities all across northern Ohio with some fireworks of its own. Up to 15 inches of rain washed out 292 bridges and thousands of picnics. A ship on Lake Erie registered a sustained wind speed of 100 mph.

April 3–4, 1974—The greatest tornado outbreak of all time raked a thirteen-state area from Mississippi to New York and Ontario. In twenty-four hours, 148 tornadoes killed 315 people and

Melissa L. Pearce

DEADLY SWIRL—This swirling cloud mass is one of the most powerful tornadoes ever to strike the East. Eighteen people died during its rampage from Niles, Ohio, to Wheatland, Pennsylvania, on May 31, 1985.

injured 5,500 others. Most of the tornadoes dipped down from twenty or more long-lived supercell thunderstorms.

June 25, 1975—On its final approach into Kennedy International Airport in New York City, an Eastern Airlines 727 encountered heavy rain and shifting microburst winds. The plane crashed a half-mile short of the runway; of the 124 people aboard, only twelve survived.

July 7, 1976—America's Bicentennial tor - nado passed the Statue of Liberty on its track up the Hudson River toward mid-Manhattan.

July 19–20, 1977—In a classic flash flood situation, a nearly stationary "cold front" of downdraft air from earlier thunderstorms kicked off a nine-hour-long series of new thunderstorms. Held in place by the Appalachians, the overnight storms dumped 12 inches of rain just upstream from Johnstown, Pennsylvania. Eleven dam failures added to the flood that washed through Johnstown and drowned seventy-seven people. In the more famous Johnstown Flood of 1889, heavy rains and another dam failure killed over twenty-two hundred people.

May 6–October 6, 1978—A five-month total of fifty-two tornadoes—forty-six in Ontario alone— made this eastern Canada's busiest twister season ever. Fortunately, none of the tornadoes killed anybody.

September 5–6, 1979—Hurricane David spun off thirty-four tornadoes along its path from Florida to Vermont. Most of the tornado damage was relatively light, but wind damage from the hurricane extended as far north as Maine.

November 20, 1981—A tornado touched down on Concourse B at Atlanta International Airport, tearing an engine off a DC-8 and damaging twenty other jetliners.

August 1, 1983—Just six minutes after President Reagan landed aboard *Air Force One*, a potent downburst raked Andrews Air Force Base, outside of Washington, D.C., damaging two buildings and three airplanes. The peak gust sent the wind gauge off the top of the scale at 150 mph, one of the highest thunderstorm winds ever recorded.

March 28, 1984—A persistent supercell generated twelve tornadoes along a 320-mile swath across the Carolinas. One tornado near Laurinburg, North Carolina, left a damage path 2.5 miles wide.

July 7, 1984—Shifting microburst winds exceeding 70 mph capsized a sternwheeler boat on the Tennessee River near Huntsville, Alabama, drowning eleven of the eighteen passengers on board.

May 31, 1985—Forty-three tornadoes in one afternoon killed eighty-eight people in Ontario, New York, Pennsylvania, and Ohio. The largest of the tornadoes destroyed eighty-eight thousand trees in a 7,500-foot-wide path of total devastation in Pennsylvania's Moshannon State Forest. A tornado outbreak in the same area killed 150 people in June 1944.

June 9, 1989—After touching down in Philadelphia, a tornado crossed the Ben Franklin Bridge into New Jersey (without paying the toll, local wags noted), where it demolished several abandoned homes.

August 18, 1989—Thunderstorms swamped the Delmarva Peninsula of Delaware, Maryland, and Virginia with as much as 20 inches of rain. Nearly one million chickens drowned.

July 5, 1990—Shortly after departing Newark, New Jersey, an Eastern Airlines DC-9 took what one passenger called a "twilight zone" ride into a hailstorm. As coffee cups sailed around the cabin, hailstones dented the wings, fuselage, and jet engines, and removed the nose cone. The plane made a successful emergency landing, and there were no injuries.

HURRICANES

Warmest climes but nurse the cruelest fangs . . .

—Herman Melville, *Moby Dick*

THE GREATEST STORM ON EARTH

To the Indians of the Caribbean, they were known as *Huracan*—the Storm Devil. The Indians of India call them *cyclones*, a word of Greek heritage passed on by the British. In Chinese the name is *typhoon*, meaning "great wind." And Australians, for some peculiar reason, have been heard to call them *willy willies*. We call them *hurricanes*, and in any language they are the Greatest Storm on Earth.

Frightful stories of the hurricane's power and destruction abound in the annals of history. Columbus lost two ships to a hurricane during his second voyage to the New World in 1494. Four and a half centuries later, on December 18, 1944, the U.S. Third Fleet was attacked by a small, but intense, Pacific typhoon named Cobra. In a few hours, the tempest had claimed three destroyers, 146 aircraft, and 790 sailors. It was one of the greatest disasters inflicted on the American Navy during the final year of the war.   Many a survivor of a hurricane at sea will share Shakespeare's account of Casca's stormy premonition of Caesar's death: "I have seen the ambitious ocean swell, and rage, and foam, to be exalted with the threat'ning clouds . . ."

It is when hurricanes leave the sea and come ashore that they unleash their greatest wrath on humanity. A hurricane from the Bay of Bengal drowned three hundred thousand people in 1737. In 1970, another hurricane killed half a million citizens of the then-soon-to-be nation of Bangladesh, and, as recently as 1991, another storm in that country drowned at least 125,000 people. The greatest natural disaster ever to befall the United States was the devastation of Galveston, Texas, by a hurricane in 1900. One-sixth of the city's forty thousand residents perished when the storm pushed the Gulf of Mexico several miles inland. The power of storm waves striking the east coast shores was so great during the New England hurricane of 1938 that seismographs—designed to measure earthquakes—in Alaska detected the rumble of the crashing seas. Hurricanes are truly earth-shaking storms! They are earth movers, too—several times in recent years the coastal charts of Mississippi, North Carolina, New Jersey, and other states have been redrawn as hurricanes created new islands and inlets and erased old ones.

Fortunately, hurricanes are relatively rare. In an average year, only six of them form in the entire Atlantic Ocean, including the Caribbean and Gulf of Mexico. Of these, only one or two are likely to strike the North American mainland. However, for storms so rare, they have a tremendous impact on the climate of the entire coastal region from Texas to Newfoundland. Most areas within 200 miles of the sea receive 10 percent or more of their summer rainfall from hurricanes (or weaker tropical storms). That 10 percent often arrives all at once, and many of the worst floods in the history of the East have been brought on by hurricanes. Even places as far inland as Chicago and Toronto have been deluged by hurricane rains. Hurricane rains have also worked for the benefit of humankind by breaking many a drought.

Although their rains have the largest impact on the climate of the East, and their waves and storm tides cause the most damage, it is the hurricanes' winds that leave the most lasting impressions. Full force hurricane winds have smashed every state and province along the Atlantic and Gulf coasts at some time in the past fifty years, and there are even instances of winds exceeding *twice* hurricane force—an incredible 150 mph. The memories of these events are etched in the minds of their many survivors, and even the landscape recalls the power of the winds. Take a stroll through any eastern woods and the odds are you'll come across a tree felled by a hurricane ten, thirty, or even fifty years ago.

ANATOMY OF A SEA MONSTER

Hurricanes are fundamentally different from the multitude of other storms that darken our skies. They are creatures of the sea. Their breeding grounds are the warm oceans of the tropics, and they grow as long as their travels continue to take them over the tepid seas. Unlike mid-latitude cyclones, which draw their power from the temperature differences across frontal boundaries, hurricanes thrive on undiluted warmth. Warm water feeds tremendous volumes of water vapor into the tropical atmosphere. This moisture-laden air is the fuel that drives hurricanes; without it, the great storms weaken and die. Like many other sea creatures, hurricanes soon expire when they leave the sea and go ashore.

The hurricane season begins in earnest during late summer, when the tropical Atlantic (between 10 and 30 degrees north latitude), including the Gulf of Mexico and the Caribbean, warms to its highest temperatures of the year. Several months of a nearly overhead sun has heated the water to 85 or 90 degrees; at these temperatures water readily evaporates into the overlying atmosphere. The dew point of the tropical atmosphere may rise above 80 degrees, making it even muggier than the muggiest days of the summer in the eastern states. The huge volume of water vapor in tropical air contains a tremendous amount of energy in the form of *latent heat*—heat stored in the molecules of water vapor when they evaporated from the surface of the ocean. When vapor condenses back into liquid water, the latent heat is released back to the air.

The air overlying just 1 square foot of the tropics may hold enough energy as latent heat to drive an automobile 2 miles. Multiply this by tropical oceans covering tens of millions of square miles! In the tropics, latent heat is normally released back into the atmosphere by the same process of convection that gets thunderstorms going. The moist air of the tropics needs to rise only 1,000 or 2,000 feet before condensation creates cumulus clouds. The release of latent heat warms the air, and the clouds grow into towering cumulus and then go on to become cumulonimbus clouds. The cycle of evaporation, rising streams of air, and condensation is the driving force behind hurricanes. Like the ignition of gasoline vapor inside the cylinders of an automobile engine, this is the way hurricanes use their fuel to create motion.

For months, from late summer well into the fall, vast reaches of the tropical atmosphere are ripe

88

DIANA BY MOONLIGHT—Hurricane Diana spins off the North Carolina coast on September 11, 1984. The moonlit eye and spiral cloud bands are clearly visible in this remarkable nighttime satellite image; also visible are the lights of cities and towns from Detroit, Michigan (upper left) to Atlanta, Georgia (lower left). Norfolk, Virginia, is directly north of the hurricane, while Washington, Baltimore, Philadelphia, and New York City appear as bright patches (upper right). Fortunately, Diana's 130 mile-per-hour winds weakened considerably before she came ashore near Wilmington, North Carolina.

NOAA

CROSS SECTION OF A HURRICANE—Moist air spirals into the storm at low levels, then corkscrews upward near the center. The rising currents near the center form enormous rainy clouds that surround that bizarre feature of all hurricanes—the clear eye.

for hurricanes to form. But each year only a few dozen hurricanes are born worldwide. It takes more than hot, muggy air to give birth to a hurricane—something needs to lift the air to its condensation level. Even this lifting is not enough, though, since cumulus clouds are commonplace in the tropics.

Although many cumulus clouds grow into thunderstorms and even huge masses of thunderstorms hundreds of miles across, these thunderstorm masses usually lack the intense, swirling winds of a hurricane. Early in the life of a hurricane, conditions must be just right or the great storm will never develop.

Forecasters at the National Hurricane Center in Miami, along with other hurricane researchers, have found that hurricanes need some sort of "seed" disturbance—a slight swirl in the atmosphere—to get things going on the right track. If the winds near the thunderstorm tops are too strong or blow in a different direction than the low-level winds, the developing thunderstorms will be torn apart as they reach into the upper atmosphere. Hurricanes indeed have difficult childhoods.

Sometimes a twist in the trade winds, a weakening cold front from the north, or even a windy dust storm heading west from the Sahara Desert provides the initial impetus. Whatever its origins, the incipient hurricane starts as a slowly rotating collection of thunderstorms. Warm, moist air from outside the disturbance spirals slowly in, replacing the air that rose upward in the thunderstorms. The Coriolis effect assures that this spiral will, in the Northern Hemisphere, turn counterclockwise. Like an upside-down version of a draining bathtub, the inward flow spirals faster and rises as it approaches the center—similar to a tornado, but on a much grander scale. On their way to the storm center, the winds evaporate more moisture from the ocean surface; this moisture then drives the convection at the core of the spiral. The cycle continues to accelerate until the swirling winds reach gale force (39 mph), and the tempest becomes a *tropical storm*. When the winds reach 74 mph the storm attains hurricane status.

The circular motion in a hurricane is so fast the winds can't go inward any farther, and a calm area—the eye—forms at the center. Although the eye of a hurricane is a mysterious and awesome place to those that find themselves within it (see end of chapter), the calm spot results from the same forces and motions that create the little funnel of air in a draining bathtub.

A fully grown hurricane is a marvel of natural engineering. In a continuous, mechanical cycle it

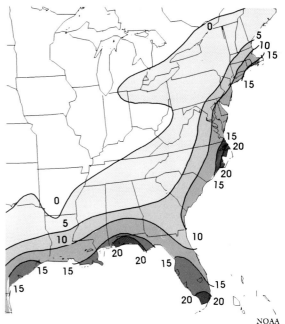

NOAA

HURRICANE THREAT—The number of times that hurricanes caused damage from 1901–1955 gives a good idea of where the hurricane threat is the greatest.

extracts latent heat energy from the ocean, releases the energy in the towering thunderclouds surrounding the eye, and exhausts the spent air—with much of its moisture gone—out the top of the storm. The amount of energy involved in a hurricane is almost beyond comprehension, and renders nuclear weapons feeble by comparison. The heat energy contained in the combined nuclear arsenals of the United States and the Soviet Union would not keep a large hurricane going for one day. Many will recall photographs of the 1946 underwater nuclear explosion in the Pacific, which tested the effects of the blast on captured Japanese warships. That detonation heaved ten million tons of water into the air. A good-size hurricane can evaporate that much water from the ocean in forty seconds.

NASA

HURRICANE ELENA—Hurricane Elena poses for a photograph from the Space Shuttle Discovery on September 1, 1985. At the time, Elena was in the Gulf of Mexico south of Apalachicola, Florida, on her way to landfall near Biloxi, Mississippi.

These tremendous energy releases give hurricanes their purpose in life. In the global atmospheric ecosystem, the prime function of all storms is to equalize the great heat imbalance that builds up between the equator and the poles. At higher latitudes, it is the familiar mid-latitude cyclone that does the job. In the tropics, hurricanes are particularly efficient at moving heat. They extract latent heat from the oceans, convert it to sensible heat, and lift it to the upper atmosphere, from where the heat is blown poleward.

Most hurricanes wither and die when they encounter cold water. Cold water evaporates less readily than warm water and, without the continuous supply of water vapor, hurricanes soon "run out of steam." Some hurricanes are deprived of their needed

Jack "Thunderhead" Corso

HURRICANE GLORIA—Trees bow before Gloria's 92 mile-per-hour gusts as she storms ashore near Bridgeport, Connecticut, on September 27, 1985.

vapor supply when they pass over land, and the effect is the same—they die. When hurricanes die, however, there is always something left over. Remnants may take the form of a mass of moisture-laden air, a slight residual swirl in the upper atmosphere, or both.

Although their winds have subsided, hurricane remnants may still be capable of dropping torrential rains. Many a storm has inflicted far greater damage—through flooding—during its dying stages than it did as a full-fledged hurricane. If what is left of a northbound hurricane encounters a cold (or stationary) front, the rotating remnant may combine with the temperature contrasts along the

front to generate a new storm. The new storm is a mid-latitude cyclone, with its energy coming from the clash of warm and cold air masses, and bears little resemblance to its ancestral tropical hurricane. Sometimes, however, these hurricane-induced cyclones become ferocious North Atlantic storms, on occasion causing heavy damage to such unlikely places as Scotland and Norway.

STORM SEASON

Some parts of the tropics are more amenable to hurricanes than others. There are seven regions around the globe—the northern and southern

Ronald Holle

TROPICAL CUMULUS—Moisture-laden tropical air feeds a growing cumulus cloud of the type that occasionally gather together to become tropical storms or hurricanes.

Indian Ocean, the seas northwest of Australia, the South Pacific, the western and eastern North Pacific Oceans, and the western North Atlantic (including the Caribbean and the Gulf of Mexico)—where tropical cyclones can develop. None has ever formed over the cool waters of the tropical South Atlantic or southeastern Pacific. The western North Pacific Ocean is the busiest region, with one-third of the globe's average of ninety-nine hurricanes and tropical storms per year. Hurricanes (or typhoons, as they're known locally) are an annual threat to the billion-plus residents of China, Korea, Japan, Taiwan, and the Philippines.

Ten or so storms form annually in the North Atlantic, about the same as each of the other "hurricane alleys" (outside of the western North Pacific, of course). Eight of these storms, on the average, form during the "hurricane season" of August, September, and October. In most years an early storm jumps the gun in May, June, or July; and occasionally a late one gets going in November or December. Three times in the past century there's been wintertime tropical storms in February and March, while there's never been a tropical storm born during January or April (although one of the December storms did survive into the following year).

Winter is off-season for several reasons. Most obviously, the ocean is cooler. The Bermuda High, the enormous high pressure system that spans much of the Atlantic, moves south, covering the prime hurricane breeding grounds and keeping thunderstorm development to a minimum. Finally, with the prevailing westerlies and jet stream also moving south, the winds aloft are stronger over the tropics—tearing apart what storms try to develop. These conditions linger into the spring months, but by May and June the oceans begin to warm up and the weather patterns move north for the summer. The northward advance of summer occurs more rapidly over and near the continents than over the high seas, so the fringes of the Atlantic basin—particularly the Caribbean and the

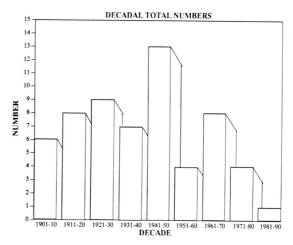

HURRICANES STRIKING FLORIDA TO MISSISSIPPI, DECADAL TOTAL NUMBERS— *Since the 1940s, Florida, Alabama, and Mississippi have seen relatively few hurricanes.*

Gulf of Mexico—become ripe for tropical storms a month or two before the mid-Atlantic does. Many, if not most, years the season's first storm forms in June or July over the Gulf or the western Caribbean. Very often the "seed" for this first storm is a late spring cold front—perhaps the last of the season—that pushes into the tropics and kicks off some thunderstorms. Although losing most of its temperature contrast, the cold front may still retain enough of a wind shift to get a spiral motion going in the atmosphere. It only happens about once a year, on the average, but it gets the season started.

During August the pattern changes dramatically. The Bermuda High shifts north, bringing heat and humidity to the eastern seaboard, while the jet stream across the Atlantic moves up to Greenland and Iceland. With the winds weakening aloft and the water warming at the surface, the mid-Atlantic between Africa and the Caribbean islands becomes the stage for most of the season's hurricanes. Every few days desert windstorms from North Africa move

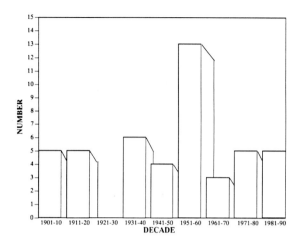

HURRICANES STRIKING GEORGIA TO NEWFOUNDLAND, DECADAL TOTAL NUMBERS— Hurricanes were unusually frequent during the 1950s for the Atlantic coast from Georgia north.

west into the Atlantic, or weak eddies form along the belt of the *doldrums* (where the trade winds of the Northern Hemisphere run into the trade winds from the south). These are the seeds of future tropical storms. Most fizzle out while crossing the ocean, but one in three or four has just the right pattern of winds, and encounters just the right conditions over the open ocean, to begin the tightening spiral toward tropical storm, and possible hurricane, status. These are the infamous *Cape Verde storms,* named after the westernmost bulge of Africa.

While the Caribbean and Gulf of Mexico continue to produce their share of storms, Cape Verde storms form the slight majority during August and September. Tropical storms develop, on the average, every ten days during these months. Averages rarely happen, though—like people, tropical cyclones have "baby booms," with two or three forming in a single week, followed by a couple of quiet weeks, followed by another outbreak. It's not

unusual to see three storms on the weather map at the same time once or twice during the season. Statistically, the season peaks on September 10— over the past century, more hurricanes have been observed on this date than any other.

The pattern changes again at the end of September. The number of Cape Verde storms drops off dramatically, and the center of action shifts back to the Caribbean. October is the busiest month of the year for tropical storms originating over the western Caribbean. Many of these storms form on the doldrum belt as it wanders north from its usual position over Panama into the still tepid waters of the Caribbean. By late October the action drops off everywhere, and the few off-season (November through April) storms that have formed have been scattered all over the tropical Atlantic, Caribbean, and Gulf of Mexico.

HURRICANE ALLEY

While it's interesting to know where hurricanes come from, it's essential to know where they go. From the moment of birth, the movement of hurricanes is guided by the prevailing winds. While still in the tropics (10 to 30 degrees latitude), hurricanes usually move westward with the easterly trade winds. Once north of the 30th parallel, though, the storms encounter the prevailing westerlies of higher latitudes, and tend to turn eastward. The typical path of a well-behaved hurricane is a sweeping arc around the Bermuda High, at first heading west, then turning north, and finally heading northeast toward the cooler waters of the North Atlantic. These guiding winds, called *steering currents,* are not always well behaved, however. Hurricanes have been known to backtrack, loop, and even stand still for days on end. Sometimes the storms hit land before they have a chance to curve north and east. A particularly interesting situation for the Northeast occurs when a hurricane gets caught up in the southerly flow ahead of a cold front approaching

Richard A. Keen

SPIRAL CLOUD BANDS—Curved bands of cumulus clouds trace the path of moist tropical air feeding into Hurricane Ella, whose eye lurks 100 miles to the left. This photograph was taken from a NOAA hurricane hunter flight on September 1, 1978.

from the Midwest. The hurricane roars up the coast at an accelerating rate, making landfall somewhere in the Mid-Atlantic states, New England, or the Maritime Provinces. The storm may move so fast—forward speeds of 60 mph have been recorded—that it has little time to weaken over the cold waters north of Cape Hatteras, and strikes land with full strength.

As a rule, and rules are made to be broken, the Cape Verde storms are most likely to follow the classic arcing path as they traverse the open ocean. Most Cape Verde storms threaten, but never strike, the North American mainland. However, on memorable occasions when the Bermuda High is west of its usual location, the great arc takes the hurricanes right into the eastern seaboard. Storms forming over the Gulf of Mexico and the western Caribbean, on the other hand, are more likely to drift to the northwest or north, and a glance at a map shows why most of these reach land. Sometimes Cape Verde storms steam across the Caribbean and into the Gulf, further increasing the number of storms that threaten the Gulf coast.

Of all the places along the Gulf and Atlantic coasts of the United States and Canada, the statistically most likely place for a hurricane to come ashore is near Apalachicola, in the Florida panhandle. Damaging winds can be expected about every two or three years, on the average. Direct hits by a hurricane's tiny eye are much rarer, and even at Apalachicola can be expected only once or twice in a lifetime. Other

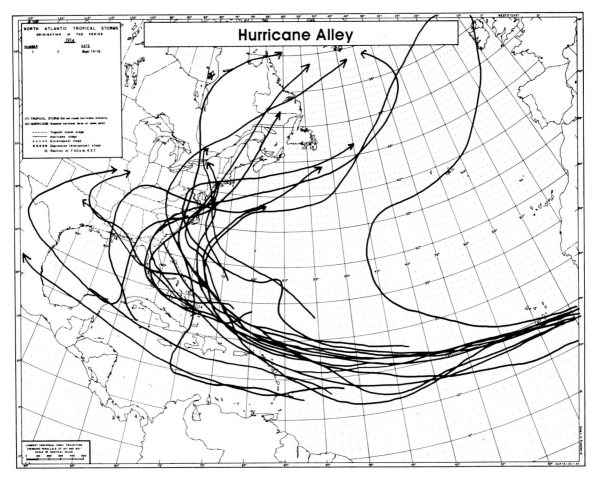

HURRICANE ALLEY—The tracks of most of the hurricanes listed at the end of this chapter are shown on this map. The Cape Verde storms travel along sweeping arcs from the tropical Atlantic, either striking North America or swerving back to sea. Storms in the Caribbean and Gulf of Mexico tend to track northward, often reaching land.

hurricane-prone locations are southern Florida, especially the stretch from Miami Beach to Key West, and Cape Hatteras, North Carolina. The *safest* places along the east coast are Jacksonville, Florida, Rehoboth Beach, Delaware, and Portsmouth, New Hampshire.

These statistics are based on a century's

worth of hurricane and tropical storm tracks, and give a fairly good idea of where these storms are common and where they aren't. However, a peculiarity of "hurricane alley" is its tendency to move from year to year. The Gulf Coast earned its statistical honors by receiving most of the United States' hurricanes during the first three decades of this

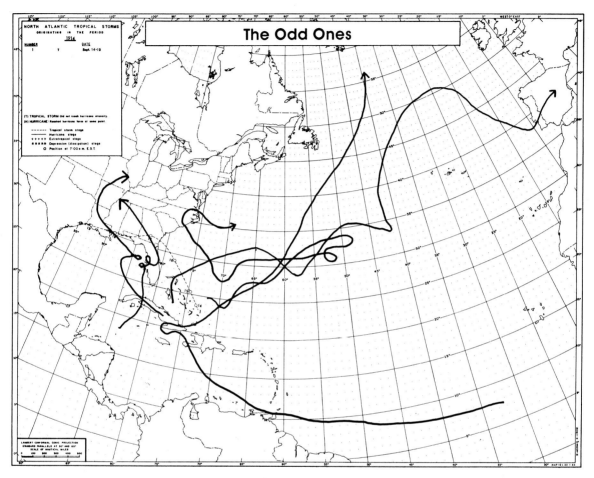

THE ODD ONES—Not all hurricanes travel in well-behaved paths. Some, like those plotted on this map, wander in all directions, and may even traverse one or more loops.

century. Florida was in the shooting gallery during the 1940s, and in the 1950s the strongest storms struck the East Coast from the Carolinas northward. The action returned to the Gulf during the 1960s and 1970s, while the 1980s saw a slight increase in the number of eastern seaboard storms. The *total* number of Atlantic hurricanes hasn't changed sig-

nificantly over the course of this century, but their tracks have.

Nobody knows why hurricane alley wanders about as it does. It seems to be related to shifts in global weather patterns—when the jet stream and Bermuda High are farther north than usual, so are the hurricanes—but then, nobody knows why *that* happens, either. There's some evidence that during North African droughts (like those that caused the famines of the 1970s and 1980s), fewer "seed" disturbances moved into the Atlantic, leading to fewer Cape Verde hurricanes. In 1957 the Weather Bureau issued monthly Hurricane Probability Statements which attempted to forecast the most likely places for hurricanes to develop and come ashore during the coming month. The forecasts were based on predictions of the behavior of the Bermuda High, upper-level winds, and the like, and weren't all that bad. However, they weren't accurate enough to be very useful, either, and received a lot of flak from coastal resort owners and chambers of commerce. The Weather Bureau dropped them after two years. More recently, William Gray of Colorado State University has issued annual predictions based on upper-level winds, the Bermuda High (of course!), and *Pacific* Ocean temperature patterns. Apparently, when the tropical Pacific warms up, thunderstorm activity there also picks up, robbing some of the energy of Atlantic thunderstorms—and leading to fewer incipient hurricanes. These forecasts are wisely limited to total hurricane activity over the Atlantic basin, and make no attempt at pinpointing where the storms may strike.

Hurricanes are, of course, individual things, and don't always feel obligated to obey the statistics. If you're really interested in the history of hurricanes and how they've affected your area, I'd suggest buying a copy of *Tropical Cyclones of the North Atlantic Ocean, 1871–1989* from the National Climatic Data Center (see the "Resources" chapter). This little book contains maps of the tracks of every hurricane and tropical storm for the past 118 years, and perusal of the variety of tracks, both "normal" and bizarre, will foster a real appreciation of the problems faced by hurricane forecasters.

THE GREATEST STORMS

Nearly five hundred hurricanes have ruffled the waters of the Atlantic since this century began, and the selection of a short list of the most interesting is not an easy one. However, here's a few of the more extreme and/or unusual storms since 1900.

September 1926—A powerful hurricane brought 132-mile-per-hour gusts to downtown Miami and put the island of Miami Beach completely under sea water. Hundreds drowned, many on the evacuee-choked causeways linking Miami Beach with the mainland. The disaster put a real damper on the 1920s land boom in southern Florida, from which the region didn't recover until the Great Depression and the Second World War were over.

September 1928—In the East's greatest natural disaster, hurricane winds drove Lake Okeechobee, Florida, over its banks, drowning 1,836 people.

September 1935—The small but exceedingly violent Labor Day Storm ripped through the middle of the Florida Keys with winds as high as 200 mph, killing four hundred people and forever removing the over-the-seas rail line to Key West. A barometer reading of 26.35 inches at Long Key remains the lowest ever recorded on the ground outside of a few Pacific typhoons. There were numerous stories of people on washed-over islands clinging to the tops of palm trees all night long to avoid being swept away, and the storm was the model for the one featured in the Humphrey Bogart and Edward G. Robinson film, *Key Largo*.

September 1938—A poorly tracked Cape Verde hurricane scored a surprise hit on Long Island and roared up the Connecticut River Valley. Winds as high was 186 mph and heavy rains caused massive wind, wave, and flood damage all over New England, and six hundred people died. The storm center was traveling northward at 56 mph when it came ashore.

September 1940—Moisture from a hurricane 200 miles offshore meeting a cold front inland produced 24 inches rain in nine hours at Ewan, New Jersey, just south of Philadelphia.

DIANA'S EYE—The bubble windows aboard a NOAA hurricane hunter plane gave this sea-to-sky panorama of the eye of hurricane Diana. The 8-mile-high "eyewall," the ring of clouds surrounding the eye, contains the strongest winds in the hurricane.

September 1947—The strongest of nine hurricanes to pound southern Florida between 1944 and 1950 ripped through Fort Lauderdale with winds gusting to 155 mph.

September 1950—Hurricane Easy, named after the fifth letter in the military phonetic alphabet, sauntered in an odd pretzel-shaped double loop in the Gulf of Mexico off Cedar Key, Florida. The storm dumped 38.7 inches of rain in twenty-four hours at Yankeetown, a record rainfall for the East.

October 1954—After wallowing in the Caribbean for a week, Hurricane Hazel suddenly turned northward, cutting across Haiti and roaring ashore near Myrtle Beach, South Carolina. Tides driven by 150-mile-per-hour winds carved new inlets along the Carolina coast, and gales shook one hundred million apples from their trees in Pennsylvania. In twelve hours Hazel sped from the Carolinas to Canada, maintaining hurricane-force winds as she merged with a strong low over the Great Lakes. The storm center had an eye-like calm as it passed over Toronto, where one hundred people died in the flooding. Ninety-five died in the United States, and hundreds more in Haiti. Hazel's remnants passed over Hudson Bay before heading off to Sweden.

August 1955—Back-to-back hurricanes Connie and Diane combined to produce the worst flooding on record along the Delaware and Connecticut rivers. Connie's rains saturated the soil after a dry summer, leaving Diane's rains nowhere to go but downstream. Among the ninety drowning victims were dozens of children at riverside summer camps. Both hurricanes came ashore in North Carolina; a month later Ione also struck the Tarheel State. The three storms dumped a total of almost 49 inches of rain on Maysville, North Carolina.

September 1955—In the forty-five years of Hurricane Hunter flights, only one plane has been lost. A Navy reconnaissance flight with a crew of nine and two reporters disappeared without a trace inside Hurricane Janet. The storm was so intense and

its pressure so low that it's possible the pilot misread the plane's altimeter (essentially a barometer), and thinking he was higher than he really was, simply flew into the Caribbean.

September 1960—Hurricane Donna went on a nine-day rampage through Puerto Rico and the Bahamas, across the Florida Keys into the Gulf of Mexico, back across Florida into the Atlantic, and up the coast, crossing North Carolina's Outer Banks before slamming into Long Island. Hurricane-force winds were recorded in every seaboard state from Florida to Maine, except Georgia, with peak gusts of 175 mph in the Florida Everglades and 130 mph at Block Island, Rhode Island. While crossing Long Island, Donna's enormous eye was 100 miles wide.

September 1961—Hurricane Debbie, born off the west coast of Africa, remained unusually far east over the Atlantic on a path that took it to the west coast of Ireland. Winds as high as 106 mph killed 11 people on the Emerald Isle and caused heavy damage across Great Britain.

October 1962—Ignoring the usual rule of losing strength over cold water, the eye of Hurricane Daisy plowed across Yarmouth, Nova Scotia, with 100-mile-per-hour winds. It was the province's most damaging hurricane since the Cape Breton storm of 1873, which wrecked twelve hundred boats. One year and three weeks after Daisy, the center of Hurricane Ginny passed directly over Yarmouth.

October 1963—Ninety inches of rain inundated Bayamo, Cuba, as Hurricane Flora lingered for four days over the eastern end of the island. Half of Cuba's sugar, tobacco, coffee, and rice crops were wiped out. Earlier, Flora lashed Haiti and the Dominican Republic with winds upward of 180 mph; the total death toll in the Caribbean exceeded seven thousand people.

August–September 1966—Hurricane Faith, a classic Cape Verde storm, spent eighteen days traversing its great arc across the Atlantic. Twice it threatened land—the Virgin Islands and the Carolinas—but veered away both times. Finally, on September 6, after traveling 8,000 miles over open water, Faith came ashore near Trondheim, Norway. One person drowned when a ferry boat sank near Denmark. Remnants of this long-lived storm were tracked another nine days and 2,700 miles, crossing northeastern Russia and finally dissipating over the ice a mere 300 miles from the North Pole.

August 1969—Camille, the most powerful hurricane ever to strike the U.S. mainland, stormed out of the Gulf of Mexico and onto the Mississippi coast with winds estimated as high as 200 mph. Damage was incredible, with buildings wiped clean from their foundations. Three days later the weakened remains of the storm suddenly unleashed torrential downpours on the mountains of western Virginia. Overnight rainfalls of up to 31 inches washed away entire hamlets. Nearly three hundred people died from this storm, half of them in Virginia.

September–October 1971—"Probably the world's longest-lived tropical cyclone," according to a National Oceanic and Atmospheric Administration report, Hurricane Ginger churned the Atlantic for thirty-one days. Born near the Bahamas on September 5, Ginger tracked halfway to Spain before stalling and then turning back toward the U.S. mainland. Ginger came ashore near Wilmington, North Carolina on October 1, bringing heavy rains and considerable crop damage, and dissipated off the Virginia coast four days later.

June 1972—Barely a hurricane, Agnes came ashore near Apalachicola, Florida, unleashing seventeen tornadoes in Florida and Georgia. Three days later her remnants stalled over Pennsylvania, where she dropped torrential rains of up to 19 inches. Overall, Agnes unloaded over 20 cubic miles of rain on the Northeast, and the resulting floods caused five billion dollars in damage and killed 118 people. On June 24 the Susquehanna River's flow exceeded one billion cubic feet per second, making it the world's second largest river (after the Amazon) that day.

July–November 1985—Six hurricanes and two tropical storms struck the U.S. coastline, matching the 1916 record. Hurricanes Danny, Elena, Juan, and Kate hit the Gulf coast, Bob came ashore in South Carolina, and Gloria crossed the Carolina capes before reaching Long Island. All of the hurricanes were damaging but none were devastating; damage totaled about four billion dollars.

August 1987—Born from a low that drifted south from the North Carolina coast, Arlene spent twenty days wandering in an erratic eastward course across the Atlantic. After briefly attaining hurricane status in the middle of the ocean, Arlene's dying remnants tracked across Portugal to near Madrid, where she dropped some rain on Spain.

September 1988—A NOAA research aircraft plying the eye of Hurricane Gilbert near Jamaica measured a sea-level pressure of 26.22 inches, the lowest ever recorded in the Western Hemisphere.

September 1989—Hurricane Hugo smashed the Virgin Islands and the north coast of Puerto Rico before heading directly into Charleston, South Carolina. Unusually warm water just off the coast gave Hugo a burst of energy before coming ashore with winds clocked at 138 mph, making it the most powerful hurricane in thirty-five years to strike the east coast north of Florida. The sea in Bull's Bay, just north of Charleston, rose to 20 feet above mean sea level, the greatest storm tide anywhere on the east coast in this century. And at a ten-billion-dollar clean-up cost, Hugo was the most damaging hurricane in history.

A TEMPEST IN A TEACUP

It's easy to demonstrate how hurricanes work by doing a little experiment right in your own kitchen. Take a cup of tea, and make sure the tea bag breaks so you get plenty of those tiny tea leaves on the bottom of the mug. Stir the tea, in a counter-clockwise direction if you like, with a spoon. If you stir it hard enough, a dip will form in the center of

Richard A. Keen

SAHARA DUST—Once or twice a year, the same trade winds that breed hurricanes send clouds of Sahara Desert dust into the skies over Florida.

the cup. Satellite photos of hurricanes show that the clouds around the eye have the same shape as the tea surface around this dip. Now look at the tea leaves. They will pile up in the middle of the cup, thanks to a current of tea moving toward the center along the bottom, just like the low-level flow into a hurricane. The lighter tea leaves swirl up around the center toward the surface, mimicking the rising air currents near the eye of a hurricane. Near the surface, the tea leaves spiral away from the "eye," and sink back down near the edge of the cup. These currents of tea are virtually identical to the motions of air in a hurricane, with one important difference. Hurricanes keep themselves going by releasing latent heat in their centers. Tea leaves contain no latent heat, so the energy must come from the stirs of the spoon.

LOOKING ELLA IN THE EYE

All sorts of superlatives can be applied to describe the power of a hurricane, but the surest way to appreciate a tempest is to encounter it personally. During World War II the Navy experimented with flights into hurricanes to pinpoint their positions. The flights began in earnest following the Third Fleet disaster in 1944, and have since become routine. Few experiences will impart one with a greater sense of awe at the majestic might of nature than a flight into the eye of a hurricane. I had the good fortune to fly on a NOAA flight into Hurricane Ella off Cape Hatteras in 1978.

The NOAA *Orion*—a military version of the *Electra*, a four-engine propjet—took off from Miami as dawn was breaking. An hour after sunrise, the first squalls on the fringe of the storm had appeared on the horizon. Below, the ocean surface was an undulating pattern of long, rolling swells fleeing from the direction of Ella. A freighter wisely fled with the swells.

Minutes later, the hurricane-hunting *Orion* began its bumpy journey through these outer fringes of Hurricane Ella. Viewed through the panoramic bubble windows of the *Orion*, the squalls appeared as long bands of billowing cumulus clouds, curving in toward the storm's center, now 100 miles away. The many scientific instruments on board the eight-million-dollar flying laboratory went into action recording temperature, humidity, wind, and even the size of the droplets in the clouds. Scientists strapped in with seat belts in front of consoles pushed buttons and flicked switches, and charts and numbers appeared on video screens.

On radar, the entire hurricane was in clear view. Its spiral pattern could have been a telescopic view of some distant galaxy, except the hurricane had a hole in its center, and it was not so far away. The *Orion* drove on toward Ella's core, sweeping in and out of the spiral rainbands; 700 feet below,

HIGH AND DRY—"Trees are in houses, houses are in the street, and cars are in the woods. Nothing is where it's supposed to be," said a Charleston, South Carolina, television news reporter, the evening after Hurricane Hugo struck, September 19, 1989. This fishing boat rode the storm 5 miles inland from its berth in Bull's Bay, north of Charleston.

turquoise streamers of underwater foam—churned by the furious winds—stretched to the horizon.

Several severe jolts announced the plane's entry into the ring of 8-mile-high rain clouds surrounding the eye of the storm. Winds of 100 mph—and momentarily gusting to 150 mph—whipped an almost solid sheet of foam across the surface of the sea. It seemed as if the waves were being flattened by the very winds that had created them.

Suddenly—within seconds—the jolts ceased. The *Orion* had entered the calm eye of Ella. Below, only a few whitecaps marred the blue waters of the sea. Above, the sun occasionally peeked through

thin clouds. And, as the *Orion* darted in and out of puffy gray clouds, the hurricane hunters on board caught occasional glimpses of the eyewall itself—an awesome amphitheater of massed clouds, dimly visible through the mists.

The respite in the 10-mile-wide eye lasted only two minutes. The plane plowed back into the violent winds of the eyewall, and for the next half an hour bounced its way back to the relatively calm fringes of Ella. It was only when the *Orion* was safely on its way home to Miami that the old-timers on board began telling their tales of lost wingtips, ruptured gas lines, and disabled navigational equipment.

105

LITTLE WINDS

If hurricanes are the Greatest Storms on Earth, perhaps we should unwind a bit and talk about some of the lesser winds that sweep the East. For the most part, these little winds are harmless, although the least wind of all—the stagnant air beneath an inversion—can be a killer. Were the world as smooth as a billiard ball, with no oceans or mountains, few of these localized winds would exist. Fortunately, the East is an intricate patchwork of oceans, bays, lakes, mountains, ridges, and valleys, each of which is capable of producing its own local wind. Many of these winds have a lot in common, including a strange resemblance to the greatest winds on Earth. Dust devils resemble hurricanes, and sea breezes are caused by the same forces that drive the world's largest wind pattern, the Hadley circulation. Perhaps the best thing about the little winds, though, is that they show these forces on a scale we can appreciate, giving us an opportunity to see for ourselves how the weather works.

MOUNTAIN WAVES

After the Atlantic Ocean, the most important geographic feature of the East is the Appalachian mountain range. By world standards the Appalachians are not very high, averaging 3,000 to 5,000 feet high and nowhere reaching 7,000 feet. It is a long range, though, and extends 1,900 miles from Birmingham, Alabama, to Newfoundland.

The ridges of the Appalachians run roughly northeast-southwest, while the prevailing winds vary in direction from southwest to northwest. A southwest wind blows along the ridge lines, never having cause to cross the ridges. But when the wind blows from the northwest, as it does a lot in the winter, it runs right up against the Appalachians, and has no choice but to go up and over. If conditions are right, the air continues to go up and down after it has passed the mountain ridge. The best way to visualize this is to watch what happens in a shallow creek when the water runs over a rock. The water goes up and over, and downstream there's a series of ripples. Air does the same thing. As far as the laws of physics are concerned, air is a fluid, just like water. Air may be lighter, and water wetter, but they're both still fluids.

These ripples of air are known as *mountain waves* or, by virtue of their position downstream from mountains, as *lee waves*. Just like the creek waves, they stand still while air flows through them.

106

Mountain waves are a lot bigger than anything you'll see in a creek. Ripples can be several miles apart, and the air going through them might rise and fall 1,000 feet or more. Mountain waves can also extend upward through the atmosphere—they've been measured as high as 15 miles above the ground, where the air is only 5 percent as dense as at sea level. Glider pilots love them because they often provide a reliable, stationary, and strong upward current of air—great for hitching a soaring ride! Many gliding records for altitude and duration came from pilots successfully "catching a wave," and their exploits have contributed greatly to our knowledge about mountain waves.

Out in the Rockies, a mountain wave wind is called a *chinook*, meaning "snow-eater," a word of the Pacific Northwest American Indian culture. These warm winds have been known to melt a foot of snow in an afternoon. One reason chinooks are so warm is that as the air goes up one side of the mountain it cools and its water vapor condenses, releasing latent heat into the air. Since the air has gained a certain amount of latent heat, it's warmer when it comes back down the other side of the mountain. It's also drier and clearer, with the clouds piled up along the upwind side of the mountains.

The northwest winds that bring mountain waves to the Appalachians make the eastern versions of chinooks a bit colder than western ones. There's not much reason to call a mountain wave in an arctic air mass a "snow-eater"! Nonetheless, arctic air does moderate a bit as it crosses the mountains, with the warming typically amounting to 5 or 10 degrees. The warming is reflected in records of all-time extreme low temperatures, with places west of the Appalachians bottoming out about 10 degrees colder than places at the same latitude east of the mountains. That 10 degrees can make a big difference if you're trying to grow peaches or azaleas or heat a home.

Bright sunshine also makes a big difference during cold waves, and there's a lot more of that east of the Appalachians. It's not unusual for Philadelphia to enjoy a brilliant sun shining through a deep blue sky with a temperature of 20 degrees, while across the ridges, Pittsburgh is cloudy with light snow and a temperature of 10 degrees. Over

MOUNTAIN WAVES—Like ripples in a creek, waves form downstream from mountain ranges.

U.S. Forest Service

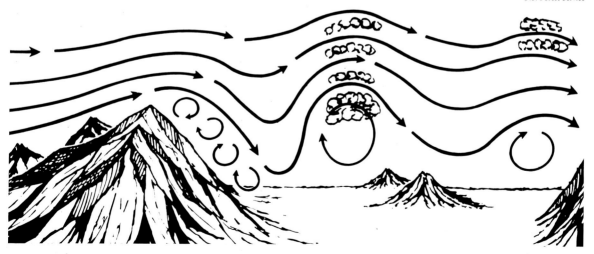

107

George Kiladis

LENTICULAR CLOUDS—So named because of their smooth, lens-shaped appearance, these lenticular clouds mark ripples in the air flow over Massachusett's Berkshire Mountains.

the course of a year, Philadelphia receives four hundred hours more sunshine than Pittsburgh, and most of the extra sunlight is courtesy of the chinook effect. Similar comparisons can be made between Charlotte and Knoxville or Portland and Montreal, or between any pair of places on opposite sides of the Appalachians.

Mountain waves are also responsible for some of the oddest clouds on Earth. As the air streaming through a mountain wave rises from trough to crest, its moisture condenses into little clouds that sit atop the waves. Because of their smooth, rounded, lens-shaped appearance, these clouds have earned the name *lenticular clouds*, although others prefer to call them *grindstone clouds*. These weird clouds will stand still for hours, even though the wind is ripping through them at 50 miles an hour or more. Look at one with binoculars; you'll see tiny shreds of cloud form on the upwind edge, blow through the lenticular, and dissolve on the downwind edge.

DUST DEVILS

Dust devils dance and twirl across beaches and parking lots, spinning dust around and around and yanking newspapers out of our hands. Sometimes they look like tornadoes, but in some ways they're more like midget hurricanes. This is why dust devils are so fascinating to watch—where else can you see a miniature storm system, compressed so small that you can run right through it?

108

Grant Goodge

SOLITARY LENTICULAR—This lonesome lenticular cloud developed downwind from the highest point in the East, Mt. Mitchell, North Carolina.

A flat bit of ground and a sunny, calm day are the main ingredients to make a dust devil. The stage is set a few hours before noon, particularly during the late spring or early summer, when the sun is highest in the sky and beats down mercilessly onto the ground.

Air warms up during the day because of the heat it gets from the sunlit ground. So, it's not surprising that the ground heats up earlier and eventually gets hotter than the air above it. It also helps to have dry ground, so you don't waste solar energy evaporating moisture. At noon, when solar heating is at its peak, the ground may get as much as 80 degrees hotter than the air. This is why sidewalks can literally get hot enough to fry an egg on (which requires at least 125 degrees), even when the air temperature is a mere 95 degrees.

Right next to the ground—an inch or two above the surface—the air can get nearly as hot as the ground. Farther up, the air gets less hot, and so on. So you end up with a thin layer of extremely hot air near the ground and cooler air aloft. At some point, a bubble of this hot air rises up into the cooler layer. More hot surface air rushes in to take the place of that pioneering hot bubble, and an upwardly mobile stream of hot air develops. These currents can go up thousands of feet, where glider pilots (once again) know them as *thermals*. Thermals are also the favorite haunts of hawks and other birds looking for a lift.

109

UPI

TIME-OUT—This dust devil forced a time-out during an exhibition game between the Orioles and Pirates in Miami.

Some thermals go straight up, while others—for a variety of reasons—start to spin. Thermals are much too small to be twisted by the same Coriolis effect that gets larger cyclones spinning; more likely the rising currents pick up small eddies downwind of small hills and buildings. It has even been suggested that coyotes and rabbits start the small swirls that grow into dust devils. In any event, the spinning goes faster as more hot air gets sucked into the base of the thermal. Mix in some dust, leaves, or any other debris, so you can see the swirling column of air, and there's your dust devil!

A typical dust devil may be 10 feet across and 50 feet tall, but in desert areas, where the heating of

the ground is stronger, the dust column may rise half a mile high. Most dust devils last a few minutes at most, but the giant ones can live much longer. In Utah some 2,000-footers have been followed for up to seven hours as they wandered 40 or so miles across the desert. These occasional giants are probably about as large as dust devils ever get—on Earth. But the deserts of Earth pale in comparison to the eternally rainless plains of Mars, where orbiting spacecraft have spotted monster dust whirls half a mile *wide* and 3 miles high!

The funnel of dust may look like a tornado, but its winds are rarely destructive. Tornado winds have been measured at over 200 mph, while typical dust devils spin at one-tenth that speed. Winds have reached as high as 90 mph in some desert giants, but that's about tops for a dust devil. Upward wind speed is likewise smaller. While tornadoes have been known to lift cows and cars off the ground, dust devils prefer smaller game, such as boxes and butterflies. The strongest dust devils have been known to launch rodents into the air; to keep such critters airborne requires a vertical wind of 30 mph.

At the same time dust and rodents may be swirling around the edge of the dust funnel, it's quite calm inside. Within this calm center, air may actually be sinking slowly back to the ground—a feature strongly reminiscent of the "eye" of a hurricane! Another resemblance between the humble dust devil and the Greatest Storm on Earth is the spiral of warm air that rises as it approaches the center, where it streams out the top of the whirlwind. Of course, there are differences. Dust devils are dry, while hurricanes thrive on moisture. There's also the obvious fact that you can fit billions of large dust devils inside a small hurricane.

LAND AND SEA BREEZES

Perhaps no wind on Earth—not even the hurricane—has caused a larger migration of humanity than the *sea breeze*. For better or worse, entire cities, from Myrtle Beach to Miami Beach and Ocean City to Atlantic City, have settled on marshes and dunes in large part because of this cooling breeze off the ocean. Millions live in the cities and villages along the seashore, and millions more migrate there for vacations and summer weekends. For a wind that rarely exceeds 20 mph, sea breezes have moved a lot of people.

Like most winds, from dust devils to the great currents that circle the Earth, sea breezes are driven by differences in temperature. In this case the temperature difference is that between the land and the sea, or, more properly, between the air above the land and that above the sea. By now it should be a familiar concept—warm (lighter) air sitting next to cold (heavier) air will begin to rise, letting the cold air creep in beneath it. Sea breezes only work when the land air is warmer than the sea air, and the greatest differentials are seen in late spring and summer, and, of course, during the day.

Let's look at an example. In July, the ocean temperature off the New Jersey coast averages about 72 degrees. Even under a cloudless sky, the ocean temperature changes very little from night to day— it took six months to warm all that water up from January's chilly 37 degrees, and it's not going to change very much in six hours. Meanwhile, the Bermuda High is pumping subtropical air up the coast to New Jersey and beyond. Inland, the solar heating of the ground pushes the daytime air temperatures toward 90 degrees, while the ocean air has a hard time getting much over 70 degrees.

By noon the land/sea temperature contrast may reach 10 or 20 degrees, enough to get a sea breeze going in earnest. Often the breeze starts rather suddenly, and comes ashore like a miniature cold front. Depending on the speed and direction of competing wind currents, like those around the Bermuda High, the sea breeze front may rush on in, providing instant relief to thousands, or its progress may be painfully slow. Some days the breeze stays out to sea.

The onset of a sea breeze can drop the temperature 15 or 20 degrees in half an hour. Once over land, the 1,000-foot-deep layer of air from the ocean begins to heat up and the breeze starts losing some of its punch. Most sea breezes peter out within 20 miles of the coast, confining the natural air conditioning effect to a narrow strip along the shore. On a typical July afternoon, downtown Atlantic City gets no warmer than 79 degrees, but only 7 miles inland, the city's airport averages 84 degrees. Sixty miles from the sea, well beyond the reach of the cooling breeze, Philadelphia simmers at 86 degrees. Another way to look at it is to count the number of days with temperatures of 90 degrees or higher, weather most people consider uncomfortably hot. Philadelphians see twenty-one hot days a year, unless, of course, they spend the summer at the shore, in which case they count only four. In between, the Atlantic City airport has twelve 90-degree days.

Summertime ocean temperatures along the Atlantic coast range from 50 degrees around Newfoundland to 60 degrees off Maine to 70 degrees along the Jersey shore, providing that whole stretch of coast with plenty of free air conditioning. South of Cape Hatteras the ocean is a lot warmer, 80 degrees or higher, and where you need it the most, the cooling is less. By the time you get to Florida, the ocean is about 84 degrees in July. Even at these temperatures there's a sea breeze effect, although not a whole lot— July's daytime average of 88 degrees at Miami Beach is only 2 degrees less than at Miami International Airport, 10 miles inland. More important than that 2 degrees, though, is the breeze itself.

The opposite of a sea breeze is a *land breeze*. At night, when the land may get colder than the ocean, the winds blow out to sea. Along much of the Atlantic and Gulf coasts, land breezes waft across miles of marsh as they head to the sea, picking up thousands of mosquitoes along the way—yet another reason the crowds leave the beaches when the sun goes down!

111

H. Michael Mogil

SEA BREEZE—A cool breeze off the Atlantic keeps the sky cloud-free over Myrtle Beach, South Carolina, but a line of cumulus is growing where the sea breeze meets hot, humid air a few miles inland.

Sea breezes aren't only seen around seas, either. Lakes the size of Erie, Ontario, and Okeechobee generate *lake breezes* nearly every summer day, as do large bays like the Chesapeake and Delaware, and other large water surfaces such as Pamlico and Long Island sounds. Smaller lakes and rivers can also send cooling breezes several hundred yards from their shores, and I've even detected ever-so-slight zephyrs blowing off of swimming pools! As long as the water is cooler than the air, and all other winds are light enough, sea breezes (or lake breezes, etc.) can blow from virtually any watery surface.

MOUNTAIN AND VALLEY WINDS

Those who live far from the ocean can take heart—they, too, have their version of the sea breeze. These winds are driven by the uneven heating and cooling of mountain slopes and valley floors, and so we call them *mountain and valley winds.* Because these winds are as varied as the

H. Michael Mogil

POLLUTED SUNSET—The setting sun sinks into a layer of man-made smog and natural haze trapped beneath an inversion. The sun is both dimmed and reddened by minuscule particles suspended in the atmosphere.

shapes of the terrain that cause them, let it suffice here to point out a few generic features.

Mountain and valley winds rely on the way air right next to the ground heats up faster by day and cools off faster at night than air farther off the ground. Remember this from dust devils? During the day, warm, light air near the ground drifts up hills and the sides of valleys, to be replaced by cooler air that sinks down into the centers of the valleys. The warm air currents rising above the hills can lead to clouds and, sometimes, thunderstorms.

At night the opposite happens. Layers of cool air that form on hillsides slide into the valleys, creating air currents commonly called *drainage winds*. If the hill is steep enough, drainage winds may start right after sunset, but on gently sloping terrain the cold air may have to build up for several hours before it starts moving. Being heavier, the cold air eventually finds itself in the lowest place around, which is the valley floor. This is why night

113

temperatures are almost always colder in valleys than on mountain tops.

If you live in a valley or near a mountain, take note of how the wind direction changes from day to night. No matter where you live, the surest way to appreciate these fickle little winds is to camp in the mountains. When that first cool breeze slides down the valley during your evening meal, you'll know it.

INVERSIONS

The end result of nighttime valley breezes is often a valley full of cold air. If the breezes are doing their job, the coldest air is right at the bottom. This is an *inversion*, a word derived from Latin and roughly meaning "upside down." Since air cools as it rises, in most situations the atmosphere is colder aloft than it is near the ground. With inversions, however, the atmosphere gets warmer with altitude.

This inverted atmosphere has one particularly unsavory feature: If you give the cold heavy air near the ground an upward kick, it will come right back down. In other words, the air is extremely stable, and it's not easy to get the cold air out of the valley. Whatever we put into the air—exhaust, smoke, dust, and the like—stays right there with us. Virtually all heavy pollution comes from the concentration of pollutants in a thin, inverted layer of air near the ground.

Inversions don't just happen in valleys at night. Los Angeles' famous smog is kept in by a shallow layer of cool air that drifts in from the sea and backs up against the surrounding mountains. Southern California's smog is an inevitable consequence of the mellow climate that drew all those people there in the first place. Easterners may gripe about their blustery winters and rainy summers, but this stormier climate means that Eastern cities have better natural ventilation—and less smog—than Southern Californian cities.

The most persistent inversions in the East are usually the remnants of arctic cold waves. Once or twice a year, often in late fall, a cold layer lingers in mountain valleys and along the coastal plain for several days as warmer air streams in aloft. The inversion remains until either the sun heats the cold layer into oblivion (a slow process in November), or another weather system arrives to blow the mess away.

More unpleasant, perhaps, are the summertime inversions in which warm (and usually quite humid) air near the ground is capped by even hotter air aloft. The inversion inhibits the development of thunderstorms that might otherwise draw up and disperse a polluted layer of air, and relief from both the heat and the pollution usually awaits the arrival of a cold front.

SOME BIG LITTLE WINDS

October 26–31, 1948—Steel mill smoke trapped by a persistent valley inversion beneath an Indian-summer high caused twenty deaths at Donora, Pennsylvania, near Pittsburgh.

July 25, 1956—Two passenger liners, the Italian *Andrea Doria* and the Swedish *Stockholm*, collided at the edge of a dense fog bank in an ocean-chilled air layer off Nantucket Island. The *Andrea Doria* sank twelve hours later with a loss of fifty-one lives.

April 21, 1963—Beneath a clear sky, a dust devil described as "a black spiral, easily one-half mile high" uprooted trees, downed power lines, and tore bricks from the side of a school in Reading, Pennsylvania.

November 20–25, 1966—More than 120 people died of respiratory problems during one of New York City's worst smog episodes.

October 24, 1973—Moist air and smoke from garbage dump fires trapped beneath an inversion combined to form dense fog along the New Jersey Turnpike, leading to a sixty-five-car wreck near Newark that killed nine motorists. Four years earlier, similar conditions near the southern end of the Turnpike caused a pileup of twenty cars and a propane truck, killing six.

H. Michael Mogil

INVERSION—Cumulus clouds dot the top of an inversion viewed from an airplane window. Above the layer, the air is warmer, drier, and (of course) cleaner than the visibly polluted air beneath.

April 25, 1983—Powerful northwesterly flow behind a passing coastal cyclone set up a strong and persistent mountain wave along the length of the Appalachian Mountains. Thomas Knauff caught this wave over Williamsport, Pennsylvania with his glider, *Nimbus III,* and sailed above the ridges to North Carolina and back. The 1,023-mile-long glider flight set a world record.

July 17, 1987—A small, fair-weather water-spout—the marine equivalent of a dust devil—spun off Chesapeake Bay onto a beach near Havre de Grace, Maryland. Before dissipating seconds later, the whirlwind lifted a small sailboat 10 feet off the sand and dropped it on its side, damaging its mast.

December 11, 1990—Once again, fog created havoc on the highways, this time on the Hiwassee River bridge on Interstate 75 northeast of Chattanooga, Tennessee. Morning valley fog, enhanced by moisture from the river and smoke from a nearby pulp mill, slowed some motorists but not others. Chain-reaction pileups in both directions involved a total of eighty-three vehicles and left thirteen motorists dead.

HOW HOT, HOW COLD?

We find at New York the summer of Rome, and the winter of Copenhagen, at Quebec the summer of Paris, and the winter of St. Petersburg.

—Alexander von Humboldt,
Essay on Isothermal Lines, ca. 1828

The climate of North America often had a few surprises for the early settlers from Europe. The prevailing theory at the time was that climate depended mostly on latitude, which was a fair—but by no means perfect—approximation to reality. A simple glance at the map showed Quebec at nearly the same latitude as Paris and New York on the same parallel as Rome, and there was little reason to suspect the climates would differ greatly. When the settlers arrived (usually in summer) they found everything, in explorer Samuel Champlain's words, "very pleasant on account of the woods, the beautiful landscapes, and the fine fishing," along with very familiar, splendid summer weather.

After wintering over along what is now the Maine–New Brunswick border, Champlain realized that "it was difficult to know this country without having wintered there. . . . There are six months of

winter in that country!" Sometimes winter was reason enough to call it quits. Following his first winter (1607 to 1608) in Maine, Raleigh Gilbert declared that because of "the fear that all the other winters would prove like the first, the company would by no means stay in the country." Fortunately for us (now in our heated homes), many other settlers stuck it out and adapted to the rigorous climate.

Farther south the new settlers saw the New World's climate differently. The Swedes who settled along the Delaware River were not impressed by the cold. "The winter begins in December, and ends in January, continuing only seven, eight, or at most nine weeks," commented a resident of New Sweden. To the Swedes, though, summer was the season that required some getting used to. "August and September . . . are the hottest parts of the year," wrote John Companius, keeper of the New World's first regular weather records, "and in some years it is so warm that people long for rain and wet weather."

Well, you can't please everybody, but what the transplants from Europe found was a climate that was much more changeable than that of their homelands. If the summers were like home, the winters were much colder, and if the winters were

116

tolerable, summer was too hot. In much of the East, the seasonal swing, measured as the difference between the average temperatures of July and January, is around 40 to 50 degrees—nearly twice that of most places in western Europe. The extreme ranges between the highest and lowest temperatures ever recorded are likewise greater in the New World. Plymouth, Massachusetts, has seen the temperature cover a 123-degree span, while the range at Plymouth, England, is a mere 72 degrees. Indeed, the 179-degree range registered at Iroquois Falls, Ontario, on the rail line between Toronto and Hudson Bay, is the greatest in the world outside of some Siberian valleys.

The New World's climate is so extreme for the same reason Siberia's is: its location on the eastern edge of a large land area. Riding the prevailing westerlies, most of the East's air masses arrive overland and free of the moderating influences of any oceans. Europe receives these same air masses, but only after they have crossed 3,000 miles of the Atlantic Ocean. Within this region we call the East, the range of climates from north to south is as impressive as the range from summer to winter. The temperature at Key West, Florida, has never even come close to freezing, while the year-round average temperature on the summit of Mount Washington is 5 degrees *below* freezing. There are many extremes in the East's varied climates; let's look at some of them and their causes. You'll find that the causes can be as interesting as the records themselves, because there's at lot to be learned from looking at these freaks of weather.

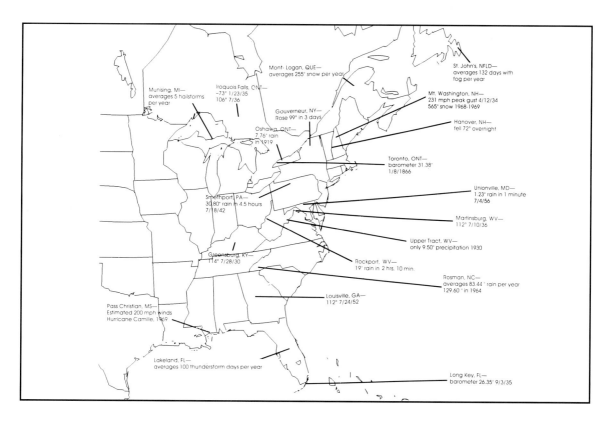

HOW HOT?

Although some of the earliest settlers kept meticulous journals of the weather, another century passed before they could attach real numbers to their records. Thermometers didn't arrive in the New World until 1717, when Dr. Cadwalader Colden of Philadelphia obtained one from England. After receiving several smashed thermometers in the mail (some things never change!), Benjamin Franklin finally received a working version in 1749 and began taking occasional readings. The earliest consistent temperature records began in 1737 at Charleston, South Carolina, in 1742 at Cambridge, Massachusetts, and in 1743 at Quebec City. In 1820, the U.S. Army Medical Department set up a weather reporting network at hospitals and forts from the coast to the frontier. Fifty-one years later national weather services were organized in the United States and Canada, and the era of widespread, continuous, and—most important—consistently measured weather records across North America began.

It didn't take long for the early thermometers to get a workout. Ben Franklin reported 100 degrees the first year his thermometer was in operation. However, for some reason—either the climate changed or thermometers were set up and read differently, or both—100-degree readings remained quite rare in the East until the latter part of the nineteenth century. Even at places with two hundred years of records, most of the highest temperature readings on record are in the present century. Following Franklin's hot day in 1749, Philadelphia's temperature stayed below 100 degrees until 1876, a period of 127 years! In the 115 years since then the century mark has been reached no less than forty-eight times.

As it stands now, most cities in the East have reached 100 degrees at one time or another. The extreme highest temperature ever measured east of the Appalachians is 112 degrees at both Martinsburg, West Virginia, and Louisville, Georgia. West of the mountains, but still within the East, temperatures 1 or 2 degrees higher have been recorded. From there it becomes a matter of how we define the East, since the extremes increase steadily as you head west, reaching 120 and 121 degrees in the states from North Dakota to Texas. East of the Mississippi (but just barely!), the highest heat extreme recorded is 117 degrees at East Saint Louis, Illinois. Death Valley, California, holds the North American record of 134 degrees (although the accuracy of this reading has been disputed), and the world record is 136 degrees at the oasis of Azizia, Libya.

More remarkable, perhaps, than these high temperatures is the uniformity of the extremes across the region. Key West and Goose Bay, Labrador, share the same all-time high—100 degrees. No major eastern city has ever exceeded 110 degrees. This tells us that the same hot air masses that frequent Florida can also reach into Labrador and every point in between with little moderation of temperature. Of course, farther north hot air is much less common, but when we're talking about extremes, once is enough.

There are two general exceptions to the uniformity of extreme heat across the East. Within a given air mass, higher places are cooler by 3 to 5 degrees per 1,000 feet. Thus, atop 6,262-foot Mount Washington the high of 72 degrees is 32 degrees lower than Boston's 104 degrees, and the 100 degrees at Asheville, North Carolina, is 5 degrees less than the 105 degrees at Raleigh, North Carolina, 1,700 feet lower. Also, offshore islands don't get as hot as the mainland or even coastal locations. The 95 degrees at Block Island is 9 degrees lower than the high of 104 degrees at Providence, Cape Hatteras' 97 degrees is 8 degrees less than Raleigh's 105 degrees, and Sable Island's 86 degrees is 13 degrees lower than the 99 degrees recorded at Halifax, Nova Scotia. Even on the island of Miami Beach, a mere 3 miles from shore, the record high of 98 degrees is 2 degrees less than mainland

FRYING EGGS—A crowd gathers on a Philadelphia street corner on a 94° afternoon to watch an egg fry on the sidewalk. The August sun heated the concrete to the 125° (or higher) temperatures required to cook the proteins in the egg whites.

Miami's 100-degree record. The reason, of course, is that the hot air mass *must* cross open water to reach an island, and its lower layers get chilled along the way. While coastal towns are cooled by sea breezes much of the time, once in a while hot air blows directly off the land. Again, extremes only have to happen once, and the highs at most coastal locations are just as hot as at inland towns.

119

HOW COLD?

It didn't take long for early American thermometers to get workouts on their low end, either. David Ludlum, in one of his several books on America's weather history, chronicled the progression of ever lower temperatures recorded in the United States (and former colonies). At New Haven, Connecticut, Yale's President Clap recorded 5 degrees in 1741—*inside* his house! A reading of 3 below zero came from Newport, Rhode Island, in 1752; 9 below was recorded at Boston in 1765; and 22 below was the reading at Hartford, Connecticut, in 1780. The settlement of interior New England brought even colder records: 29 below at Rutland, Vermont, in 1792, and 34 below at Hallowell, Maine, in 1807. The mercury froze at 40 below zero at several towns in northern New England during a bitter cold spell in 1835, and lower readings had to await the invention of the alcohol thermometer (which doesn't freeze at 40 below). A 52 below zero reading at Bath, Maine, in 1857 remained the United States' record low until 1885, when the extreme moved to Montana (63 below zero)—where it has been ever since (excluding Alaska, of course).

That 52 below in Maine ties the upstate New York records set at Stillwater Reservoir in 1934 and Old Forge in 1979 as the lowest temperature ever recorded in the eastern United States. They are all put to shame by eastern Canada's record lows of 66 below at Doucet, Quebec, in 1923, and 73 below at Iroquois Falls in 1935. If we include Greenland as part of North America, the East's—and entire continent's—record is 87 below zero recorded at the Northice station high on the ice dome in January 1954. By the way, the world record is 128 below, recorded at the Soviet Union's Vostok station, 11,000 feet up on the Antarctic Plateau.

On the high end of the low temperature scale, Key West, Florida, has never chilled below 41 degrees—making it the only city in the United States (outside of Hawaii) that has never frozen.

Clearly, the uniformity of extreme highs across the East is not mirrored in the distribution of low temperatures. Quite simply, the air masses that invade Labrador in the winter are much colder than those that make it into Florida. The air masses start out the same, but as they head south across lower latitudes, increasing sunlight warms them. In summer the amount of sunlight doesn't change much with latitude, as longer days up north compensate the lower sun angles to keep the hot air hot.

Cold air masses responsible for the low temperatures at any location in the East form over the arctic regions of the Northwest Territories, Alaska, and Siberia. While these areas receive virtually no sunlight during the winter, their snow-covered surfaces radiate heat off into space. As a result, any air that passes over the Arctic will find itself losing heat and getting colder. The longer it stays, the colder it gets. Eventually, these refrigerated air masses are taken south by cyclones forming along their southern boundaries.

The normal west-to-east flow of jet streams across North America brings a stream of relatively mild air from the Pacific Ocean, and keeps arctic air from moving south. As the arctic air continues to chill, however, the temperature difference grows between the Arctic and the tropics. With this temperature difference, the strength of the jet must also increase. When the jet blows too fast, it starts to buckle. The buckling takes the form of troughs and ridges in the upper atmosphere and as fronts, cyclones, and anticyclones in the lower atmosphere. And the frigid mass of arctic air begins to move south.

The path of the cold air outbreak depends on where the buckles form on the jet. A common pattern is for the ridge to develop over the Yukon and the trough over the Great Lakes. This pattern sends the cold wave into the Midwest, where it may moderate slightly before reaching the Atlantic seaboard. Overall, winters are about 5 degrees colder in

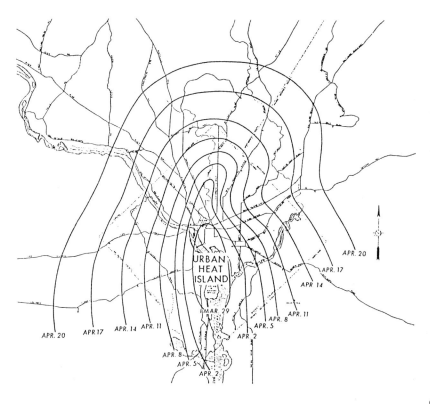

WASHINGTON, D.C. HEAT ISLAND—The average date of spring's last overnight freeze gives a good idea of when the growing season may begin. Gardeners near downtown Washington, D.C., can plant tomatoes three weeks before their suburban colleagues can, thanks to the urban heat island effect.

the Midwest than at the same latitude along the East Coast. Less frequently, the ridge and trough pattern shifts east, and the cold air tracks farther north across Canada before plunging south directly into New England. This is the pattern responsible for most of the cold records in the northeastern states and Maritime Provinces.

Once the cold wave has overrun the East, local factors like terrain and snow cover take over. Cold air is heavy, and extremely cold air tends to hug the ground. So, the coldest air masses moving south

from the Arctic often extend upward only 2 or 3 miles. But within the depth of the air mass, the air near the top is colder than that near the surface, due to the familiar decrease of pressure with altitude. Once the cold air settles in over the mountains and valleys, locally chilled air at night has a habit of sinking into the valleys. If the valley has a thick blanket of snow on the ground (which effectively insulates the air from the residual heat in the ground, and vice versa), a thin layer of air near the ground can cool off extremely rapidly after sunset, leading to

121

very low overnight temperatures. The ideal conditions for extreme cold temperatures, then, are clear, calm nights in valleys with deep snow on the ground.

Even if you don't live in a mountain valley, a foot of snow on the ground can still chop 5 or 10 degrees off your overnight low. If your desire is to *raise* the low by 5 or 10 degrees, move your thermometer downtown. Mobile meteorologists with car-mounted thermometers have found local warm spots enclosing city centers and even shopping malls. Averaged over the course of a year, these "urban heat islands" average 1 or 2 degrees warmer than the surrounding countryside, with greater differences at night and in the winter. There are several reasons for the *heat island effect*, all of which involve the ultimate causes of all temperature differences—radiational balances and imbalances.

Trees use sunlight to make food and to release water, leaving only part of the incoming solar radiation to heat the ground and air. Sunlight striking concrete and asphalt (particularly black asphalt!) goes mostly into heating the mass of human-made material. When the sun goes down, trees and fields readily radiate their heat into space, and being relatively lightweight, their excess heat is soon gone. Buildings and parking lots hold a lot more heat, and all night long act like huge space heaters to warm the nearby air. Meanwhile, smog and haze over cities blocks some of the radiation that tries to get out. Under the clear, calm conditions characteristic of extreme low temperatures, I've seen readings in downtown Philadelphia 20 degrees higher than those at the airport 5 miles away, and 30 degrees warmer than the countryside a bit farther out.

RANGES AND CHANGES

Putting together the extremes, we find that temperatures in the East have ranged from 114 above to 73 below, an amazing 187-degree spread. Incredibly, all but 8 degrees of that spread have been recorded at one spot—Iroquois Falls, Ontario. As mentioned earlier, the 179-degree range at Iroquois Falls is exceeded only by the 188-degree range at Verkhoyansk, Siberia The all-time high at Iroquois Falls, 106 degrees, was during a widespread heat wave in July 1936—only eighteen months after their lowest reading! The 1930s, and particularly the period from 1934 to 1936, was an exceptionally volatile epoch in North America's climate. From Alaska to Florida there were many extremes of both heat and cold that have not been equaled since.

One hundred seventy-nine degrees is a huge spread, but eighteen months is a relatively long time. To find really large, quick temperature changes we must go south a bit to the battleground of the air masses—New England and the Great Lakes, Ohio Valley, and Mid-Atlantic regions. Tropical and arctic air masses can—and do—meet anywhere on the continent, but this is the area where the meetings are most frequent. The sharpest temperature changes are the falls that follow cold front passages in the winter and spring. Once or twice a year, most places experience an overnight drop of 40 degrees or more due to a cold front. One of the strongest cold fronts on record swept into New England on February 7, 1861, dropping the temperature at Gouverneur, New York, from 30 above zero to 40 below—overnight. The actual low was probably even colder, since the mercury in the thermometer froze at 40 below and didn't thaw out until 9 A.M. The temperature at Hanover, New Hampshire, plunged from 40 above to 32 below, a fall of 72 degrees in half a day! Equally remarkable was the subsequent return of mild air. By February 11, Gouverneur recovered to 59 degrees above zero, a rise of at least 99 degrees in three days. More recently, Washington, D.C., cooled from 85 to 26 degrees when a front cut short an early summer in March 1921.

Even stagnant air masses can produce large and rapid temperature changes. Under the clear and still conditions near the center of a slow-moving or stationary high pressure system, temperatures may plummet at night and quickly rebound under the next morning's sun, only to plummet again the following evening. The ideal situations are most common in spring and fall, when day-to-night temperature excursions of 40 to 50 degrees (occasionally greater in favorable valley locations) might happen. Unfortunately, these same weather situations may also cause the accumulation of smog.

Less dramatic are the records for the *smallest* changes of temperature. On April 21–22, 1964, Philadelphia's thermometer was stuck at 43 degrees for twenty-four continuous hours. The weather situation was not a rare one, with drizzle and a steady breeze off the ocean, and there have doubtlessly been other instances of twenty-four-hour temperature fluctuations of zero degrees. But for the smallest range of all-time extremes at any one location, we return to the island city of Key West. In the 120 years on record, the temperature has never exceeded 100 degrees or fallen below 41 degrees. The 59-degree spread is the smallest in the "lower forty-eight" states and Canada. Over the course of a century, Key West has experienced a change of temperature far smaller than Hanover, New Hampshire, has seen overnight.

FROM HERE TO THERE

Some of the temperature differences between places a few miles apart can be as impressive as the changes over short periods of time. Mount Washington is frequently 20 to 30 degrees colder than Gorham, 12 miles north and 1 mile lower. However, this is cheating a bit—we expect it to be colder in the mountains.

The largest *horizontal* temperature differences occur along fronts. One of the mightiest cold fronts in recent history was the one that whipped up the Buffalo Blizzard on January 28, 1977. Just before the front struck Philadelphia at 7:00 P.M. the thermometer read 44 degrees, while Pittsburgh had already plummeted to 10 below. That's a 54-degree

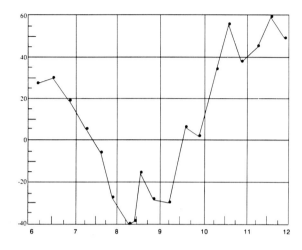

David Ludlum

TEMPERATURE GYRATIONS—The temperature at Gouverneur, New York, fluctuated rapidly in February, 1861, as a cold front came and went.

difference over 250 miles. Even sharper temperature contrasts are seen across the *backdoor fronts* that often separate spring from winter along the Atlantic coastal plain. These fronts originate from cold air masses centered over New England or the Maritime Provinces, and get their name by backing in from the northeast rather than from the usual westerly direction. The upper wind pattern that brings the backdoor front down the coast may also bring early spring heat from the southwest. As a result, once or twice a year temperatures in the 80s or 90s are separated from the chilly, drizzly 40s by no more than 50 miles—about the distance between New York City and Trenton, New Jersey.

It may be academic, perhaps, but the greatest temperature difference ever recorded across eastern North America probably occurred on the morning of January 23, 1935. This was when the weather observer at Iroquois Falls read 73 below from his thermometer. At that same moment, far south of

123

the cold front, Key West read 66 degrees. Over a distance of a 1,660 miles, the temperature difference was 139 degrees.

What is the *least* temperature difference the East has ever seen? Some help in figuring this one comes from the fact that at the farthest corners of the region, Goose Bay, Labrador, has been hotter and colder than Miami Beach has ever been. Consequently, it is unavoidable that at some time both places, 2,100 miles apart, have recorded the same temperature at the same time.

The eastern third of North America harbors places where the temperature has fallen 72 degrees overnight, and places where it hasn't nudged a degree. At any moment the weather may range from arctic to tropical across the thirty eastern states and provinces, or it may be identical at locales 2,000 miles apart. This, in a nutshell, is the varied weather of the East.

Following is a list of the some of the extremes of heat and cold to visit the East over the past century or so. The selection was a difficult one, since nearly every year some location in the East experiences record-breaking heat or cold. The events chosen here are based as much on their extent as their severity.

GREAT EASTERN HEAT WAVES

August 18–19, 1935—The normally cool Maritime Provinces of Canada had their hottest days in history as the mercury reached 101 degrees in Nova Scotia and 103 in New Brunswick.

July–August 1936—All of the summers of the Dust Bowl Decade (1930–1939) were on the warm side, but the summer of 1936 takes the cake as the most severe and widespread heat wave in North American history. Fifteen states from Texas to North Dakota (where it was 121 degrees!), to West Virginia (112 degrees), Pennsylvania (111 degrees), New Jersey (110 degrees), and New York City (106 degrees), along with the Canadian prov-

inces of Ontario (108 degrees), and Manitoba (112 degrees) had their hottest days ever. From the Ohio Valley to the Great Plains it was the hottest summer (measured by average temperature) in the history of thermometers.

June–August 1954—It was déjà vu all over again as another hot decade withered crops and people. In the peak of the heat during the summer of 1954, six states from Nevada (122 degrees) to North and South Carolina (109 and 111 degrees, respectively) and Virginia (110 degrees) saw their highest temperatures on record. In terms of average temperature, it was the Southeast's hottest summer, while the Northeastern states and southeastern Canada got their turn just a year later, in 1955. Both summers ended with a round of drought-busting hurricanes.

July 1966—"Hot town, summer in the city . . ." went the hit tune during the summer of 1966, and the mercury cooperated by soaring to 107 degrees at New York's LaGuardia Airport, downtown Philadelphia, and Harrisburg, Pennsylvania, the highest temperatures ever reported in those metropolitan areas.

August 2, 1975—New England's "Hot Saturday" sent the mercury to 107 at Chester, Massachusetts, and 104 at Providence, Rhode Island, both state records. Normally cool Nantucket, Massachusetts, had its hottest day ever, an even 100 degrees, and high atop Mount Washington the temperature reached "room temperature"—72 degrees—for the first time.

April 1976—Summer arrived in spring as an April heat wave sent the thermometer soaring as high as 98 degrees at Providence, Rhode Island. In much of the Northeast it was the hottest weather of the year.

June–September 1988—Persistent heat and drought scorched the country from coast to coast. Two cities recorded their hottest days ever—Cleveland (104 degrees) and San Francisco (103)—and many towns in the northeastern United States had more 100-degree days than they had ever seen before in one summer. By August the relentless heat had warmed the normally brisk waters of Lake Erie to a tropical 80 degrees—another all-time record, and nearly warm enough for tropical storms to form!

April–September 1991—Summer came early and stayed long past its welcome. The East's two largest metropolitan areas—New York and Philadelphia—sweltered under more 90-degree-plus days (thirty-nine and fifty-three, respectively) than ever before.

GREAT EASTERN COLD WAVES

February 1899—The most widespread outbreak of extreme cold ever to visit the United States set cold records—most of which still stand—in such far-flung places as South Dakota, Texas, Michigan, Florida, and New Jersey. Perhaps the most remarkable reading was 2 below zero in Tallahassee, Florida. The cold wave ended with a massive blizzard along the Mid-Atlantic coast.

January 5, 1904—At 34 below, the town of River Vale recorded New Jersey's lowest temperature in history. Only 17 miles away, the low temperature at New York City's Central Park was 30 degrees warmer—the heat island effect when it was needed the most!

December–January 1917–1918—In many cities in the eastern half of the United States this was the coldest winter (in terms of average temperature) on record until the winter of 1976–1977. Combined with a deadly flu epidemic and wartime fuel shortages, it was also one of the most miserable on record for millions of Americans.

February 1934—After freezing Alaska for most of January (66 below at Fairbanks), arctic air poured into the northeastern states, giving places like Buffalo, Boston, Providence, New York City, Philadelphia, Mount Washington, and Sault Saint Marie (Michigan) their coldest weather in history.

Bottom honors went to Stillwater Reservoir, New York, at 52 degrees below, and Vanderbilt, Michigan, at 51 below. An earlier cold wave during the last days of 1933 set city records in Ottawa and Montreal and a state record of 50 below at Bloomfield, Vermont.

January 23, 1935—The thermometer at Iroquois Falls, Ontario, sank to 73 below zero—eastern North America's all-time coldest temperature reading (excluding Greenland).

January 1966—On the tail of a Mid-Atlantic states blizzard, cold air poured into the heart of Dixie. Twenty-four below at Russellville was Alabama's coldest recorded temperature, and state records were broken in Mississippi and North Carolina.

January 1977—Repeated arctic outbreaks made this the coldest month on record across much of the Ohio Valley and Mid-Atlantic region. Cincinnati's average of 12 degrees was a whopping 19 degrees colder than normal, while Philadelphia's 20-degree average was the coldest in two hundred years on record. Some locations ended up with their coldest winter ever. The following two winters were nearly as cold (or colder in some spots) as that of 1976–1977, leading to an unprecedented three abnormally cold winters in a row for the East.

February 18, 1979—Bitter cold air and a clear, calm night led the temperature to plummet to 52 below zero at Old Forge, New York, tying the all-time record low for the eastern United States.

January 1982—Cold waves struck on consecutive Sundays—January 10 and 17. On January 10, thousands of Cincinnati fans shivered at 9 below during the Bengals–Forty-Niners playoff game, the second coldest professional football game ever played—it was 13 below at a Green Bay (Wisconsin) Packers game in 1967. On the second Sunday the mercury sank to 5 below at Washington, D.C., its first subzero reading in forty-eight years, and gave Philadelphia its coldest afternoon ever—an even zero.

January 1985—The Southeast's coldest cold wave of this century sent the freezing line south into the Florida Everglades. In central Florida's citrus belt, the double whammy from this cold wave and the Christmas freeze of the previous winter destroyed entire groves, pushing the citrus belt south 50 to 100 miles. Before the similar back-to-back freezes a century earlier in 1894 and 1895, oranges were grown in far northern Florida, 150 miles north of the northernmost surviving groves after 1985. Up in the Northeast, it was 4 below in Washington, D.C., where President Reagan's inaugural parade was canceled, 8 below in Atlanta, and 34 below atop Mount Mitchell, North Carolina.

January 28, 1986—For the third winter in a row, freezing weather invaded central Florida. This time the major casualty was the space shuttle *Challenger*, whose explosion at 47,000 feet was blamed, in part, on the effect of the 28-degree overnight cold on rubber seals in the booster rockets (as well as on the decision to launch in the cold weather). The commission investigating the accident also suggested that the seals "could have been affected . . . by changing winds aloft" as the shuttle flew through jet stream turbulence (associated with the cold wave) around 35,000 feet.

EL NIÑO

Californians are becoming concerned that the dreaded "El Niño" is again about to strike their shores . . .

The above comment from a 1986 television documentary illustrates some of the apprehensions—and misconceptions—that many have about the weather upheaval known as *El Niño*. Recent history makes it clear that the Niño phenomenon is one of great concern and interest to weather watchers. The winter of 1982–1983 brought a Niño that has been rated the biggest in a century. Three times the usual number of cyclones—some with hurricane-force winds—pounded the Gulf Coast. Several cities along the Mid-Atlantic coast were buried by their heaviest snowstorm on record. Spring was the wettest ever for much of the eastern seaboard, and widespread flooding wreaked billions of dollars in damage. Despite this, winter temperatures were exceptionally mild. Meanwhile, the Atlantic hurricane seasons of 1982 and 1983 were exceptionally quiet, with only half the usual number of tropical storms. For better and worse, the weather of 1982–1983 was odd by any standard, and if it was caused by the "dreaded Niño," then it behooves us to understand what the Niño is and what causes it.

Sometimes it is easier to tell what something isn't rather than what it is, and El Niño is *not* a storm that strikes the coast. As a matter of fact, the phenomenon that is correctly called El Niño happens thousands of miles from our shores, and has little, if any, impact on eastern weather. However, it's a catchy name, and in the absence of a better one, it appears that whatever it *is* will be called El Niño for some time to come.

In its original sense, El Niño is the name given by the fishermen of coastal Peru and Ecuador to a warm ocean current that shows up every so often. Normally, the western coast of South America is swept by a current of cold water from the Antarctic. Cold water drawn up from the depths mixes with this current, keeping the water good and chilly. This is the Southern Hemisphere counterpart of the current that keeps San Francisco in cool fog all summer. The fresh supply of deep water brought to the surface by this upwelling is loaded with organic nutrients, which feed the plankton and, in turn, the swarms of anchovies that populate the area. As a result, these Peruvian and Ecuadoran coastal areas are among the richest fishing grounds in the world, although in recent

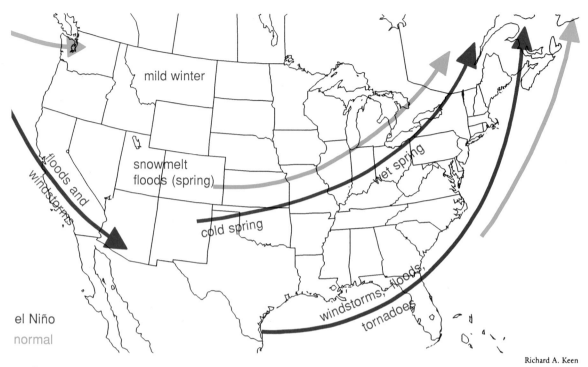

mild winter

snowmelt
floods (spring)

floods and
windstorms

wet spring

cold spring

windstorms, floods,

tornadoes

el Niño

normal

Richard A. Keen

*NIÑO-RELATED WEATHER ANOMALIES AND THEIR STORM TRACKS—The strange weather
of the 1982-1983 El Niño can be explained, for the most part, by the shifted storm tracks.*

years they have been severely depleted by overfishing.

The coastal current and its attendant up-welling vary according to seasons. In December, at the height of the Southern Hemisphere summer, the current usually weakens and the coastal water warms up a little. Some years the current ceases or reverses direction, and the water warms up a lot—as much as 10 degrees or more. In these years the nutrient-loaded upwelling ceases, dwindling the fish population. Since these warmings often begin around Christmas, the locals have dubbed the warm current El Niño. The Spanish translates to "The Child," referring to—without implying blame—the Christ child. Recent Niños occurred in 1957, 1972,

1976, 1982, and 1987. Combined with the over-fishing that has taken place, these Niños have become increasingly disastrous for the local fishing industry, not to mention for the fish themselves and for the birds that feed on them.

The phenomenon doesn't end with dead anchovies littering the beaches of Peru and Ecuador. The warm water may spread, reaching westward across the tropical Pacific and northward along the west coast of Mexico. At this point the warming becomes a global concern, since its worldwide climate effects can be enormous. However, out of due respect for the fishermen who coined the name, remember that El Niño really applies to the

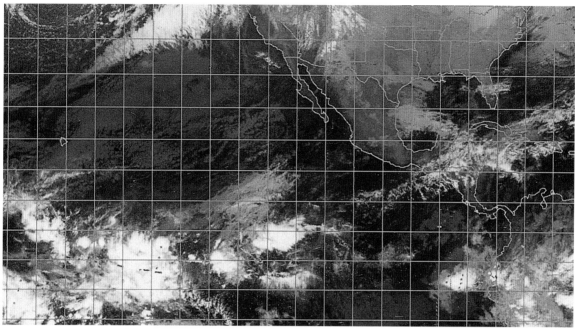

El NIÑO: THE VIEW FROM SPACE—This sequence of images from a NOAA weather satellite graphically demonstrates how thunderstorms spawned by an El Niño in the Pacific Ocean can result in storms over the East. On January 17, 1983, at the height of the largest El Niño of the century, thunderstorms blossom over the Pacific Ocean south of Hawaii.

warming of the ocean water off the South American coast. It is, to say the least, stretching it a bit to apply the name to storms in New Jersey, Alabama, and California, but again, for lack of a better name, let's use it.

The variety and scale of the worldwide weather freaks that occurred during the 1982-83 Niño are truly impressive. Elsewhere during that Niño year, California was slammed by a relentless series of Pacific storms, and snow dusted the cacti of northern Mexico. Around the globe, torrential rains flooded desert areas of Peru and Ecuador, while droughts struck Brazil, Africa, and Indonesia, and the life-giving rains of the Indian monsoon arrived late. A long, hot summer led to terrible brush fires

that consumed thousands of square miles of Australian bush, along with several small towns. Many meteorologists—but not all, mind you—believe that all of these weather disasters were related, and that the massive warming of the Pacific Ocean provided the common link.

Let's slow down a bit. Could all this bad weather really be the fault of some warm water? The last Niño before 1982 was in 1976, and the following winter was nothing at all like the mild and wet one of 1982–1983. The winter of 1976–1977 was the driest winter in recent memory across most of the United States, while the 1982–1983 winter was one of the wettest. The bicentennial winter was also one of the bitterest in history. It was the winter of

129

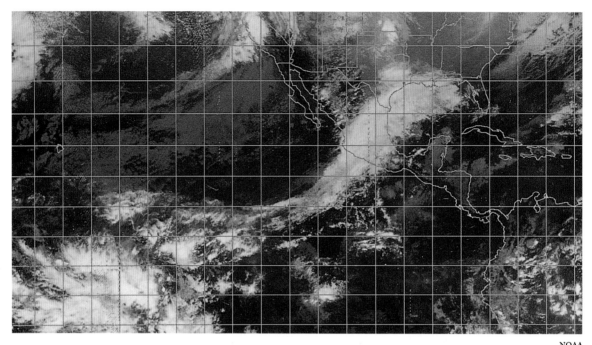

CLOUDS STREAM INTO THE GULF—One day after the previous image, a thick batch of cirrus clouds from the Pacific thunderstorms streams northeastward across Mexico. The cirrus clouds mark the location of 120-mile-per-hour jet stream winds blowing into the Gulf of Mexico.

the savage Buffalo Blizzard in upstate New York, and snow even fell on Miami. However, there were few coastal storms on either side of the continent. What happened to the storms striking the coasts of North America from all directions? Why was it so cold? Was the 1976 Niño different from that of 1982, or is it all a bunch of bunk?

The reason for the differences between 1976–1977 and 1982–1983 lies in the misuse of the term El Niño. True, both years saw Niños off the coast of Peru. However, this relatively local phenomenon is not the global upheaval that sends storms spinning in the Gulf of Mexico. Rather, it is the warming of large areas of the rest of the Pacific Ocean—and especially the tropical Pacific—that

upsets the weather. These warmings were quite different between the two years.

CHANGING THE WIND

To paraphrase certain stockbrokers, when the Pacific warms up, the world listens. Indeed, a warmer-than-usual tropical Pacific Ocean can disturb the most fundamental forces that drive the world's weather. The most powerful and persistent winds of the world—the subtropical jets of the Northern and Southern hemispheres—result from the upward and outward flow of air in the huge thunderstorm masses that cover Africa, South America, and Indonesia. North of the equator, air streaming north from the upper levels of these

NOAA

GULF COAST CYCLONE—Two days later, on January 20, 1983, the cirrus clouds and jet stream winds consolidate into a cyclone over Mississippi. The Gulf Coast endured three times its usual number of cyclones during the 1982-1983 winter, making it one of the wettest and stormiest winters ever.

thunderstorms turns into an eastward-blowing jet stream, thanks to the slower speed of the underlying ground at higher latitudes. The predominant patterns of the subtropical jet result from the locations of the thunderstorm masses, with the jet being farther north and stronger due north of the storms. South American thunderstorms strengthen the jet over eastern North America and out into the North Atlantic. The next jet to the west—the one that develops north of Indonesia—usually cuts northeast across the Pacific Ocean.

Normally, when the tropical thunderstorms are dousing Indonesia, New Guinea, and other islands at the western limits of the Pacific, the subtropical jet is strongest from eastern China to the western Pacific south of Japan. This jet stream is so persistent across most of the Pacific that during World War II, the Japanese used it to float balloon-borne bombs to the United States. However, the jet has a tendency to peter out by the time it reaches North America. This kept most of the Japanese balloons from ever reaching the United States, although a few did make it, causing several deaths and minor damage.

The thunderstorms that drive the subtropical jet are fed by the latent heat evaporated from the surfaces of the warm tropical seas. These thunderstorms prefer to build up over the equatorial land masses, where the overhead sun is most effective at directly heating the ground and causing the rising

131

EL NIÑO YEARS

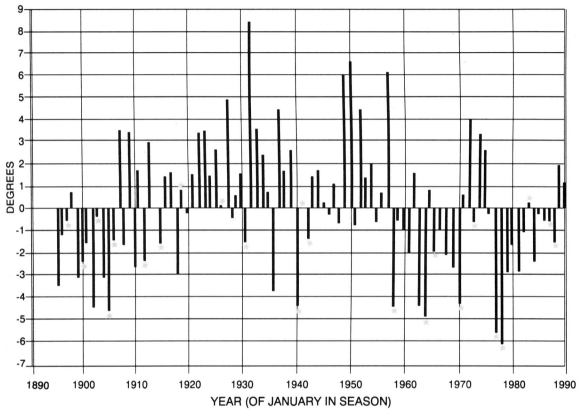

National Climatic Data Center/NOAA

SOUTHEAST U.S. WINTER TEMPERATURES, 1895–1990—Ninety-six years of winter (December through February) temperatures, averaged over a five-state area (Alabama, Florida, Georgia, Mississippi, and South Carolina), are shown here as departures from the long-term mean. Overall, winters during El Niños (marked with stars) average 3° colder than non–El Niño winters.

currents of air that trigger the storms. Of the three major land masses along the equator, Indonesia is the smallest, being in reality a bunch of islands. Most of its surface area is water. However, Indonesia is surrounded by the most extensive and warmest of all the tropical ocean areas, and this makes it the thunderstorm capital of the world.

When the tropical Pacific Ocean gets even warmer than usual, as happens during some Niños, a major shift in the position of the Indonesian thunderstorm mass can take place. Sensing the large supply of latent heat energy lying over the open ocean, and not feeling as bound to form over the islands as would its African and South American counterparts, this mass of storms may move east. The bulk of the thunderstorms can shift several

EL NIÑO YEARS

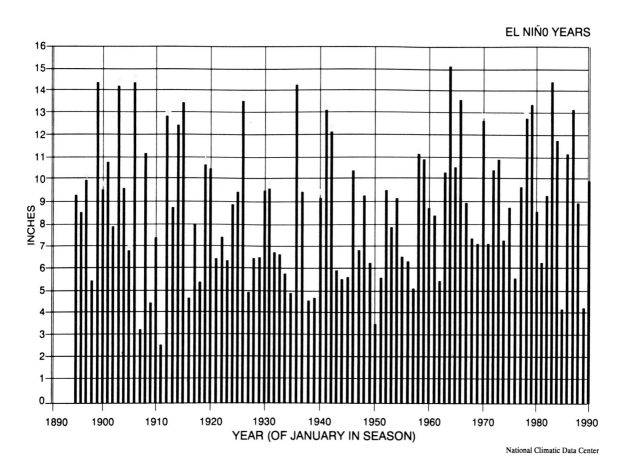

National Climatic Data Center

FLORIDA WINTER RAINFALL, 1895-1990—The Sunshine State is a bit less sunny when an El Niño is in progress. Florida's December through January rainfall increases by 52 percent, on the average, during an El Niño.

thousand miles to the east. At the height of the 1982–1983 Niño, it strayed 5,000 miles from its normal location. When the largest source of energy release into the atmosphere moves one-fifth of the way around the world, things are bound to happen!

What did happen when the thunderstorms moved east was that the subtropical jet stream likewise extended farther east. In 1982–1983, the jet knifed into California at full strength, and floods sent hot tubs floating into the sea. When the thun-

derstorms occasionally moved even farther east, at times all the way to South America, the Pacific jet blew into the Gulf of Mexico, generating those powerful cyclones.

NIÑO WEATHER

The storms of 1982–1983 illustrate the classic pattern of Niño weather. The subtropical storm track continued across the southern United States from November through March, unleashing high

133

winds, floods, and even some tornadoes along the California and Gulf coasts. Meanwhile, the northern states were high and dry, well north of all the action; parts of southern Canada had one of their warmest winters on record.

The arrival of spring brought no real relief from the ravages of the subtropical jet, just a change of targets. The jet performed its normal seasonal swing to the north, and frequent storms began dumping rain up the Atlantic coast. Farther west, the storm track moved north into the Rockies, dumping massive snows. The jet disappeared during the summer, as it usually does, but the excess thunderstorms over the tropical Pacific remained, apparently sapping the strength of their counterparts over the tropical Atlantic and Caribbean and depriving these seas of their usual hurricane season. By autumn, the mass of Pacific thunderstorms had returned to its usual home near Asia, and the Niño was over.

The weather patterns of 1983 were similar in many ways to those of 1878, 1941, 1958, and 1973, all years with large Niños. Each of these years featured stormy winters across the South and mild winters across the northern states, followed by soggy springs from the Rockies to the Atlantic. But there were important differences among these Niño years, particularly in the timing and duration of the unusual weather—sometimes the stormiest weather started a year early!

An explanation is needed for the cold, dry winter of 1976–1977. Although a Niño year, this winter's weather was nearly the exact opposite of the one experienced during the 1982–1983 and earlier Niños. Once again, the Niño off the coast of Peru was not the problem. The western part of the tropical Pacific did *not* warm up like it did in 1982. There was a slight warming, and the Indonesian thunderstorms did move east a little. But they did not move far enough east to steer the subtropical jet directly into the southern United States. Instead,

the jet veered far to the north, crossing into the Yukon before plunging back south into the heart of Dixie. This enormous bulge in the jet, with its western ridge and eastern trough, led polar air deep into the southeast. The result: frozen oranges.

A NIÑO IS BORN

We have seen that thunderstorms and ocean currents in places as distant as New Guinea and Micronesia can do strange things to the weather. Accordingly, a few words are in order about the tropical Pacific Ocean and why its currents fluctuate. It begins with the sun heating the ocean's top layer. Being lighter than cold water, the warm water stays on top. Most of the time, winds in the tropics blow from the east—these are the *trade winds* of sailing fame. The trade winds blow the warm water to the west, toward New Guinea, where it starts to pile up. This leaves cooler water in the eastern Pacific; this pattern of warm water to the west and cool water to the east is the normal situation in the tropical Pacific.

If the trade winds should slacken, all that warm water piled up around New Guinea starts to slosh back toward Peru. Sometimes, the trade winds actually reverse and blow from the *west*; this gives the pile of warm water an extra push toward Peru. When this happens, the normally cool eastern Pacific gets overrun by warm water, and El Niño is in progress. Eventually, the easterly trade winds return, and the warm water heads back toward New Guinea.

This, in the simplest terms, is the cause of El Niño. The real details are not so simple. The patterns of warming and cooling differ from one Niño to the next, as do the timing, duration, and strength of the events. One very basic question remaining for researchers is, why do the trade winds weaken? When this and other still-open questions are answered, we may be able to forecast winter weather patterns months—if not years—in advance.

FIRE AND ICE

Evidence . . . shows a cooling trend over the Northern Hemisphere since around 1940, amounting to over 0.5 degrees.

—Ernest M. Agee, Purdue University, 1980

In the next few decades, we can expect a significant global warming . . .

—American Meteorological Society Council, 1988

Some say the world will end in fire, some say it will end in ice.

—Robert Frost

Way back in 1980, following three of the coldest winters in a row in the history of the East, the talk among climate researchers and in the media was of future ice ages. There was even a novel that described the burial of the Capitol building in Washington by a nonstop snowstorm. Less than a decade later, after several mild winters and a few of the hottest summers in history, the talk had turned to global warming and the melting of what snow and ice there is on our planet. What had changed? Is the climate really different than it was ten years ago, or is the change mostly in our perceptions—and expectations—of the what the climate is, and what it will do?

There is no doubt the climate changes. The glaciers that covered half of North America eighteen thousand years ago, and are now gone, provide the most dramatic example of climate change. On a more personal level, many of us can recall how there used to be more (or fewer, depending where we live) hurricanes or snowstorms when we were kids, and our grandparents claiming that "winters aren't like they used to be." In 1781, Thomas Jefferson wrote: "Both heats and colds are become much more moderate within the memory even of the middle-aged. Snows are less frequent and less deep." Of course, weather is never *exactly* the same from year to year, but some of the fluctuations of temperature, storm patterns, and such over the years certainly suggest that something is happening to the climate. The trick is to pin down *what* is happening (the evidence is far from unanimous), and then—this is the clincher—explain *why*.

Before we talk about *climate change*, we'd better make it clear what is meant by the word *climate*. It's not the same as *weather*. The latter is the

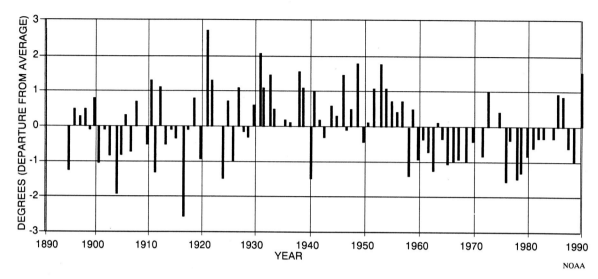

EASTERN CLIMATE: THE PAST 96 YEARS—Annual temperatures have a large year-to-year variability. The decades of the 1920s through the 1950s were warmer than the decades before and since, but overall there is no evidence of any warming or cooling trends.

day-to-day, even hour-to-hour, fluctuations of clouds, winds, temperature, and the like due to the passages of such things as thunderstorms, fronts, and cyclones. Climate is the sum total of all this weather over a period of time.

There are many ways to express this thing called climate, depending on the information on hand. Lacking barometers, our ancestors used descriptive methods, recording crop successes and failures, freezes and thaws, and great deluges. This being the age of computers and weather instruments, though, the preferred method nowadays is to use numbers—lots of them. There are a bewildering variety of things in the atmosphere that can be measured, and new ones are being thought up all the time. The most useful measurements for observing climate are the basics—temperature and precipitation. Long records of both are the cornerstone of climate studies; in the East they go back over two centuries. For earlier periods of time, we must rely on evidence supplied by

tree rings, silt deposits in lakes, features gouged in the ground by now-gone glaciers, and even comments written by the earliest settlers.

Many folks like to think of their climate in terms of a "normal" about which the weather fluctuates. *Normal* is usually taken to mean the average temperature, or whatever, over a suitably long period of time (ten years or more). However, these averages depend on the selection of years that go into them, and, like the weather itself, are always changing. The truth is that there really is no exact normal. What we call normal today would have been considered quite unusual during the Ice Age or back in the days of dinosaurs, or even a century ago. So, as the climate changes, so does our perception—and definition—of what is normal.

The shortest period of time that can be realistically called climate is a year, and the quickest kind of climate change is the variability between one year and the next. On the other end of the scale is the

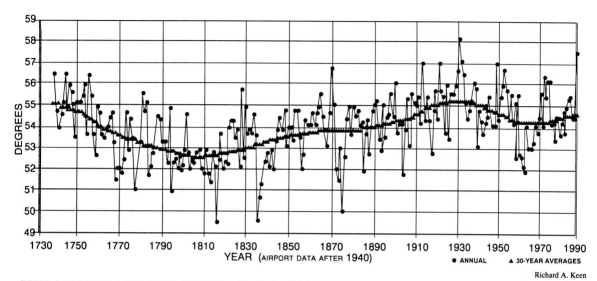

PHILADELPHIA TEMPERATURES: THE PAST 250 YEARS—One of the longest temperature records in North America is Philadelphia's, which began in 1737. The heavy line shows the trend of thirty-year average temperatures.

five-billion-year evolution of our planet's atmosphere, from a steamy soup of poisonous gases to the life-sustaining air of today. You can read about the history of the atmosphere in the "Why Is There Weather" chapter; let's look at some of the things the climate has done since.

WHAT A DIFFERENCE A YEAR MAKES

For us mortals whose lives span less than a century, the most familiar and noticeable versions of climate change are the differences between one year and another. One summer may kill crops with drought, while the next drowns them with incessant rains. Some winters you may ski a trail that other years is better suited for hiking. Over the past century, average winter temperatures up and down the East Coast have varied by as much as 15 degrees, and average yearly temperatures have fluctuated by half that. The East Coast has one of the most reliable rainfall rates in the world, but yearly totals can be twice as high in wet years as in dry ones. New York City's annual rainfall has ranged over a nearly three-fold difference, from 26 to 67 inches.

This variability of the climate is enormous. In terms of temperature, the year-to-year fluctuations are equivalent to moving from Atlanta to Boston, or, in terms of precipitation, from Rochester to Tucson, Arizona. In fact, the changes are nearly as big as those that occurred during the Ice Age! The distinction is, of course, that the Ice Age went on for thousands of years, while the current fluctuations last a year or season at a time. Nonetheless, we are talking about a rapid and large climate change.

The year-to-year climate fluctuations can have enormous economic consequences, in large part due to the very rapidity of the changes. Agricultural practices, for example, can adjust to the slower climate trends lasting decades or more. However, imagine suddenly moving an Orlando orange grove to Cape Hatteras, or a South Jersey cornfield to the

137

Painted Desert, for a year. They wouldn't do very well, would they? That's what an extremely cold winter in Florida, or dry summer in New Jersey, can be (and has been) like.

In the previous chapter we saw the marked effects of El Niño on the climate of parts of the East. However, Niños are relatively rare, and ten years may pass between the really big ones. What happens the other nine years? The most plausible possibilities invoke some changes in the amount of heat entering the atmosphere. Remember, the need to carry heat to the poles is what drives the weather in the first place. El Niño is an example of how huge shifts in the heat contained in the tropical ocean can affect climate.

Similar shifts of warm and cold water can take place in the North Pacific and Atlantic, and no doubt affect the weather of the East. The Pacific is the source of most of the storms that cross North America, and many of these storms pick up steam from the warm waters of the Gulf of Mexico and the Gulf Stream. When the temperature contrast of the Pacific between Alaska and Hawaii is exceptionally great, the air above will tend to take on the same contrast, strengthening the jet stream. A stronger Pacific jet stream sends more and stronger storms ashore to cross North America and affect the weather of the East. On the other hand, a weak temperature contrast weakens the jet. If the Pacific is cold to the west and warm to the east, the jet will tend to follow the boundary by veering to the north, and the storms plow into Canada and Alaska instead of the "lower forty-eight." Back east, if the Gulf Stream meanders farther from the coast, the storms that form off Cape Hatteras tend to track out to sea, leaving fewer northeasters for New England. And so on. If it has nothing better to do, the jet tends to follow the boundaries between areas of warm and cold ocean water. The important words here are *tends to,* because sometimes it happens that way; often it doesn't. From day to day the jet stream can, and does, stray far from its "expected" position.

Snow on the ground can also influence the heat balance of the atmosphere. Fresh snow is quite good at reflecting away sunlight that would otherwise heat the ground. It is also an excellent radiator of heat out to space. Furthermore, a deep, insulating blanket of the white stuff prevents the residual warmth of the ground from seeping into the atmosphere. If Canada is covered with heavy snows early in the winter, polar air masses forming over the north country get a little colder than they would otherwise. Cold waves headed for Florida nip the citrus a bit harder if the states to the north lie under a good blanket of snow. Snow cover can affect local climate, too. A 6-inch coating of snow can easily knock 5 or 10 degrees off the overnight low temperature, and turn an ordinary cold wave into a record-breaker.

Six times the size of New England and 1,000 miles to the northwest, the huge inland sea of Hudson Bay has its influence on the climate of the East. Until it freezes over in November or December, the open water of the bay moderates polar air passing south. If the bay freezes unusually early in the fall or the ice lingers late into the spring, early- and late-season cold snaps in New England and the Maritime Provinces can be more severe than usual. As farmers and gardeners know, these unseasonal frosts can be devastating.

All these explanations for climate variability have one problem in common—they don't really account for much of the variation that is actually seen from one year to the next. Every so often there is a winter or summer that looks like it suffered from one or another of these influences. Most years, though, the weather acts in strange ways without any unusual blankets of snow and ice, errant ocean currents, or El Niños to blame.

If the climate is not reacting all that often to outside forces, like oceans and snow on the ground, what is left? Can it be that it changes on its own whim? This may sound silly at first, but it is a possibility—which brings us to an elusive concept called *autovariability*. This has nothing to do with cars; it comes from the Greek prefix *auto,* meaning "self," and translates to "self-changing." So what does it mean?

We know that today's weather pattern—the positions of highs, lows, jet streams, and the like—depends very much on what yesterday's pattern was. And tomorrow's will depend on what is happening today. This concept is the essence of weather forecasting. By using the laws of physics and lots of calculations, we can predict what that change will be from one day to the next. Carrying this idea further, we realize that the weather pattern, say, six months from now will be affected by today's weather map. And so will every day in between now and then. Certainly, the effect gets smaller as the interval gets longer, but it's still there. Remember, a single storm can be the most important feature of an entire winter, and a 100-mile difference in its track can make all the difference for your town. A severe winter may result from the weather "getting off on the wrong foot."

To put it in different terms, the whole sequence of fronts, cyclones, and anticyclones—the exact tracks they take and the specific dates and times they pass certain points—depends on their positions on the first day of the season (or *any* day). It's like rolling a boulder down a hillside. The law of gravity and the shape of the hill guide the path of the boulder once it's rolling, but the precise point of departure—the exact position of the rock when you shoved it—decides which of the infinite possible paths that the rock actually takes and where it finally lands.

Unfortunately, our knowledge of the atmosphere isn't complete enough to allow forecasts to be made very far in advance. It's tough enough going five days into the future, much less six months. In effect, we know neither the shape of the hill nor the initial position of the rock accurately enough to

do better. This leaves us with the prospect that seasonal forecasts, those predictions of general weather patterns made a month to a year in advance, may never be as correct as we would like.

Again, autovariability is an elusive concept, and difficult to understand. It's not as easy to deal with as some clear-cut, identifiable cause such as ocean temperatures or volcanoes. But it's there, and because of it, don't expect perfect long-range seasonal forecasts any time soon.

CYCLES AND SPELLS

There will come seven years of great plenty throughout all the land of Egypt, but after them there will arise seven years of famine.

—Genesis 41:29-30

Cycles of rain and drought, and of heat and cold, are nothing new. They plagued the pharaohs of Egypt in the times of Genesis, and today they plague the presidents and prime ministers of nations from Africa to North America. North America had its share of problems during the lengthy drought that desiccated the central states and prairie provinces during the 1930s, and at times extended to the East Coast. The drought area became known as the Dust Bowl, and, curiously, it lasted seven years—from 1933 to 1940. A four-year drought in the Northeast during the 1960s dropped reservoirs to perilously low levels. Another northeastern drought in the early 1980s had a similar effect, and hot and dry weather scorched the Southeast in the mid-1980s.

The perception that droughts seem to occur every eight, twenty, or whatever number of years has prompted researchers to look for "cycles" in the climate record. In the East at least, there's no evidence of these cycles. Rather than being the dry side of a regular rainfall cycle, droughts are more properly thought of as "spells" of below normal precipitation, usually lasting a few years. Droughts could be five years apart, or they could be fifty. A twenty-year cycle does appear in the records of major droughts in parts of the Midwest and Great Plains, but only if you let the drought areas move a little from one cycle to the next. The similarity between this twenty-year cycle and a twenty-two-year cycle of storm activity on the surface of the sun, known as *sunspots*, has led to speculation that sunspots may, in some way, cause droughts. However, this theory is very controversial, partly because the timing between sunspots and drought isn't always right, and partly because nobody has any idea how sunspots could cause droughts in one particular part of the world.

Droughts aren't the only things that come in spells; mild and severe winters and even busy hurricane seasons have come in bunches. Anyone over forty years old from South Carolina northward remembers the spate of hurricanes in the mid-1950s, the likes of which haven't been seen before or since. The same years saw mild winters from Miami to Montreal, in contrast to the bitter winters of the 1960s. Florida frosts, which have since become all too common, were rare, and summers were hotter.

Many of these climatic oddities fit together in a coherent pattern. As the Bermuda High expanded to the north and west during the 1950s, the coastal storm track moved inland to the Appalachians. With more storms passing west of the coastal plain, the major metropolises of the eastern seaboard often found themselves in the warm and rainy southeastern sector of the cyclones. Coastal northeasters of the kind that bring the big snows were few and far between. When summer came, the strong Bermuda High brought persistent heat waves, and hurricanes that normally would have headed straight out to sea or toward Florida were diverted straight north up the coast. After 1958, the storm track moved back offshore, and for a while, the storms tended to be so far out to sea that they missed the seaboard entirely—causing the Great Northeastern Drought of 1963–1966.

The wanderings of the east coast storm track have continued, although not as dramatically as during the 1950s and 1960s. The cool conditions that began in 1958 have more or less persisted, with a respite in the early 1970s, a return to colder years after 1976, and milder conditions again in the late 1980s. Generally, warm years bring the storms inland, and cold years send them offshore. It's all part of the larger scheme of things, with a general northward shift of jet streams and storm tracks observed all around the Northern Hemisphere during the globally warm 1950s, and a southward shift since then. Eastern China and Japan, whose climates are similar in many ways to eastern North America, saw many of the same strange weather patterns (including lots of typhoons) at the time. I wish I could tell you *why* these global changes in weather patterns happen, but I can't—even though I wrote my doctoral thesis on the subject! It's been suggested that ocean temperatures and arctic ice could each play a role, but these could as easily be a result of the climate shifts as a cause. Whatever the cause, the climate has swung between warm and cold in the past, will continue to do so in the future, and is doing this on its own volition. We should take note of the climate's past behavior before blaming many of the future changes that are bound to happen on ourselves, the Russians, or humanity in general.

THE LITTLE ICE AGE

The longest spell of odd weather in the recorded history of North America was a frosty period known as the Little Ice Age. It could be the reason this book is written in English instead of Norwegian. Let me explain.

A thousand years ago the climate was enough warmer than now—by 2 to 5 degrees—that Vikings sailed their little boats from Scandinavia to Iceland, Greenland, Newfoundland, and possibly as far south as Massachusetts. Greenland was so mild that self-sufficient, crop-raising colonies thrived for two centuries or more. Times got tough in these colonies after A.D. 1200 when a sharp downturn in the climate made agriculture iffy at best. Sailing conditions around Greenland worsened as the ice thickened, and by A.D. 1300 the Scandinavian homeland lost all contact with its colonies. Explorers returning to Greenland centuries later could find no trace of the Norse colonies. The Iceland settlements survived, although it wasn't easy, and one can speculate about the history of North America had the Greenland colonies also been able to endure and expand.

That cold spell—the Little Ice Age—persisted for four centuries, finally moderating around A.D. 1700. Thomas Jefferson may very well have witnessed its final years when he wrote that "snows are less frequent and less deep." There are no temperature records from the time, but evidence ranging from rocks left by glaciers in the Alps and Rockies, to Chinese and European harvest records, to dates of the Japanese emperor's cherry blossom festivals, as well as the sad history of the Viking settlers, indicate the cooling amounted to 2 degrees or more.

As is the case for all climate fluctuations, we don't know for sure what caused the Northern Hemisphere to cool down for four hundred years. However, scientists doing some clever detective work found that Chinese records of spots on the sun, Scandinavian sightings of the *aurora borealis,* and variations in the amount of certain kinds of carbon atoms in tree rings all strongly suggest that as Earth cooled, so did the sun. If the sun was truly sending us less energy at the time, we may need to look no farther for a cause of the Little Ice Age.

SOMETHING'S IN THE AIR

Now we get to some of the things that are more commonly thought of as climate change, such as the effects of carbon dioxide, volcanoes, and yes, even nuclear bombs. Compared to something as slippery as

Urban Archives, Temple University

DUST BOWL—What looks like a drought scene from Oklahoma is actually a dust storm on a farm in southern New Jersey in 1938.

autovariability, the influences of dust and gases in the air are refreshingly simple to grasp. The theory behind these atmospheric pollutants, some natural and some human-made, rests on how they foul up the radiation balance of the globe. Earth gains heat energy from sunlight striking the surface of the planet and loses it by infrared radiation back out to space.

The current temperature of the Earth, averaged worldwide, results from the balance between the heat gains and heat losses. Anything that changes the amount of incoming light or outgoing radia-

141

tion, or both, changes the temperature of the Earth. Yes, it's just like your checkbook—if you earn less, or spend more, or (especially) both, you go broke.

The way for planet Earth to earn less is to block out the sunshine. Volcanoes spew tremendous volumes of geologic gunk into the atmosphere, and these clouds can certainly blot out the sun. The ash cloud from Mount Saint Helens' cataclysmic eruption of May 18, 1980, kept towns from Washington state to Montana in the gloom for one or two memorable days. And these places did cool off from the lack of sunshine—afternoon temperatures were 10 degrees or more lower than they should have been. However, this was a local and short-term effect and qualifies more as a bizarre form of weather than as climate change.

To affect the climate, volcanic ash has to get high into the atmosphere and stay there for several years. Volcanic ash itself—those little particles of rock that gritted everyone's eyes after Mount Saint Helens' eruption—doesn't stay up all that long. Usually most of it falls out of the sky after a few days and never has a chance to foul the climate. What does stay up are the clouds of sulfur dioxide gas shot into the sky from erupting volcanoes. Sulfur dioxide is the same noxious gas that comes from coal-burning factories and power plants and gives us acid rain. Mount Saint Helens blew half a million tons of the stuff into the atmosphere.

Mount Saint Helens had relatively little sulfur, however, and much more of the stuff went skyward when the Mexican volcano El Chichon (meaning "The Bump") blew in April 1982. The 1,000-degree heat of the gases combined with their muzzle velocities out the volcano's throat shot tremendous amounts of sulfur dioxide into the stratosphere. The stratosphere is that part of the atmosphere lying between about 8 and 30 miles up. It is a pretty quiet place, and once gases get there, they stay for months or years.

As a gas, sulfur dioxide is transparent, but in the stratosphere it combines with water vapor to form little droplets of sulfuric acid—the same corrosive material that forms the clouds shrouding the planet Venus. Fortunately, Earth's sulfuric acid clouds never get as dense as Venus', although after El Chichon they were thick enough to blot out 2 to 5 percent of the sun's rays. Similarly thick clouds formed after the eruptions of Krakatoa in Indonesia (1883), Santa Maria in Guatemala (1902), Katmai in Alaska (1912), Agung, also in Indonesia (1963), and Pintatubo in the Philippines (1991). In 1815, Indonesia was also the home of the most recent really big blow, when Tambora exploded with fifty times the force of Mount Saint Helens. The sulfur cloud from Tambora is estimated to have been ten times as thick as those from El Chichon and Krakatoa, and may have cut the solar energy reaching the ground by as much as 20 percent.

It's not hard to see these clouds of sulfuric acid if you look at the right time. At 15 miles up, they catch the last rays of sunlight long after the ground has slipped into darkness, resulting in brilliant lavender twilights about twenty minutes before sunrise and after sunset. Spectacular twilights were seen worldwide for several years following all the big eruptions of the past century.

Theoretically, trimming the amount of sunlight by 2 or 3 percent should cool the surface of the Earth. The amount of solar energy reaching the latitudes of the United States and southern Canada drops off by 3 percent every two days during the autumn, due to the lowering sun angle. Over these two days, the East's average temperature normally cools about three-quarters of a degree, so we might expect a similar cooling following a big eruption. The volcanic cooling, though, should last as long as the volcanic cloud—one or two years.

Like so many ideas, the concept of volcanic cooling originated with Benjamin Franklin, who suggested that the eruption of Laki in Iceland had something to do with the hard winter of 1783–1784. However, it's difficult to say whether Laki, Krakatoa, or any other volcano really cooled the climate. The worldwide average temperature actually rose a bit following 1982's El Chichon eruption. This was, however, the same time El Niño was warming the Pacific Ocean. The global climate cooled about half a degree around the times of the Agung, Santa Maria, and Krakatoa eruptions, but some of these cooling trends seemed to start *before* the eruption! The detonation of Tambora has been linked to the bizarre weather in 1816, "the year without a summer," an account of which you can read in the next section. Some of the scanty temperature records of the time, from places like Montreal, Quebec City, Salem and New Bedford, Massachusetts, and Thomas Jefferson's home at Monticello, Virginia, point to one of the coldest summers on record. However, it appears the summer of 1816 was the last of a string of cold summers that began in 1812, three years before the eruption of Tambora. While it is tempting to blame one unusual event on another, the blame could be misplaced. Tambora may very well have caused "the year without a summer," but then it could have been just an innocent bystander.

The jury is still out on the volcano-climate connection. Probably the only way we'll ever know how much volcanoes can alter climate is to have another titanic eruption like Tambora or the 4400 B.C. explosion of Mount Mazama (now Crater Lake, Oregon). It will be an expensive lesson to learn. When it went, Tambora took ninety-two thousand souls with it.

Believe it or not, we humans have devised an even more expensive way to find out what dust in the atmosphere does to climate. The trick is to have a nuclear war! The general idea is the same as volcanoes, except that soot, instead of sulfuric acid, from evaporated cities and forests is blown into the atmosphere. There's an ongoing debate as to how much soot would be created, how high it would go into the atmosphere, how long it would stay there, and what its effects on the climate would be. Some say a massive cooling, the *nuclear winter*, would result from blockage of sunlight; however, there's a counterpoint that there would instead be a *nuclear summer*, since all that dust would also let less infrared radiation back out. It's still just a theory, and one we never want to test.

THE YEAR WITHOUT A SUMMER

Probably the most celebrated quirk of climate in the history of eastern North America (and Europe) was in 1816, "the year without a summer." Of course, there was a summer that year, but it wasn't very warm—frequent frosts and the general lack of warm growing weather resulted in widespread crop failures north and east of the Potomac. Many farmers packed up and crossed the Alleghenies to the Ohio Valley, in the hopes of finding more reliable growing conditions. The weather was equally abominable in Europe, where the gloomy Swiss summer reportedly put Mary Shelly in the proper mood to write *Frankenstein*.

Not surprisingly, there's little in the way of precise weather records describing the weather of 1816. Perhaps the most descriptive account of that chilly summer is in Charles Peirce's *Meteorological Account of the Weather in Philadelphia*. This journal spans fifty-seven years of weather, from 1790 to 1847, but Peirce saves his strongest words for 1816. As you read his account, keep in mind that Peirce probably collected some of his frost and ice reports from country towns far from Philadelphia (where a July freeze is unheard of). Even so, the summer was clearly not normal. Here are a few of Peirce's descriptions of the summer of 1816.

April. "The medium temperature of this month was 47. It commenced mild, but did not maintain its credit; as Jack frost came along mounted upon a cold, boisterous northwester, and made every thing tremble and shiver before him. The blustering snow squalls which followed would have been more suitable for January than April. After the wind lulled, ice formed on several nights, half an inch thick, which destroyed all the buds, and almost every green thing."

May. "The medium temperature of this month was 57, and she was really a frosty jade. Her frowns were many, and her smiles few. Northerly winds, with cold frosty nights prevailed, until every green thing was either killed or withered. A melancholy hue appeared to seal the fate of all vegetable life. Buds and small fruit froze upon the trees. On some mornings there was ice from a quarter to half an inch thick, in exposed situations. Corn was replanted two or three times, and very little ever came to perfection. Westerly and south-west winds prevailed but seven days during the whole month. There were two north-east rain storms."

June. "The medium temperature of this month was only 64, and it was the coldest month of June we ever remember; there were not only severe frosts on several mornings, but on one morning there was said to be ice. Every green herb was killed, and vegetables of every description very much injured. All kinds of fruit had been previously destroyed, as not a month had passed without producing ice. From six to ten inches of snow fell in various parts of Vermont, three inches in the interior of New York; and several inches in the interior of New Hampshire and Maine."

July. "The medium or average temperature of this month was only 68, and it was a month of melancholy forebodings, as during every previous month since the year commenced, there were not only heavy frosts, but ice, so that very few vegetables came to perfection. It seemed as if the sun had lost its warm and cheering influences. One frosty night

VOLCANIC TWILIGHT—Several times this century, volcanic eruptions around the world have sent massive clouds of sulfurous gases into the stratosphere. These gases remain for years, causing brilliant lavender sunsets and sunrises (such as this one two years after the 1963 eruption of Agung) and possibly affecting the global climate.

Richard A. Keen

was succeeded by another, and thin ice formed in many exposed situations in the country. On the morning of the 5th there was ice as thick as window-glass in Pennsylvania, New York, and through New England. Indian corn was chilled and withered, and the grass was so much killed by repeated frosts, that grazing cattle would scarcely eat it. Northerly winds prevailed a great part of the month; and when the wind changed to the west, and produced a pleasant day, it was a subject of congratulation by all. Very little rain fell during the month."

August. "The medium temperature of this month was only 66! and such a cheerless, despond-ing, melancholy summer month, the oldest inhab-itant never, perhaps, experienced. This poor month entered upon its duties so perfectly chilled, as to be unable to raise one warm, foggy morning, or cheer-ful sunny day. It commenced with a cold north-east rain storm, and when it cleared the atmosphere was so chilled as to produce ice in many places half an inch thick. It froze the Indian corn, which was in the milk, so hard, that it rotted up on the stock, and farmers mowed it down and dried it for cattle-fodder. Every green thing was destroyed, not only in this country but in Europe. Newspapers received from England said, 'It will ever be remembered by the present generation, that the year 1816 was a year in which there was no summer.'"

GREENHOUSES AND OUTHOUSES

We've found ways to keep the sunlight out. How about keeping the Earth's heat in? The way to do this, of course, is to block the escape of infrared radiation. Several trace constituents of the air, such as water vapor and methane (the flammable gas that rises from swamps and outhouses), are quite effective at doing this. Another gas that works well is carbon dioxide. Being transparent, these gases let sunlight in; however, they do not let infrared radiation out. It works just like the glass covering of a greenhouse, and so the idea has been coined the *greenhouse effect.* We know the greenhouse effect works; just look at Venus,

whose carbon dioxide atmosphere has raised its air temperature to 850 degrees.

Carbon dioxide is of particular interest. Its amount in the atmosphere has been increasing over the past century because of the burning of coal and oil. Burning wood doesn't really add carbon dioxide to the air; it merely returns the carbon dioxide taken from the air by the trees when they were growing. Burning coal and oil releases carbon dioxide that was removed hundreds of millions of years ago, when the Earth's atmosphere was full of the stuff.

So far we have burned up about 10 cubic miles of oil, raising the amount of carbon dioxide in the atmosphere about 20 percent above its natural content of a century ago. Theoretically, this amount of additional carbon dioxide might warm the Earth a fraction of a degree. The degree of warming would be easy to calculate if the greenhouse effect raised the temperature, but left everything else in the atmosphere the same. It's not that simple, though. A warmer atmosphere evaporates more water from the oceans, which in turn could form more clouds. More clouds reflect more sunlight, *reducing* the amount of solar energy reaching the planet and limiting the carbon dioxide warming. However, the point at which clouds cause the warming to level off, if at all, is a hot topic among researchers, and predictions of the greenhouse warming over the next few decades range from nothing (or even a slight cooling!) to 3 or 4 degrees. These predictions are global averages; some parts of the Earth might feel the heat more than others, and some places might actually cool.

The greenhouse effect was first predicted in 1863, and meteorologists have been looking for it ever since. The first announcement that the warm-ing was here came in 1939, at the end of the hot Dust Bowl Decade. The subject was dropped dur-ing the cool years that followed—indeed, during the 1970s there were predictions that dust and soot from industry and farming would act like a perpetual volcanic cloud, and, outweighing the greenhouse effect, actually cool the planet. The warm 1980s revived the fame of carbon dioxide. Most recently, the hot summers of 1988 and 1990 prompted all sorts of discussion among scientists, politicians, and the media that the greenhouse effect had finally arrived.

It's not coincidence that "greenhouse effects" seem to appear after warm spells, only to quietly disappear several years later. It's simple statistics. Scientists want to use the best and the latest data available. For studies of the global climate, this usually means looking at temperatures from 1870 or 1880 (the start of reasonably complete worldwide temperature records) up to the present. If the latest years in the temperature records are particularly warm, as they were in the 1930s and 1980s, the overall tendency for the whole period of record will be upward. This is especially true since at the beginning of the recordings, the 1870s and 1880s, it was relatively cool. The 1960s and 1970s were also on the cool side, and at that time it appeared that the climate was stable, if not cooling. It's sort of like the on-again, off-again connections between coffee drinking and health, with different studies giving different conclusions. However, if the heat of the 1980s persists through the 1990s and into the next millennium, then we may have a real problem. Until then, we just can't tell the greenhouse effect from everything else that goes on with the climate. A fraction of a degree is awfully small compared to the larger effects of El Niño and autovariability. However, at the rate we're burning oil, it may not be long. . . .

CAVEAT EMPTOR

This is a good time to warn you about climate data. It's tempting to gather as much temperature and rainfall data as can be found, compute a grand average, and look for minuscule differences to call climate change. Statistically, there's safety in numbers—the more numbers you average, the more accurate that average is. That's only true if your data

can be taken at face value, which, unfortunately, in meteorology is not always the case. Over the years, techniques and technology of weather observing have changed drastically. Thermometers are made differently now (they're electronic, not mercury in glass), located differently, and often read differently. The favorite place for thermometers a century ago was atop the highest building in town, the idea being to measure the air free of obstructions by trees and other buildings. That all changed with the rapid growth of aviation during the 1930s and 1940s. Pilots needed frequent weather reports from the places where they were landing and departing, so official weather stations began moving to airports, where the thermometers were placed out on the grass between the runways. The temperature can easily differ by several degrees between the top of city hall and the airport. In fact, so many weather stations moved from downtowns to airports that some of the cooling observed after 1940 should really be called the *airport effect*.

Even such a simple thing as the time of day the thermometer is read can affect a place's average temperature—read all about that in the "Watching the Weather" chapter. I've seen false climate changes of 2 to 4 degrees caused entirely by changes in location and reading time of the thermometer. Rainfall records are even worse, climatologically speaking, since the measured amount of rain and (especially) snow depends so much on the design of the gauge. The same goes for wind speed observations. A wind gauge commonly used decades ago is now known to read 20 to 30 percent too high. And so on. This doesn't mean the climate doesn't change; some changes are indisputable. Just think twice before believing every half-degree temperature difference you hear.

THE GREAT ICE AGE

Now it's time to talk about the granddaddy of all climate changes—the Great Ice Age. We don't have to worry about inaccurate thermometers and half-degree temperature differences here; the evidence is literally carved in stone all across the continent. To anyone standing on a Manhattan street corner on a sweaty August afternoon, it might seem absolutely inconceivable that just eighteen thousand years earlier (a mere blink of an eye, geologically speaking), that same spot was buried under several thousand feet of solid ice. In January, however, it might seem a little more believable, but still incredible. Other ice sheets covered parts of Europe, from Britain to the Soviet Union, and Antarctica.

The greatest ice sheet of all time was the one that initially formed around Hudson Bay, and spread over the northeastern half of the continent. Sheets of glacier ice extended as far south as New York City, Williamsport and New Castle, Pennsylvania, Cincinnati, and Saint Louis; in the Midwest, the Ohio and Missouri rivers form the approximate boundaries of what was the ice sheet. Long Island, Nantucket, and Cape Cod are giant banks of gravel pushed there from the north, and mark the southern limit of the glaciers along the eastern seaboard. Some of this gravel was scoured from the pits that later became the Great Lakes.

Needless to say, the climate of the East was vastly different from today's. One way to visualize the differences is to exaggerate the unusual weather conditions of cold years in the recent past, such as 1962 and 1978. Other evidence is provided by the kinds of plankton left in layers of silt that settled to sea bottoms during the Ice Age and by the geologic residue of the glaciers themselves. Combining the clues shows that the East was colder, drier, and windier than today.

Since New York City was at the edge of the ice, we'd expect its year-round temperature to average close to the freezing (or melting) point, 32 degrees. That's about 20 degrees below today's annual normal. Farther south, average temperatures above 32 degrees would melt the ice. In Florida and

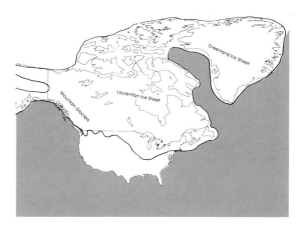

THE GREAT ICE AGE—At its peak 18,000 years ago, ice up to 2 miles thick covered half of North America.

elsewhere in the tropics, temperatures probably averaged about 10 degrees colder than today. North of the Big Apple, on the ice, the climate probably resembled modern-day Greenland.

Since the Arctic cooled off more than the tropics, increasing the equator-to-pole temperature difference, the jet stream and prevailing westerlies were stronger. This would have pushed coastal cyclones out to sea (like during the 1960s drought), and most of the United States east of the Rockies was much drier than now. Huge clouds of dust picked up from the Great Plains (a desert then) swept eastward; much of the soil in the Mississippi and Ohio valleys is made of this dust. Once out to sea, the storms probably turned north toward eastern Canada, where they replenished the glacier with heavy snows.

Ice-Age Florida may have been a near-desert. Today, the state usually receives plenty of rain from daily thunderstorms in the summer and occasional hurricanes in the fall. The warm ocean that feeds moisture to these storms was not so warm back in the Ice Age, and the supply of moisture was stingier. Furthermore, the peninsula was twice as wide then,

Richard A. Keen

ICE-CARVED VALLEY—Mile-deep ice crossing the Island of Newfoundland flattened the plateau at right; after the ice melted, a smaller glacier carved the lake-filled valley.

since sea levels were 100 or 200 feet lower than now (all the water was piled up as ice on the continents), and the interior of the peninsula was farther from the already reduced moisture source.

When did all this happen? Apparently, there have been a whole series of ice ages, beginning several million years ago with the growth of the Antarctic ice sheet. For the past seven hundred thousand years, ice sheets have grown and melted in the Northern Hemisphere at one-hundred-thousand-year intervals, and lasted several tens of thousands of years each. Between each of these ice ages, the climate was much like it is today. The last ice age began seventy-five thousand to ninety thousand

years ago, and the ice sheets grew to their maximum extent eighteen thousand years ago. Four thousand years later—around 12,000 B.C.—the world's climate suddenly warmed up to near-present temperatures. It took another five thousand years to melt the huge mass of ice over North America, and the last patch disappeared from northern Quebec around 5000 B.C. The Ice Age continues in Antarctica and Greenland, and remnant ice caps are still found on some of the islands of northeastern Canada.

There are many theories about the cause of the ice ages. One plausible theory was put forth in 1920 by a Yugoslavian named M. Milankovitch and concerns the wobbles of the Earth and its orbit. Like a spinning top, the axis of Earth's poles wobbles around and changes its tilt in cycles of twenty-six thousand and forty thousand years, while the shape of the Earth's orbit around the sun changes over several longer cycles—up to one hundred thousand years. The actual size of the orbit never changes, and, over an entire year, the total amount of sunlight reaching the Earth never changes. Thanks to these wobbles, however, the solar heating of the different hemispheres during different seasons varies by 5 or 10 percent over thousands of years. If the Northern Hemisphere gets less sunlight during the summer, that season is cooler. As it is now, the winter snows that cover far northern Canada barely melt before summer is over; if summers were 5 degrees cooler, the snow might not melt at all from some places. That means the snow would build up year after year. Once the snow cover gets thick enough, it can increase the cooling by reflecting sunlight back into space. Keep that up, and in a few thousand years there's an ice sheet.

The Milankovitch theory predicts several cycles that might affect the buildup of snow, and some of them do fit the cycles of the Ice Ages. The theory also predicts that the past Ice Age was not the last one. So, if you thought the winter of 1977 was bad, just wait until 11,977!

148

LIGHTS IN THE SKY

Long before flying saucers were first reported in 1947, humans have looked up at lights in the sky with attitudes ranging from amusement to awe. It's a good thing, too, because that's how meteorology began. Even if we choose to ignore that bit of the universe that lies above and beyond the atmosphere and confine ourselves to things within the earth's sheath of air, there's still a fantastic variety of visual phenomena. Here are a few of my favorites.

METEORS

This might seem like good place to begin, because what would meteorologists study if not meteors? Well, we've all taken high school science and know that meteors are pieces of space dust burning high in the atmosphere that are sometimes called "shooting stars." Of course, meteorologists study other stuff, right? Wrong! The dictionary defines *meteor* as, among other things, "a phenomenon in the atmosphere, such as lightning, a rainbow, or snow." "Shooting stars" also occur in the atmosphere, so we may add them to the list. It just happens that this last definition has become the one most commonly used nowadays.

Most of the confusion comes from the fact that meteorology has changed somewhat since it became a science and received its name some twenty-five hundred years ago. The name is Greek, and comes from *meteoros,* meaning "high in the air," and originally *anything* that appeared in the sky was fair game for meteorologists. We now associate meteorology with things in the lower part of the atmosphere, and the higher stuff—like shooting stars—belongs to astronomers.

However, since I brought up the subject, I should say something about it. Meteors, and now I'm using the common definition, are indeed pieces of space dust burning up in the atmosphere. The study of these meteors is called *meteoritics.* The dust particles range in size from microscopic to basketball-size, with "typical" shooting stars being about the size of a pinhead. Anything larger than a basketball is likely to reach the ground and become a *meteorite.* Most appear to be the remains of disintegrated comets. Space probes to Halley's Comet in 1986 revealed that comets are mountain-sized masses of ice and dirt, much like that found in urban snowbanks, that become visible when the ice evaporates and forms a cloud of sunlit water vapor and

Gary Emerson

METEOR SHOWER—On November 17, 1966, meteors from the constellation Leo fell at a rate of forty per second. *A repeat performance is possible in 1999.*

other gases. As the ice evaporates over millions of years, leftover dust is strung out along the comet's orbit. The comet disappears when all the ice is gone, leaving an orbiting stream of dust. When our planet plows through the dust, we see meteors.

The combined orbital velocities of the Earth and ex-comet send the meteor particles into our atmosphere at speeds of 10 to 45 miles per *second.* For comparison, space shuttles come back in at 5 miles per second, and even at that speed they glow red hot. Meteors get white hot, briefly reaching temperatures of 5,000 to 10,000 degrees before they're gone. They first appear at altitudes of 70 miles or so, and most burn up completely in a second or two, by which time they're down to 40 or 50 miles above the ground.

The bright thing we see as the meteor or

shooting star is not so much the burning pinhead of dirt as it is a glowing ball of air surrounding the particle. The collision of dust particles and air molecules heats the air, too, causing it to shine—just like the extremely hot air inside a lightning flash. Some of the larger and faster (and therefore hotter) meteors leave long, glowing trails of hot gases and burnt meteor dust in their wake. These trails can last for minutes, sometimes even an hour, after the meteor has gone, by which time they've become contorted into fantastic shapes by the winds way up there. Scientists have used observations of meteor trails to measure these winds, and have come up with speeds of 100 mph and higher. This is how the earliest measurements of high-altitude winds were made, which gets us back where we started—meteorologists *do* study meteors!

WHY IS THE SKY BLUE?

Probably the first thing we ever notice about the sky is that it is blue. We certainly get used to the fact, and would surely consider any other color odd. But always at the back of our minds the question nags, ever so slightly: Why is the sky blue? The answer has to do with sunlight and molecules, and with a process called *scattering.*

Spend a day on a fishing pier, and if the fish aren't biting, you might notice what happens when waves strike the pilings. Big waves splash against the pilings, but most of the wave continues on its way. Small waves, or more like ripples, bend around the pilings, with the ripples rounding either side of the post heading off in opposite directions. Since the waves and ripples go off in various directions, their bending is called scattering.

Light is also a wave, but its waves are made of electric and magnetic fields instead of water. Waves of visible light are quite small, too, with their ripples being about one fifty-thousandth of an inch apart (this distance is the *wavelength*). Like all waves, light scatters, but the bending is caused by things like molecules of air. And again like waves in the ocean, shorter wavelengths of light (ripples) scatter more than longer wavelengths (waves). One way to visualize it is that to shorter waves, molecules look larger and present more of an obstacle to their forward motion.

To us sunlight appears white or pale yellow, but its light is really a mixture of all colors, from blue to green, yellow, orange, and red. Blue light has a shorter wavelength than red light, so when a sunbeam shines through the molecules of air over our heads, blue light is scattered the most while red light, which is scattered the least, continues in a straight line. When you look at the sky away from the sun, then, more blue than red, yellow, or green is being scattered in your direction. That's why the sky is blue!

TWILIGHT

When you look at the sun, your eyes take in a beam of light that has had more blue light than red light scattered out of it. So the sun, which looks white in outer space, appears slightly yellowish. When setting, the sun shines through twenty to forty times as much air as it does when it's high in the sky, and proportionately more blue light is scattered away. That's why the setting sun appears red. (The same is true for the rising sun, of course.)

Long after the sun has set its light continues to scatter off the molecules of the upper atmosphere. Twilight can last an hour or two after sunset, by which time the glow you see low in the west is sunlight scattered by molecules 40 to 50 miles high and 600 miles away. Even though the light reaching these molecules from the distant setting sun is red, the molecules still prefer to scatter blue light. The result is a mixture of red, greens, and blues.

Light waves are small, but molecules are even smaller. A typical air molecule is about one hundred-millionth of an inch across, or less than a thousandth the size of a wavelength of light. Particles that are larger than one or two wavelengths,

like dust and cloud droplets, scatter light quite differently—these particles look big to all wavelengths of light, and all wavelengths of visible light are scattered equally well. That's why clouds look white.

Most clouds are confined to the lower atmosphere, but on occasion clouds can form in the stratosphere, 15 to 40 miles up. Ice particle clouds occasionally form high above the Arctic in the summer, but these are extremely rare south of 50 degrees latitude. At lower latitudes, the most common stratospheric clouds are the layers of sulfuric acid droplets spewed out by exploding volcanoes. These larger particles scatter the setting sun's red light much more effectively than do molecules, and twilights take on a different hue. Instead of greens and blues we see much brighter yellows, reds, and purples scattered by the globe-circling layers of volcanic acid. Sometimes you'll even see shadows of distant clouds cast on the volcanic layer, creating dark rays on the bright twilight sky. These spectacular twilights usually last two or three years after major volcanic eruptions, of which there have been only five in the past century (some on the other side of the world!).

AURORA BOREALIS

Of all the lights in the sky, none can give the cool shivers like the *aurora borealis*, or *northern lights*. They often begin as a pale green arch hugging the northern horizon, but then searchlight beams crisscross the sky and multiply and merge into red and green curtains that march overhead and off to the south. At times, the entire sky shines and shimmers like an incongruous mixture of fire and jello. Watching an outbreak of the northern lights is one of the most memorable ways one can spend a clear night.

For centuries no one could figure out what was going on. *Aurora* means "dawn" in Latin and *borealis* means "north"; down under, the southern equivalent is called the *aurora australis*. Over the years the

Richard A. Keen

AURORA BOREALIS—A gigantic solar flare bathed most of North America with brilliant, multicolored auroras on the night of March 13, 1989. A reddish glow was seen as far south as Guatemala and the Caribbean.

most popular explanations of the "northern dawn" involved peculiar kinds of twilight—for example, sunlight reflecting off the polar ice back into the sky. Sometimes the aurora was blamed on distant forest fires lighting the sky, or even the spontaneous combustion of the air itself. The correct answer, of course, is none of the above.

The aurora works on the same principle as fluorescent or neon lights, or outdoor mercury and sodium vapor lamps. The idea is to run energetic,

high-speed electrons through a gas. In the case of the aurora, the gases are mostly oxygen and nitrogen. The high-speed electrons strike the gas molecules, shaking the molecules' electrons out of their little orbits. When the molecular electrons drop back to their original orbits, they lose the energy they picked up from the high-speed electrons. This energy radiates away as light.

Fluorescent lights get their electrons from the house current, with an extra kick given by the lamp's ballast mechanism. The aurora is lit by electrons from the sun, which need no boost. Electrons thrown out by hot spots in the solar atmosphere known as solar flares can travel the 93,000,000 miles to Earth in less than a day.

The solar electrons never quite make it to Earth, however. Several thousand miles up they get caught in our planet's magnetic field. Earth's magnetic field looks just like the familiar magnetic pattern around a bar magnet, with broad loops connecting the North and South poles. The electrons are deflected north or south along these loops, and as they approach the poles they dip down into the atmosphere. To an electron, the magnetic field looks somewhat like an apple, with electrons on the surface of the apple forced to moved "north" or "south" into one of the dimples. The electrons are finally funneled into the top of the atmosphere in a ring (called the *auroral oval*) surrounding each of the magnetic poles.

Electrons are always funneling down to Earth, and there's always an aurora—albeit faint most of the time—along the auroral oval. After a solar flare the solar electrons are much more energetic and penetrate much deeper into the magnetic field before getting caught. Their trajectories bring them into the atmosphere farther from the poles, the (northern) auroral oval expands south, and we see the northern lights.

The aurora gives us a chance to glimpse the very highest reaches of our atmosphere. Most auroras shine between 60 and 200 miles up, but occasionally a really big show can reach as high as 600 miles—higher than most satellites! In contrast to these enormous vertical dimensions, the curtains themselves are only a few thousand feet thick. Often the curtains shade from greenish on the bottom to red at the top; both colors come from oxygen atoms. Occasionally a deep violet glow from nitrogen atoms appears in the higher reaches of the aurora.

The North and South poles of Earth's magnet—the dimples on the apple, so to speak—are not

Pekka Parviainen

NORTHERN LIGHTS—A small, greenish-blue curtain shimmers in front of the Big Dipper. The curtain was blurred slightly by its motion during this time exposure.

exactly at the geographic North and South poles, but about 1,000 miles away. That places the magnetic North Pole over Ellesmere Island in the Canadian Arctic. This quirk of our magnetic field is a boon for eastern aurora watchers, since it brings the magnetic North Pole—and the auroral oval—1,000 miles closer, increasing the frequency of auroras. At the same geographic latitudes in Asia, auroras are much less frequent than they are in North America.

Pekka Parviainen

NOCTILUCENT CLOUDS—These clouds resemble cirrus in appearance and, probably, in composition (ice crystals). However, they float an incredible 50 miles above the ground, so high, in fact, that they remain sunlit for one to two hours after sunset and before sunrise, earning them the name noctilucent, *meaning "shines at night." Noctilucent clouds are extremely rare, and are sighted only north of 50 degrees latitude and usually in late summer (when they may shine all night long!).*

Over North America the auroral oval usually runs from northern Alaska, across the northern Northwest Territories, into northern Quebec and Labrador. That's the place to go if you want to see the aurora almost every clear night. Farther south the frequency drops off—to thirty nights per year at Montreal, ten at Boston, five at Norfolk, one at Jacksonville, and once every five years at Miami. (Remember that about half of these auroras will be clouded out.) The southernmost aurora borealis on record was seen from the Cayman Islands (19 degrees north) in the Caribbean in March 1989. The frequency of auroras closely follows the eleven-year cycle of solar activity known as the *sunspot cycle.*

The last peak was in 1989, when several spectacular shows lit up the East; the next peak should arrive around 2000.

REFRACTION

Light does not always travel in straight lines, nor does it always travel at the so-called "speed of light," 186,283 miles per second. This number is actually the speed of light in a vacuum. However, light slows down when it goes into something thicker than a vacuum, like air, water, or glass. In water or glass light slows to two-thirds its vacuum speed, but in air the deceleration is much less—about 50 miles per second out of the 186,283.

154

Besides slowing down, light also changes its direction when it goes from a vacuum into glass or air. It's very much like the uncomfortable experience of running the right wheels of your car off the edge of a paved road onto a muddy shoulder. The resistance of the mud slows the right side of the automobile, pulling the car off the road. If you didn't steer back to the left, your car would end up in the mud. Light beams don't have anyone on board to steer them back, so they simply change direction when they enter the glass or air—just like your tire tracks.

The bending of light is called *refraction*, and the amount of bending depends on several things. Generally, the denser the material (glass is denser than water, which is denser than air), the more the bending. Refraction is also greater if the light rays strike the surface of the glass or air at more of a glancing angle, like your car just edging off the road. The smaller the angle between the incoming light and the refracting surface (or edge of the road), the greater the bending. If the light strikes the surface head-on, there's no bending—just as if you drove straight off the end of a parking lot into the mud, you'd slow down, but you'd still be going straight. Finally, shorter wavelengths of light (like blue) bend more than longer wavelengths (like red)—in our automotive analogy, a short wheelbase Volkswagen gets tugged off the road faster than does a Greyhound bus.

HARVEST MOON

When the moon hits your eye like a big pizza pie,
That's amore!

—Spike Jones

Of the twelve or thirteen full moons every year, there's something special about the first one of autumn—the *Harvest Moon*. Astronomically, October's (or late September's, sometimes) moon is quite ordinary, but after a summer of leaf-filled trees it's the first full moon we can easily see as soon as it comes over the horizon. In milder climates the leaves don't leave until November, and the spectacle is saved for the *Hunter Moon*. In either case, the rising Harvest (or Hunter) Moon does indeed look huge, like a 16-inch pizza. And if you catch the rising moon when it's sitting right on the horizon, it also looks a bit squashed, like a football lying on its side (after all, it is football season!). The squashing effect is caused by the atmosphere, so let's look at that one first.

Light entering the atmosphere from any object in space is refracted toward the ground, and the shallower the angle of entry, the greater the refraction. For those of us on the ground looking up, an object appears *higher* in the sky than it would without refraction—the only exception being an object directly overhead at the zenith, which cannot appear any higher! The lifting effect is greatest for objects on the horizon, where it amounts to half a degree, or just about the apparent diameter of the moon. Refraction actually causes the moon (and sun) to rise earlier (and set later) than they would on an airless Earth.

The angle of refraction decreases for objects progressively higher above the horizon. When the moon is sitting on the horizon, then, its top edge is refracted less than its lower edge. This compresses the apparent distance between the top and bottom of the moon. Meanwhile, the moon's horizontal width appears its normal size, since atmospheric refraction works only in the up-down direction. The result is a squashed moon.

None of this explains why the moon should appear so big when it rises, however. Refraction actually *shrinks* the overall size of the rising moon. Even without refraction the moon should appear slightly smaller when it is on the horizon, since is almost 4,000 miles (half the Earth's diameter) farther away than when it is overhead. However, the moon's average distance from the Earth's center is 239,000 miles, and that 4,000 miles doesn't make a noticeable difference in the moon's size. The "pizza

Richard A. Keen   Richard A. Keen

LUNAR ECLIPSES—The bright coppery luster of a normal lunar eclipse (left) comes from sunlight refracted through Earth's atmosphere. The dull grey eclipse of December 30, 1982 (right), darkened by volcanic dust from El Chichon, required such a long time exposure that stars appear as dashes.

pie" effect is an optical illusion created by our mind's interpretation of what the eye sees. When the moon is high in the sky, we (consciously or not) compare its size with nearby objects such as branches, roofs, and streetlights. When the moon sits on the horizon, the comparison objects are more distant (but larger) things like houses, hills, and trees. So the moon, instead of appearing as big as a leaf, looks more the size of a house. The effect strikes us in October because, once again, it's the first time we've seen the moon on a clear horizon in a while. Doubters can prove it for themselves by taking photographs of the moon at different elevations above the horizon, or, more cleverly, by comparing the moon's apparent size with that of a small (one-third of an inch) object taped to the end of a yardstick.

LUNAR ECLIPSES

There's another special kind of full moon that occurs about once a year, on the average,

although it's just as likely to happen in March, or any other month, as in September or October. Rather than stunning us with its size or brightness, though, this full moon nearly disappears by passing into the Earth's long, tapered shadow, or *umbra*. It is, of course, an eclipse of the moon (or *lunar eclipse*). Although lunar eclipses are slightly less common than the more dramatic eclipses of the sun, they can be seen from the entire half of the Earth from which the moon is visible at the time. Most of you have probably seen a lunar eclipse at one time or another, while very few have found themselves within a total solar eclipse's narrow path of visibility.

The moon is completely outside of the Earth's atmosphere, so it may seem that its eclipses belong entirely to the realm of astronomy, rather than meteorology. However, the Earth's atmosphere, along with such phenomena as refraction, scattering, and even volcanic eruptions, play important roles in the phenomena we see during a lunar eclipse.

156

Normally the eclipsed moon shines a bright copper-orange, or, as one nineteenth-century observer wrote, "like a glowing iron." Once in a while the moon turns dark and grayish or even disappears completely. Although the dark eclipses are the unusual ones, it is really the bright orange luster of "normal" eclipses that require some explaining. During a total eclipse the moon is completely immersed in the umbra, and, one might expect, totally cut off from sunlight. Then, why doesn't the moon *always* disappear during an eclipse? The answer lies in the Earth's atmosphere: Like a thin lens encircling our planet, the atmosphere refracts rays of sunlight as they pass by the edge of the Earth, focusing them into the umbra. As at sunset, scattering reddens the rays as they pass through the atmosphere, except here the red sunlight shines on to the moon.

The degree of refraction depends on the density of the air the sunlight passes through—the denser air in the lower atmosphere refracts sunlight deep into the umbra, while the thin air higher up bends light rays only slightly. At the distance of the moon, most of the light refracted into the umbra passes through the stratosphere, 15 to 40 miles up. Since the stratosphere is normally cloudless, the umbra (and therefore, the eclipsed moon) is relatively bright.

The robot lunar lander *Surveyor III* observed a lunar eclipse in 1967 from a completely different perspective, and photographed the passage of the sun behind the Earth. At mid-eclipse the night side of the Earth was surrounded by a thin—but brilliant—ring of sunlight, broken here and there by the tops of the highest clouds. The total brightness of this ring was ten to one hundred times that of the full moon as seen from Earth. When future astronauts and cosmonauts (none of the *Apollo* astronauts were so fortunate) witness this spectacle, they will, in a way, be gazing upon a most memorable sunset, with the setting sun stretched all the way around the horizon that is the edge of the planet Earth.

If the atmospheric lens that illuminates the moon becomes dirty enough, light will be blocked from entering the umbra. Volcanoes are the most common source of stratospheric dirt. One of the most recent large eruptions was that of the Mexican volcano El Chichon in March 1982. By December, when there was a total lunar eclipse, El Chichon's 5-mile deep cloud of sulfuric acid had spread around the globe. More a haze layer than a cloud, the volcanic cloud was fairly transparent compared to most earthly clouds. However, light rays grazing the Earth's edge on their way into the umbra passed nearly horizontally through the haze layer. After a 500-mile passage through the haze, only 1 percent of the light remained to enter the umbra. When the moon crossed the umbra on December 30, 1982, it appeared dim and gray, and observers in cities had trouble seeing the moon at all!

El Chichon was by no means the first volcano to tarnish the coppery glow of a lunar eclipse. Dark eclipses followed major eruptions in 1902, 1912, and 1963. The infamous paroxysms of Tambora (1815) and Krakatoa (1883) preceded dim, almost invisible eclipses. In 1620, the great astronomer Johannes Kepler observed an eclipsed moon so dark that "nothing could be seen of it, though the stars shone brightly all around," and although he was unaware of any volcanic eruptions, he correctly attributed the darkness to "mists and smoke" in the Earth's atmosphere. It may have been another unknown volcanic upheaval around A.D. 753 that ultimately led a reporter for the *Anglo-Saxon Chronicle* to describe the eclipsed moon that year as "covered by a horrid black shield," in contrast to a more normal eclipse appearing "sprinkled with blood" thirteen years earlier.

Volcanoes are one of nature's most awesome phenomena. In seconds they can reduce cities and countryside to steaming mounds of dust, and globe-girdling volcanic clouds can change the color of the

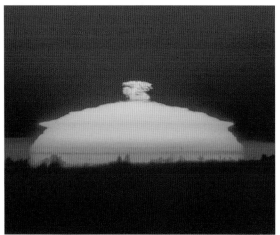

Pekka Parviainen

SETTING SUN—Refraction by the atmosphere puts a green fringe on the sun's upper edge.

Richard A. Keen

GREEN FLASH—The Green Flash lingers briefly after the rest of the sun has set.

sky and may, perhaps, even influence our planet's climate. Now we see that volcanic eruptions can literally cast shadows on the moon, a quarter of a million miles away.

THE GREEN FLASH

It sounds like a comic book super-hero, but the *green flash* is really just the sun (a super-hero of sorts!) putting on a rare, but spectacular, show at setting time. The cause is the same one that lifts the squashed moon off the horizon—refraction—but with an extra twist. Refraction bends blue light more than red, so at sunrise and sunset, the sun's blue (and green) light is lifted a little higher off the horizon than is the red and orange light. The shifting of different colors is not great, but is enough to grace the sun's upper edge with a bluish or greenish fringe. The lower edge of the sun gets a reddish fringe out of the deal, but that's not so obvious, since the whole setting (or rising) sun is tinted red. The separation of colors is exactly the same as you see when sunlight shines through a prism or crystal, except now the atmosphere is doing the job.

It's easy to see that when the sun sets, the last part to go is the blue-green fringe on top. Unfortunately, haze and junk in the atmosphere usually dull the colors, and the sun simply disappears. When the air is exceptionally clear, however, that blue-green fringe can shine alone for a second or two before it, too, disappears. The brilliant green color can appear quite suddenly, giving it the name *green flash*. Since the atmosphere needs to be clear, the best places to observe the green flash are over the ocean or from an airplane. Be patient, though. In thirty years I've seen it only three times—from Bora Bora in the South Pacific, an airplane over Pittsburgh, and Cape May, New Jersey (in case you were wondering).

RAINBOWS

Rainbows, and theories attempting to explain them, have been around for a long time. To Noah, the rainbow at the end of the Great Flood was God's message that it would never again rain quite so much. In the fourth century B.C., Aristotle, who didn't know about refraction, attributed rainbows to sunlight reflecting from clouds only at one particular angle. He had little to say about the rainbow's colors, but he did correctly explain the bow being an arc of a certain angular diameter. Two thousand years after Aristotle, Isaac Newton finally—and correctly—explained the colors of rainbows in terms of refraction, much to the dismay of his contemporary poets.

Contrary to popular conception, raindrops are *not* teardrop-shaped. Most drops are almost perfectly spherical, but drops larger than a sixteenth of an inch or so actually flatten out as they fall. It's the little spheres that make rainbows. When sunlight shines into a raindrop, refraction bends its path and breaks it up into its component colors. The light may exit the backside of the drop and continue on its way, or it may reflect off the inside of the drop and exit the drop heading back in the general direction of the sun. For a perfect sphere, reflected light can deviate as much as 42 degrees from the line pointing directly back toward the sun, with light being reflected at all angles up to 42 degrees.

Most of the sunlight comes back at angles near zero degrees, or straight back toward the sun. Because these light rays go straight into the drop and straight out again, there's not much refraction (mostly reflection), and the light does not separate into colors. This kind of reflection is quite bright, though—just like the glass beads on stop signs reflecting your headlights. At increasing angles, the reflected light becomes relatively dim, until becoming bright again as the angle approaches 42 degrees. Increasing angles also bring greater refraction and color separation. To an observer with his or her back to the sun, refracted light coming back at *any* angle will form a colored ring of that angular diameter surrounding the point opposite the sun.

We now have rainbows forming at all angles up to 42 degrees. However, at angles less than 42 degrees the rainbows overlap and their colors wash out. Only the last—and brightest—bow, the one at 42 degrees, survives to become a rainbow. Occasionally several of the outer bows, called *supernumerary arcs*, are visible as colored fringes inside the main rainbow.

Sunlight may reflect more than once inside the drop before exiting. With two reflections, the light may leave the drop at angles *greater* than 50 degrees, creating a secondary rainbow 50 degrees from the point opposite the sun. The extra reflection reverses the color sequence—red is on the inside, blue on the outside. Between the two rainbows the sky is relatively dark, since neither case reflects at angles between 42 and 50 degrees.

A third reflection within the drop sends the light in the same general direction as the original sunbeam. Therefore there's no third rainbow. Since each additional reflection further dims the light, higher order rainbows—fourth, fifth, and so on—have never been observed.

HALOES AND SUNDOGS
Dazzle mine eyes, or do I see three suns?

—Edward, in Shakespeare's
The Third Part of King Henry VI

"In this the heaven figures some event," continued Edward's brother Richard, neither apparently aware that the two extra suns were caused by ice crystals miles above the ground. Nor did they suspect that haloes, crosses, and many other omens in the sky were likewise beams of sunlight shining through ice crystals. Had they known, their minds would have been boggled by the vast variety of visual phenomena ice crystals can produce.

Most ice crystals have six sides and two flat ends, but the relative proportions of length versus width can vary greatly. Two common shapes are responsible for most of the phenomena: hexagonal (six-sided) plates and hexagonal columns. Plates look like flat, six-sided wafers and columns resemble segments of a six-sided pencil. Both shapes have eight surfaces that can refract and reflect light. The

159

Paul Neiman

MOON HALO—Ice crystals floating within a thin veil of cirrus clouds produce a ring around the moon, along with two moon dogs on either side. The bright horizontal line between the moon and both moon dogs is a parhelic circle, which appears curved in this wide-angle photo.

most common form of refraction through a hexagonal shape bends light at angles of 22 degrees and greater. It's much like light shining through a three-sided prism. If the sky is full of hexagonal columns, those oriented at right angles to the sun refract sunlight into a 22-degree halo surrounding the sun, with red on the inside and blue on the outside.

As they fall, ice crystals more than a few thousandths of an inch across orient their longest dimensions horizontally. Plates fall flat and columns lay on their sides. Horizontal hexagonal plates are capable of the same refraction by which columns create the 22-degree halo, but only if they are at the same elevation above the horizon as the sun. This produces bright, colored spots 22 degrees to the left and right of the sun known as *mock suns* or *sundogs*.

Along with the real sun in the middle they made Edward's three suns.

Ice crystals reflect, too. Like a myriad of mirrors, horizontal plates may reflect the setting sun into brilliant pillars extending above and below, but no wider than, the sun. Vertically oriented reflecting surfaces, like the end faces of horizontal columns or the edges of plates, can generate a band of light extending horizontally from the sun. Sometimes this band extends all the way around the horizon at the same elevation as the sun, and is called a *parhelic circle*. The horizontal band and vertical pillar occasionally combine to form a cross centered on the sun. Unlike refracted sundogs and haloes, these reflection phenomena are mostly colorless—unless, of course, the setting sun is turning red.

160

Paul Neiman

SUNDOGS—Muted colors in this close-up of a sundog show the prismatic effect of the tiny ice crystals.

These examples are a mere fraction of the possible arcs and haloes that have been observed, and even more are theoretically possible. Exotic crystal shapes such as pyramids add even more variety to the picture. And just as there are sun haloes and sundogs, night owls can enjoy *moon haloes* and *moondogs*.

TWINKLING

Twinkle, twinkle, little star

How I wonder what you are

—Anonymous

Sorry, kids, but the stars' twinkling actually tells us very little about what they are and, as far as astronomers are concerned, it merely confuses the issue and hinders their studies. True, some stars do vary their brightness, but that takes hours or days or, in some cases, years. The rapid flickering many call "twinkling," and scientists call *scintillation*, originates not in the stars, but in the air surrounding our own planet.

Our atmosphere is riddled with temperature contrasts, and the temperature changes from place to place within the atmosphere are not always smooth. Between the ground and the beginning of the stratosphere, 8 or 10 miles up, the temperature may drop from 60 degrees above zero to 60 below. The vertical rate of cooling comes out to 12 or 15 degrees per mile, but very rarely is that rate a steady one. Somewhere in that 120-degree spread there's bound to be several layers of relatively warm air overlying a layer of cooler air. Winds in the warm layer blowing across the top of the cool layer can create waves, just as winds in the atmosphere create waves on the surface of the ocean. And just like ocean waves, waves in the atmosphere can grow and break, mixing turbulent bubbles of cold and warm air. Jet streams, with their strong winds and temperature contrasts, are just about the best places in the atmosphere for these bubbles to form.

Cold air, being denser, refracts light more strongly than does warm air, so cold bubbles act like weak lenses and focus light rays together, while warm bubbles spread light rays apart. The temperature differences between the bubbles are usually quite small, a degree or two, so the bending of the light rays is very, very slight. However, if the bubbles are 8 or 10 miles up, the light can be deflected several feet. The net effect of the spreading and focusing of starlight by hot and cold bubbles is a blotchy pattern of light and dark moving along the ground with the same speed and direction as the winds aloft that blow the bubbles around. When bright and dark parts of the pattern pass by your eyes, you see the star flash accordingly—this is twinkling.

We don't see starlight patterns on the ground at night because individual stars aren't bright enough, and the combined patterns from the thousand or so naked-eye stars average each other out. If there were a single, extremely bright star overhead, the ground would shimmer like the bottom of a swimming pool on a sunny day. We do have an extremely bright star—the sun—but it does not twinkle. Neither does the moon except during eclipses of the sun

when the visible disk of the sun is reduced to the thinnest of crescents, creating ripples of sunlight that often dance across the ground. It's one of the many rare phenomena you can see during a solar eclipse, and one of the reasons eclipse watchers travel thousands of miles to see an event that lasts a few minutes at best. Nor do any of the planets, like Jupiter or Mars, twinkle very much, and when they do it's in a more sedate manner. That's because all these objects appear as sizeable disks in the sky, although it takes a telescope to see the planets as disks. Stars, even through a telescope, always look like brilliant points of light. Light rays reaching our eyes from a planet arrive from a variety of slightly different directions and pass through slightly different places in the atmosphere. At jet stream levels, the slightly different places are 5 or 10 feet apart. For a planet not to twinkle, then, the twinkling effects for light rays even a few feet apart must cancel each other out, and that means the blobs of hot and cold air are typically no bigger than a medicine ball!

The very slight refraction by the hot and cold bubbles causes noticeable focusing only at very large distances, and most of the twinkling we see comes from the very highest bubbles, those in and near the jet stream. Knowing this, astronomers made some of the first measurements of jet stream wind speeds by simply timing twinkles from a star as they appeared in two telescopes several yards apart. Twinkling may still leave us wondering what stars are, but it tells us a surprising amount about the atmosphere!

WATCHING THE WEATHER

"I wish you had a thermometer. Mr. Madison of the college and myself are keeping observations for a comparison of climate." These words were written in 1784 by Thomas Jefferson to the other Mr. Madison, James Madison, the fourth president of the United States. Jefferson had been keeping weather records since 1777 and continued to do so for fifty years. He logged his valuable account of early American weather into his *Weather Memorandum Book*, now on file at the Library of Congress and the Massachusetts Historical Society. James Madison took Jefferson's advice and soon began taking thermometer readings at his home. For his last thirty-three years, George Washington kept an "Account of the Weather." Thus, the first, third, and fourth presidents of the United States knew the joys (and importance) of watching the weather. They understood that the best way to learn about something is to participate in it, and to participate in the changing weather means to observe it closely.

Humans haven't always known what makes the weather work. That knowledge came over the centuries by paying close attention to the passages of clouds, wind, and rain, and to the vagaries of temperature, humidity, and pressure, and finally fitting all the observations together until they made sense. There is no need for you to recreate these early days of discovery, of course, but if you watch the skies carefully enough and long enough you will find that you understand the weather in a way no book can teach you.

Yogi Berra understood these great truths, and even said so: "You can observe a lot by just watching." Baseball managers aren't meteorologists, but in many ways, weather is like baseball. The ever-changing action is fascinating and fun to watch. The more you know about what you're watching, the more rewarding it is. If you know more than the umpire (or any other expert), it's even more fun yet! How do you keep score? By taking records of temperature, rain, snow, or whatever else suits your fancy. (Whether your daily temperatures look more like baseball, football, or basketball scores depends on where you live.)

Observing the weather is an activity that can be done at nearly any level of dedication and expense. On one extreme, you can simply watch the clouds and what falls out of them and note what kind of weather occurs each day. You don't need to spend a cent on weather instruments, since you already have the most remarkable weather instrument ever devised—a pair of eyes. On the other extreme, you can invest thousands of dollars in automatic weather recording devices, perhaps even hooked up to a home computer. Most of you will fall somewhere in between these two extremes; you may want to watch the weather with the help of a thermometer and rain gauge. After all, it is in some strange way satisfying to be able to put numbers to things. To measure something is to understand it a little bit better, and being able to compare one weather event with another makes both all the more familiar. Weather is indeed like baseball; we all want to know how yesterday's snowfall stands in the all-time ratings.

Now that you're convinced you want to set up a small, inexpensive weather station, what instruments should you get? Should you buy them or make them yourself? Where do you put them and how often do you read them? And what do you do with your records? Of course, your choices are individual ones. But perhaps this veteran weather buff can give you some hints and cautions to ease you into a fascinating hobby that only gets more captivating with time.

No matter how big or small your weather station is, or even if you're using no instruments at all, keep in mind that some form of record keeping is essential. Memories change with time, with big storms getting bigger and small storms smaller. Most days disappear entirely. Twenty years from now, you probably won't remember what today's weather was. Write it down, and two decades from now your notebook will be one of your prized possessions. If you only have a dollar to spare, invest in a notebook. Roomy calendars and appointment books work just fine, as do business ledgers and cash books.

Now for the instruments. It pays to be somewhat picky in your choice of instruments and to be careful about how and where you set them up.

You want your records to be as accurate as possible. Not only is it a matter of personal pride, but accurate records can be of use and interest to others. The following suggestions should help you get the best weather records for your dollar.

TEMPERATURE

The most basic instrument—and one that most people already own—is a *thermometer*. However, most household thermometers don't give very accurate readings. This is not to say the thermometers themselves are inaccurate, but rather they are situated where their readings are not representative of real weather. A window mounted thermometer picks up some heat from the house and may read 5 or 10 degrees higher than the actual outside air temperature. A thermometer sitting in the sun's rays might read 50 degrees too high. While temperatures "in the sun" may mean *something*, it is difficult to say what. Consider that the reading of a thermometer set in the sun is affected by wind speed, angle of the sun, where the thermometer is mounted, type and brand of thermometer, and, last and least, the actual air temperature. In other words, you don't learn much from thermometer readings taken in the sun. That is why meteorologists around the world have chosen to take readings "in the shade." If your thermometer readings are taken the same way, they can be compared directly with temperatures from, say, Bangkok or Siberia, or even from a spacecraft on the surface of Mars.

To a meteorologist, "in the shade" doesn't necessarily mean under a tree. In fact, it has been found that thick groves of trees generate a local *microclimate* that is substantially cooler than surrounding areas. Good locations for thermometers are on the north sides of buildings or under porch roofs, although even here reflected sunlight can affect the readings by a few degrees. The best location for a thermometer, and the one chosen as an international standard by the World Meteoro-

Paul Neiman

DOUBLE RAINBOW—A rain shower near State College, Pennsylvania, ends with a spectacular double rainbow. Note that the sequence of colors reverses between the inner and outer bows.

logical Organization, is in a white louvered box at eye level above open ground, as far as possible from trees, walls, buildings, or other obstructions. While setting the thermometer out in the open may seem to contradict the "in the shade" requirement, the louvered box (called an *instrument shelter* in the business) actually provides more effective shade than any tree or wall, while still allowing free flow of air around the thermometer. Anybody willing to invest thirty dollars and a day's work can build a suitable box. A design that has served me well for many years is described in Appendix 2. Making one would be an easy project for a novice do-it-yourselfer.

Whether or not you make a box, weather watching is a lot easier if your thermometer can tell you what the temperature *has been*, as well as what it is now. The simplest (and cheapest) way to do this is to get a *maximum-minimum thermometer*, called simply a *max-min* in the trade. This kind of thermometer indicates the highest and lowest temperatures that have occurred since you last checked it. Simply read the high, low, and current tempera-

165

tures, reset the high and low indicators, and come back the next day. The most reliable (invented in 1782!) max-min thermometers are the liquid-in-glass type, and good ones made by Taylor and Airguide are sold in hardware and department stores for twenty to thirty dollars. Radio Shack has a battery-powered digital max-min for about the same price. Don't forget to keep the battery up to snuff, or you'll lose irreplaceable data. There are cheaper max-min thermometers of the coiled-metallic-spring type, but their metal springs have a tendency to shift and stretch with time and cause the temperature readings to lose accuracy. For one hundred dollars and up you can get chart recording or computerized memory thermometers that give you the same information and more. However, these expensive gizmos are also complicated, and can sometimes break down. For example, computerized thermometers are very susceptible to lightning and power outages. The basic max-min thermometer is a glass tube with some mercury and alcohol in it, and about the only way to make it malfunction is to take it out of its box and hit it.

Temperatures are best recorded on a daily basis. With an ordinary thermometer, readings made at the same time every day, say 7:00 A.M. or 6:00 P.M., give a good account of the day-to-day excursions of the weather. By taking twenty-four readings—one every hour on the hour—and averaging them, you get the average temperature for the day. That's a lot of work. Fortunately there's a better way. Nearly two centuries ago, weather watchers found that the average of readings made at sunrise, 2:00 P.M., and 9:00 P.M. came reasonably close to the actual average temperature for the day. After max-min thermometers became widely used in the mid-1800s, an even easier way to figure the average temperature was discovered: Simply average the high and low temperatures for the day! All you have to do is read your max-min thermometer once a day and you've got the day's average. Read it each day

for a month and you can figure the average for the month, and so on.

Even with a max-min, there are good times and not-so-good times to read your thermometer. For example, if you read your max-min every day at 6:00 A.M., the temperature is near the minimum for the day. If that minimum was, say, 48 degrees, the temperature when you take the reading may be 50. When you reset the thermometer, it remembers that 50-degree temperature. Now imagine that the weather warms up over the next twenty-four hours (probability says this happens about half the time!), and the next morning's minimum is 60 degrees. When you take the reading, however, the thermometer will show a low of 50, left over from the previous, cooler morning. This happens often enough that your computed averages can be as much as 2 degrees lower than the actual average temperature. The opposite problem occurs if you take your daily readings in the afternoon—your averages will be 1 or 2 degrees too high. The best time to read a max-min thermometer is when the temperature is normally midway between the high and low. Studies of this problem have shown that these times are about 9:00 A.M. and 10:00 P.M. The National Weather Service has chosen the calendar day—midnight max-min readings—for their weather stations. Your choice of a time depends on your lifestyle. One important thing to remember is that the key to good and useful records is consistency. Pick a time that you can stick with over the long run. There are a lot of false climate changes in weather records the world over that are really changes in weather station locations or observation procedures. Try not to change your horse in midstream, and your records will be all the better for it.

HUMIDITY

Much of what we call weather—clouds, rain, snow, frost, fog, and so on—is caused by moisture in the atmosphere. This is why humidity is so important. Humidity is also difficult to measure accurately. Most common humidity indicators, or *hygrometers*, use hair and paper to measure humidity and they rely on the fact that these materials expand when they absorb moisture from the air. Unfortunately, these materials also attract dust and bugs and tend to stretch over time. As a result, the humidity readings are not a whole lot more accurate then noting how clammy your skin feels when you're outside.

Another problem with hair or paper hygrometers is that they measure *relative* humidity, which is the amount of moisture in the air expressed as a percentage of the amount the air could hold at that temperature. However, the real interesting thing to measure is the *absolute humidity*—the actual amount of moisture in the air. Meteorologists prefer to express absolute humidity as the *dew point*. If you take outside air and cool it, the dew point is the temperature at which the water vapor in the air condenses. In other words, when night cooling drops ground temperatures to the dew point, dew forms. Higher dew points mean more moisture in the air.

The most economical way to measure the dew point is with a *wet-bulb hygrometer*, available for thirty or forty dollars. If you don't like the price, it's easy to make your own for about five dollars. This little gadget consists of two thermometers mounted side by side. One thermometer has a wet cotton wick attached to its bulb; the other end of the wick is dipped in a small reservoir of water. The dry thermometer reads the ordinary air temperature, or *dry-bulb temperature* while the wet thermometer gives, not surprisingly, the *wet-bulb temperature*. Because of evaporative cooling, the wet-bulb reading is always lower than the dry-bulb reading. Using a small chart supplied with the hygrometer, you can convert the wet-and dry-bulb temperatures into dew points.

Another version of the wet-bulb hygrometer is the *sling psychrometer*. This also has wet- and dry-bulb thermometers mounted side by side, with the whole thing attached to a hinge or a chain. Soak the wet-bulb wick, twirl the thermometers around (to get better ventilation), and read the wet- and dry-bulb temperatures. With either version, the situation gets complicated when the wet-bulb temperature is below freezing. Ice evaporates, or, more properly, sublimates, more slowly than liquid water, so when the wet wick freezes, the "ice-bulb temperature" reads higher for the same dew point temperature. There are separate charts for converting ice-bulb readings to dew points.

Watch the dew point closely, especially during the summer, and you'll see how the moisture content of the air changes with different air masses. Dew points over 80 degrees are oppressively humid, no matter what the dry-bulb temperature is. Many flood-producing rains fall with dew points in the 70s. In the winter, dew points up near 60 may mean the possibility of severe thunderstorms. Along the coast, the dew point may change sharply as winds switch to and from the ocean. Eventually, you'll find that the dew point is a handy number to know when making your own forecasts.

RAINFALL

Measuring rainfall is the epitome of simplicity. One inch of rain from a storm simply means that the ground is covered with one inch of water (assuming none of the rain runs off or soaks into the ground). Rain is a lot easier to measure than temperature and in some ways is more interesting. Rainfall rates can vary dramatically over distances of a few miles or less. Unless you live close to a weather station, you really need your own measurements to know how much rain you've had.

Official-type rain gauges cost several hundred dollars, but fortunately you can buy small gauges that are nearly as accurate for five or ten dollars. My favorite is the plastic wedge made by Tru-Chek, a company based in Albert Lea, Minnesota, but others of the same genre are just as good.

To set up your rain gauge, mount it on a fencepost, clothesline pole, or (for you apartment dwellers) on the roof. About the only rule to remember is not to place the gauge near or under anything that might interfere with the rainfall. The rule of thumb is to place the gauge at a distance from trees, buildings, and the like that is at least equal to the height of these obstructions. Read the rainfall at the end of each storm (don't wait too long, or some rain might evaporate), or, if you like, make daily readings when you check your thermometer. Don't forget to empty the gauge each time, and above all, remember to write the amount down before you forget it.

SNOWFALL

Although snowfall is one of the trickiest of weather phenomena to measure, its measuring instrument is certainly the simplest and most commonplace of all weather instruments. Believe it or not, even the pros at the National Weather Service use an ordinary ruler (or yardstick) to measure snowfall. The difficulties arise because of what happens to snow after if falls. If it's warm, snow melts as it hits the ground; if it's windy, snow drifts; and if snow accumulates over 4 to 6 inches, it settles under its own weight. Because of these varied fates that can befall grounded snowflakes, snow depth on the ground sometimes decreases even as the snow continues to fall. So really, there are two things to measure. One is *snow depth*; the other is *snowfall*.

To measure snow depth, simply go out and stick your ruler into the snow in several places and take an average depth. If there has been a lot of drifting, take more measurements until you feel confident you've got a good average. This technique is simple and straightforward. Snowfall, on the other hand, requires an attempt to measure the amount of snow that would have accumulated had there been no melting, drifting, or settling. To do this, measure snow depth on a surface with relatively little melting—wooden decks and picnic tables are favorites. Some people prefer to use a special "snow board," a white painted piece of wood set on the ground. Measure the snow every few hours, or whenever 4 to 6 inches accumulate, and write down your measurement. Clear off the table or set the snow board back on top of the snow. Let the snow start accumulating again and take another measurement in a few hours. This eliminates the settling problem. Your snowfall total is the sum of the individual measurements. It's not really all that difficult, once you have the procedure down.

Measurements of snow depth and snowfall often differ, particularly in bigger storms. Snowfall is always the larger of the two. The National Weather Service measures both, but uses snowfall for the official record of a storm. If you live near an official weather station and wonder why it always has more snow than you, it may be because you're comparing its snowfall with your snow depth.

HAIL

For a while, during the 1940s and 1950s, hail was considered a form of snow for measurement purposes. If hail piled an inch deep, it went down in the records as an inch of "snow, sleet, hail." Unfortunately, this confused the situation. Places in Florida, for example, were having "snow" recorded in July, and the practice was dropped. The depth of hail covering the ground is still interesting, though, if for no other reason than its rarity. Even if the hail is only sprinkled across your lawn, you can still measure the size of the hailstones (get an average size, along with the largest). Should the stones measure three-quarters of an inch or more in diameter, call the Weather Service immediately. Hail that large is considered "severe weather" and potentially damaging, and forecasters want to know about it. If the stones are 17 inches or more in circumference, put it in your freezer and protect it with your life—you may have a world record!

An aid to those who aren't always at home to measure their hail is an inexpensive device called a *hail pad*. It's nothing more than a slab of beaded Styrofoam (like the stuff cheap picnic coolers are made of) wrapped in heavy-duty aluminum foil. Set it outside, weigh down the edges with bricks to keep it from blowing away, and when hail strikes, the cratered surface of the pad vividly records the storm. This delightfully simple instrument was perfected by hail researchers in Illinois, who found it more reliable than high-tech instruments with lasers and sound recorders.

WIND

Wind can be as tricky to measure as snowfall and a lot more expensive. There is an incredible variety of wind gauges—or *anemometers*—available on the market, most of them of the familiar three-rotating-cup variety. For about one hundred dollars you can buy one that tells you wind speed; for twice that they throw in wind direction. For three hundred dollars there are anemometers that recall the peak gust since you last reset it, sort of like a max-min thermometer. For the same amount of money you can get one that gives a continuous chart recording of the wind speed. On the opposite end of the price scale is an elegant little device that measures wind speed by using the pressure of the wind to push a red fluid up a tube. Made by Dwyer (P.O. Box 373, Michigan City, IN 46360), this gauge sells for forty dollars. Whichever design of wind gauge you may decide to buy, remember to place it high enough that trees and buildings don't interfere with its readings. Rooftops are great locations, as long as the anemometer mast is at least 10 feet tall. Otherwise, air flow over the roof crest may cause erroneously high readings. Above all, ground it well to protect from lightning.

Anemometers, with their rapidly fluctuating dials, are fun to watch. However, you don't absolutely need to buy one to measure wind speed. You may very well have one or more anemometers growing in your back yard, because trees are fairly accurate indicators of wind speed. The idea of watching the effects of wind to estimate wind speed was first formalized in 1806 by Sir Francis Beaufort of the British Navy. Beaufort tabulated descriptions of the state of the sea—wave heights, roughness, whitecaps, and the like—corresponding to different wind speeds, for use by mariners. Later, Beaufort devised a similar table for land use. More recently, Theodore Fujita of the University of Chicago expanded the scale to the extremely high wind speeds found in tornadoes and severe hurricanes. These wind scales are described in Appendix 3. You can use them to make surprisingly good estimates of wind speed.

If you are a diehard do-it-yourselfer you might want to make your own anemometer. It's not impossible, as the basic concept is really rather elementary. The wind pushes on the three round cups and makes them spin about the axis. This in turn rotates a small electric generator which creates a voltage (proportional to wind speed) which moves the needle on a *voltmeter*. A small direct-current motor from a hobby shop works just fine as the generator, and a *milliammeter* makes a great readout dial. Making the cups and attaching them securely to the motor can be tricky, as can waterproofing the motor from the rain. An effective way of calibrating the device is to drive a car at specific and constant speeds while holding the cup mechanism out the window and comparing the current readout with the speedometer. Enlist a friend to help you with the driving.

The not-quite-so-diehard do-it-yourselfer may prefer to build a wind vane, which simply indicates wind direction. The standard design is essentially a large-tailed arrow balanced on a pivot, so the arrow always points into the wind. This can be as simple as a plywood arrow that pivots on a nail. Let your imagination run free on this project. When you record wind directions, though, remember that meteorologists always talk about the direction the wind blows *from*.

BAROMETRIC PRESSURE

The most popular instrument for do-it-yourself weather forecasters is undoubtedly the *barometer*. Many weather books contain tables describing tomorrow's weather based on today's barometric readings. Sometimes these rules of thumb are right on the barometer dial. It's a good way to begin understanding your barometer, but be sure to remember the times those rules of thumb *don't* work. We all know that falling pressures mean stormy weather, and rising pressures mean clearing, right? Not necessarily so! A rapidly intensifying storm that's moving away can cause your barometer to fall, even though the skies are clearing, and many heavy lake effect snowstorms occur as the pressure rises after the passage of a cold front.

Buy a barometer—decent ones are twenty dollars and up—and read it once or twice a day (preferably at the same time each day). Don't forget to write your readings down, along with the rest of your observations. You might want to consider purchasing a chart recording barometer, or *barograph*. They're expensive—two hundred dollars and up—but they tell at a glance what's happening.

THUNDERSTORMS AND LIGHTNING

Here's something you can record with no instruments at all! All you need are ears. Officially, a thunderstorm occurs and is recorded when the weather observer hears thunder. It doesn't have to be raining, or even threatening. If it doesn't thunder again for fifteen minutes, the next rumble (should there be one) is considered a separate thunderstorm. However, if you happen to go inside for 20 minutes and miss a few peals of thunder before going outside again, that doesn't mean the next

boom is another thunderstorm. Fortunately, most thunderstorms are fairly obvious, and the fifteen-minute rule is usually academic and shouldn't be applied too strictly. What hour of the day has the most thunderstorms at your home? Keep records for a year, and you'll get a pretty good idea. Perhaps you can also figure out *why* your storms happen when they do. It's an easy, interesting, and cheap weather project.

As mentioned in the "Thunderstorm" chapter, an easy way to judge the distance of the storm (in miles) is to count the seconds between the flash of lightning and the arrival of the thunder, and divide by five. Usually thunder can be heard up to 8 to 10 miles away, depending on the lightning's altitude and intensity, wind direction, terrain, general noisiness around your ears, and whether or not you are paying attention. To detect thunderstorms at greater distances, listen to the crashes of static on an ordinary AM radio. After a while, you'll be able to gauge the distance and intensity of the storm from the loudness and frequency of the static crashes generated on your favorite local station.

If you want to get scientific about it, tune the radio between stations, take the audio output from the earphone jack, rectify it (from AC to a DC signal) and filter it with a capacitor (a couple of millifarads will do), and read this rectified, filtered output on a milliammeter. If your radio has a signal strength meter, you don't need to tinker—just read the strength of the static on the meter. Radio static can give advance warning of an approaching storm long before you hear the thunder, and the meter indicates how close the storm is. Another trick is to rotate the radio until the static level drops off or disappears. At that point, the radio's antenna (usually a black rod with copper wire coiled around it, running lengthwise inside the case) points directly at the storm. You'll have to guess *which* end of the antenna is doing the pointing. Years ago the U.S. Forest Service used direction-finding radios to locate lightning storms for fire-fighting purposes. Now, you can use your radio to wisely decide when to shut off your computer or get out of (or off of) the water.

Commercial lightning detectors use a lower and more reliable radio frequency than ordinary AM radios, but, for the most part, are dreadfully expensive. However, you can buy a detector that picks up lightning strikes up to 50 miles away for under fifty dollars from McCallie Manufacturing Corp., P.O. Box 17721, Huntsville, AL 35810.

WHERE TO GET 'EM

I've already noted a few addresses where you can find some of the more specialized devices. Some of the more common instruments, like thermometers, barometers, and rain gauges, are carried by hardware and department stores. For a wider selection, try the catalogs available from:

•American Weather Enterprises, P.O. Box 1383, Media, PA 19063;

•Edmund Scientific, 101 E. Gloucester Pike, Barrington, NJ 08007;

•Robert E. White Instruments, Inc., 34 Commercial Wharf, Boston, MA 02110;

•Science Associates, 31 Airpark Rd., Box 230, Princeton, NJ 08542;

•Weathertrac, P.O. Box 122, Cedar Falls, IA 50613;

•Weatherwise Books and Instruments, Main St., New London, NH 03527; and

•Wind & Weather, P.O. Box 2320, Mendocino, CA 95460.

WHAT TO DO WITH YOUR WEATHER RECORDS

When you first start taking weather records, the satisfaction you gain will be a personal one. Each time you watch, measure, and record some weather phenomenon, you notice details about the event that would have otherwise escaped you. You may certainly have some fun gathering our own statistics. After a while, you'll have enough statistics to start tinkering with them. Plotting temperatures, pressures, rainfall, snow depth, and snowfall on graph paper is an engaging way to display your data, and gives you a real feel for how the weather varies from day to day. This job is easier if you have access to a computer with a spreadsheet and graphics software, but plotting it by hand lets you appreciate the data more. After all, the computer doesn't care what these numbers mean! When you have several years of records, you'll be able to calculate "normal" temperatures, rainfall, and snowfall for, say, April, and have a record of all-time highs and lows.

Don't forget that there are others who also like statistics. They may be interested in yours. Just look at a newspaper. Check the sports page, business section, or even the weather column, and what do you see—statistics! People love statistics, so don't be shy about sharing yours with them. How you go about doing this depends on where you live. If you're in a city or near an official weather station, you don't want to compete with the official records. However, the public, media, and even meteorologists are interested in how the weather varies across town, especially during storms. Let your newspaper, radio, or television station, or National Weather Service office know you're keeping records. You may be pleased to find they're interested in your reports. This will be particularly true if you live in a small town or in the country away from the nearest weather station.

The National Weather Service has organized a network of volunteer weather observers across the country in a program called *Cooperative Observer Network*. The role of these cooperative observers is to fill in the large gaps between Weather Service stations, which are usually located at major airports. Ideally, cooperative observers are spaced about 20 miles apart, with fifty or one hundred such observers in each state (depending on the size of the state).

171

If you live more than 20 miles from the nearest cooperative station, the National Weather Service may want *you* as an observer! The greatest need for cooperative observers is in isolated regions of the western states, but there are still gaps in rural parts of the East. If you become a cooperative observer, the Weather Service will set you up with official U.S. government-design weather equipment. Your responsibilities would include taking daily observations on a consistent basis and filling out and sending in a monthly weather summary. The satisfaction comes in seeing your data published in the government publication, *Climatological Data*, and knowing that thousands of subscribers across the country are reading and using your data.

If you like kids, this is your big chance to enrich their lives. Schools and scout groups are always looking for projects and field trips. Wouldn't you have liked to visit a weather station when you were a kid?

Sharing your interest in the weather can be rewarding. Eventually, however, your greatest satisfaction will probably come from your own growing understanding of the way the weather works. Even though the weather can cause personal hardship— from leaking roofs and snow-slick roads to planes missed because of fog—following it over the years will lead to a familiarity that breeds respect rather than contempt.

WEATHER MAPS

You can look out the window to see what the local weather is doing, but you need a broader perspective before the weather you see makes any real sense. After learning this in the nineteenth century, meteorologists developed the weather map. Since then they have devised internationally accepted ways of mapping the weather. Weather maps used by meteorologists are loaded with information expressed by hundreds of symbols and numbers. There's no need to learn all the fine details of a weather map, but you may wish to pick up some of the basics. The aim of this chapter is to point out the most important features of the weather map and to show an example of one.

Unless you're a sailor, pilot, or meteorologist, you probably don't have many chances to see a real weather map. There are the weather maps that appear every day in newspapers and on television, but, unfortunately, these media maps are often simplified to the point that they tell very little about what's really happening. You can, however, subscribe to a booklet of daily maps published weekly by the National Weather Service (see the following chapter for the address).

The first thing you'll notice when you look at a weather map is a lot of lines. Many of these are *isobars*, or lines of equal barometric pressure. They're very much like the contour lines on topographic maps. Winds tend to blow along the isobars, clockwise around highs and counterclockwise around lows, with a further tendency to angle in toward the low pressure. The closer the isobars are to each other, the stronger the pressure gradient and the faster the winds. The many isobars around an intense cyclone sometimes look like a bull's-eye.

On the weather map, isobars are labeled in *millibars* of pressure. While your barometer probably reads pressure in inches of mercury, meteorologists generally use millibars to measure pressure. The average atmospheric pressure around the world is 1,013 millibars, or 29.92 inches. A typical high pressure may be 1,030 millibars (30.42 inches) or more, while an average low has pressures below 1,000 millibars, or 29.53 inches.

Fronts appear on a weather map as heavy lines with little round or pointed bumps. Round bumps mean a *warm front*, and pointed bumps mean a *cold front*. The bumps point in the direction the front is headed. A line with both round and pointed bumps pointing in the same direction is an *occluded front*. This is where a cold front has caught

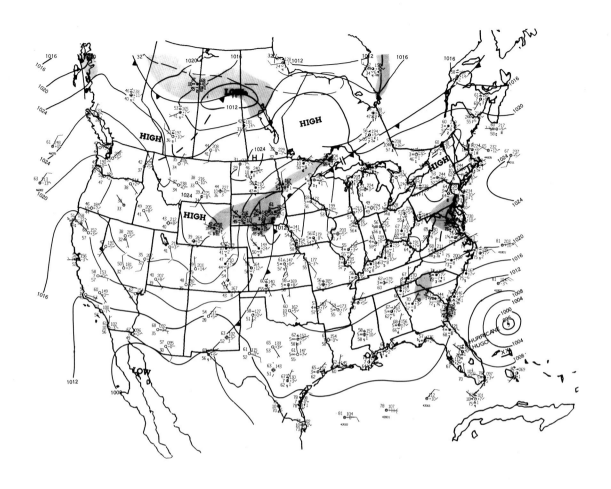

NOAA

HURRICANE HUGO BEARS DOWN ON SOUTH CAROLINA—*The weather pattern across the United States on September 21, 1989, is fairly typical for the last day of summer. Large high pressure systems centered over New York and Wyoming are separated by a cold front extending south from a low over South Dakota. The triangle symbols along the cold front point east, indicating the direction the front is headed. More high and low pressure systems, all of them weak, dot southern Canada. The grey patch over the Mid-Atlantic region is an area of light rain associated with a* trough, *shown on the map as a dashed line extending from Boston to Virginia. A trough is a region of shifting winds that lack strong enough temperature contrasts to qualify as warm or cold fronts. All in all, the map is a tranquil one—with one exception. Hurricane Hugo has just entered the southeast corner of the map. Looking like a bull's-eye on the map, the circular isobars only hint at Hugo's strength—the strongest winds and lowest pressures cover an area too small to be shown on the map. However, for 500 miles in all directions from Hugo, winds blow in a counterclockwise swirl around the center, and rain has reached the coast of Georgia. Seventeen hours later, Hugo's eye passed over Charleston, South Carolina.*

STANDARD WEATHER SYMBOLS

A, B Direction and Windspeed	C Cloud Cover	F Present Weather Conditions

A, B — Direction and Windspeed

Symbol	Speed, knots
◎	Calm
—	1 - 2
⌐	3 - 7
⌐	8 - 12
⌐	13 - 17
⌐	18 - 22
⌐	23 - 27
⌐	28 - 32
⌐	33 - 37
⌐	38 - 42
⌐	43 - 47
⌐	48 - 52
⌐	53 - 57
⌐	58 - 62
⌐	63 - 67
⌐	68 - 72
⌐	73 - 77
⌐	103 - 107

→ (wind direction)

C — Cloud Cover

Symbol	Percent covered
○	Clear
◔	Up to 10
◔	20 to 30
◑	40
◑	50
◕	60
◕	70 to 80
●	90 or overcast with openings
●	Completely overcast
⊗	Sky obscured

F — Present Weather Conditions

Symbol	Explanation
∿	Visibility reduced by smoke
∞	Haze
'	Intermittent drizzle (not freezing), slight
••	Continuous rain (not freezing), slight
••	Continuous rain (not freezing), moderate
*	Intermittent snow, slight
▽	Slight rain showers
*▽	Slight snow showers

A   Direction from which wind is blowing
B   Windspeed
C   Extent of cloud cover
D   Barometric pressure reduced to sea level
E   Air temperature at time of reporting
F   Weather condition at time of reporting
G   Visibility
H   Dewpoint temperature
I   Pressure change in the 3 hour period preceding observation
J   Height of base of lowest cloud

Missing or unavailable data are indicated by "M" in the proper location. (*Note:* Only those codes which appear on maps in this report are listed.)

NASA

up to a slower warm front. The passage of an occluded front usually brings rain or snow and a shift of the wind direction, but not much of a temperature change. If the line has round bumps on one side and pointed ones on the other, it's a *stationary front*. Warm or cold fronts may stall to become stationary fronts, and stationary fronts can start moving and turn into warm or cold fronts. Sometimes part of a front is moving as a warm or cold front while another section is stationary. If you follow the maps over several days, you'll see fronts form and disintegrate and the temperature contrasts across them strengthen and weaken.

Between all the lines on the weather map, there are little groupings of numbers and symbols. These plots of data from different weather stations are called *station plots*. At the center of each station plot is a small circle; the amount of shading in the circle shows the amount of cloudiness. An empty circle means clear skies, while a completely blackened circle means overcast. A line extending from the circle gives the direction the wind is blowing *from*, while the number of branches on the line indicates the wind speed. One branch means 10 knots or 12 mph, two branches mean 20 knots, and so on. The current temperature appears to the upper left of the circle, and the dew point temperature to the lower left. Symbols between the temperature and dew point mark the current weather. One dot means light rain, two dots mean heavier rain; a six-pointed star means light snow, and so on. Gray shaded areas on the map show where precipitation is falling at the time the map was made. Other numbers and symbols give pressures, cloud types, rainfall amounts, etc. They are all explained in a little pamphlet available from the same folks who publish the weekly booklet of weather maps.

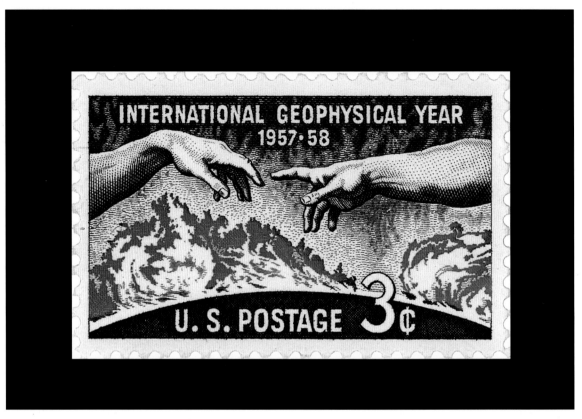

METEOROLOGY IN THE MAIL—This stamp, issued by the United States in 1958 to commemorate the International Geophysical Year, is but one of the six hundred or more stamps from over 130 countries honoring meteorologists and their profession.

RESOURCES

I hope that by reading this book, you have had the satisfaction of gaining an understanding and appreciation of the special kinds of weather we see in the East. However, weather is a fantastically complex subject, and at best, this book has just skimmed the surface. Perhaps it has whetted your appetite for more information. There are many ways to expand your knowledge about the weather, ranging from reading books and periodicals to following the daily weather maps and even taking your own weather records. Here are some suggestions for these pursuits.

BOOKS

There are many books about the weather, ranging from kids' books and photo albums to textbooks and technical reports. I'd suggest going to a library and skimming through their selection and finding a book that appeals to you. Here are some of my favorites.

Weather, by Paul Lehr, Will Burnett, and Herbert Zim (Golden Press, New York) came out in 1957 and has been updated several times since. A compact but complete overview of the weather, it is easy to read and well illustrated, and I have recommended it to audiences from Cub Scouts to mountaineers.

If you like weather facts, figures, and historical anecdotes, I recommend David M. Ludlum's series of four books—*Early American Winters* (Volumes I and II), *Early American Hurricanes*, and *Early American Tornadoes*—as well as *The American Weather Book*, available from the American Meteorological Society, 45 Beacon St., Boston, MA 02108. Along a similar vein, the Blue Hill Observatory, P.O. Box 101, East Milton, MA 02186, publishes a book and a poster about the 1938 hurricane, as well as an annual hurricane tracking chart.

The American Meteorological Society also sells the *International Cloud Atlas, Volume II*, a must for cloud watchers. Published in 1987 by the World Meteorological Organization, this lavish (and expensive) volume contains over two hundred photographs of clouds and other weather phenomena and is *the* international standard for identifying cloud types. Some of the photographs in *Skywatch East* are in this atlas. If you want something a bit less expensive, try the cloud charts (and assorted teaching aids) from How the Weatherworks, 1522 Baylor Ave., Rockville, MD 20850, and For Spacious Skies, 54 Webb St., Lexington, MA 02173. For eighteen dollars you can get *The Audubon Society Field Guide to North American Weather* (Alfred Knopf, New York, 1991), which has a beautiful selection of photographs (I know—I helped write it!).

Finally, if you're curious about the weather of western North America, I can't resist recommending *Skywatch: The Western Weather Guide*, by Richard A. Keen, published by Fulcrum, Inc. Two more weather-related books by Fulcrum are *The Avalanche Book*, by Betsy Armstrong and Knox Williams, and *Acid Rain—Reign of Controversy*, by Archie Kahan.

PERIODICALS

Weatherwise, published six times a year by Heldref Publications, 4000 Albemarle St. NW, Washington, D.C. 20016, includes articles that cover weather research, history, and recent weather events. For over forty years this has been the only magazine in America devoted solely to weather.

Science News, by Science Service, 231 West Center St., Marion, OH 43305, as the name implies, reports weekly on the latest discoveries in all the sciences, including meteorology.

American Weather Observer is a monthly tabloid that lists weather reports from amateur weather watchers around the country. You could even publish your own weather data in this publication by writing to the Association of American Weather Observers, P.O. Box 455, 401 Whitney Blvd., Belvidere, IL 61008.

Heavy weather addicts should subscribe to *Storm Track*, a bi-monthly newsletter for storm chasers and watchers published by Tim Marshall, 1336 Brazos Blvd., Lewisville, TX 75067, for ten dollars a year. It's informal and enthusiastic, and features a cartoon called *Funnel Funnies!*

The National Weather Association, 4400 Stamp Rd., Room 404, Temple Hills, MD 20748, publishes the *National Weather Digest* along with slide sets and a manual for interpreting weather satellite pictures. The *Digest* features articles written by forecasters about specific weather events, and gives you a real feel for what these people do for a living.

The *Bulletin of the American Meteorological Society* is directed more to the professional meteorologist, but amateurs will enjoy many of the articles and news notes. It's free to American Meteorological Society (AMS) members and quite expensive otherwise. Write to the AMS, 45 Beacon St., Boston, MA 02108, or check your library.

Mariners Weather Log comes out four times a year with maps of Atlantic and Pacific storm tracks, articles about the weather of the oceans and Great Lakes, and even practical advice, like how to dodge waterspouts approaching your boat. Subscriptions are six dollars a year from the Superintendent of Documents (address below), and you can get a free sample copy from the National Oceanographic Data Center, NOAA/NESDIS E/OC21, Universal Bldg., Room 412, Washington, D.C. 20235.

U.S. GOVERNMENT PUBLICATIONS

Those who relish detailed weather information will find a real gold mine in some of the publications offered by the U.S. government. Many reasonably priced publications are available from the Superintendent of Documents, U.S. Government Printing Office, Washington, D.C. 20402. Write for their general catalog, a special catalog of weather-related publications (ask for *Subject Bibliography #234—Weather*), and their monthly listing of new books. They also have walk-in bookstores in Birmingham, Alabama, Washington, D.C., Laurel,

Maryland, and Jacksonville, Atlanta, Boston, Detroit, New York City, Cleveland, Columbus, Chicago, Philadelphia, Pittsburgh, and elsewhere in the country.

The National Weather Service (NWS) has a wide selection of pamphlets and audiovisuals (slide sets and films) available to schools, groups, and individuals for purchase or loan. Their catalog, *Weather and Flood Hazard Awareness Material*, can be obtained from the National Weather Service, Disaster Preparedness Staff, Silver Spring Metro Center II, East-West Highway, Silver Spring, MD 20910, or from your local NWS office.

The National Climatic Data Center, Federal Bldg., Asheville, NC 28801-2696, publishes tons of climate data for all sorts of locations. Write for a copy of *Selected Climatological Publications*. Here are a few publications on the list.

Storm Data. Describes hundreds of storms, from hurricanes to dust devils, that strike the United States each month. There are maps, photos, and statistics—a real bonanza for storm lovers!

Local Climatological Data—your city. Monthly summaries of the daily weather for dozens of places (mostly cities with airports). All the numbers you'd ever need to know.

Climatological Data—your state. Monthly summaries of temperature, rainfall, snowfall, and other weather data at dozens of cities, towns, and even remote locations in each state.

Climates of the States—your state. Published for each state, these booklets give a narrative description of the climate of the state, several pages of tabulated statistics about temperature, wind, snowfall, and the like for selected cities, and maps of average temperatures and precipitation—very informative.

The Department of Agriculture, in cooperation with the NOAA, puts out a *Weekly Weather and Crop Bulletin* that reports on weather conditions state-by-state and around the world, with emphasis on effects on agriculture. It has been published weekly since 1872. Write to the NOAA/USDA, Joint Agricultural Weather Facility, USDA South Bldg., Room 5844, Washington, D.C. 20250.

CANADIAN GOVERNMENT PUBLICATIONS

The Canadian Climate Center, 4905 Dufferin St., Downsview, Ontario M3H 5T4 publishes a variety of periodicals, atlases, and data reports. Among these are the weekly *Climate Perspectives* and the *Monthly Record of Meteorological Observations in Canada*, which are somewhat equivalent to the U.S. *Weekly Weather and Crop Bulletin* and the *Climatological Data* series. Write for their catalog, *Selected Publications in Climate and Applied Meteorology.*

SATELLITE PHOTOS

Many of you may be impressed by the fine detail of the night-time satellite image of Hurricane Diana in the "Hurricanes" chapter. These remarkable images were taken by the Air Force's Defense Meteorological Satellite Program (DMSP) satellite. Many more DMSP images are available to the public by writing to National Snow and Ice Data Center, Campus Box 449, University of Colorado, Boulder, CO 80309. Other satellite images are available from NOAA/NESDIS, Satellite Data Services Division (E/CC6), 5627 Allentown Rd., Camp Springs, MD 20746.

AUDIOVISUALS

Films, videos, and slide sets about various aspects of the weather abound, if you know where to look. Edward A. Brotak, Atmospheric Sciences Program, University of North Carolina, Asheville, NC 28804, has put together a long list of audiovisuals that you can buy or rent. The list costs two dollars.

The Aurora Color Television Project, Geophysical Institute, University of Alaska, Fairbanks, AK 99775-0800, has a wonderful twenty-four minute video of the aurora borealis at its best (set to

classical music!). It costs a little over one dollar and fifty cents a minute—that's thirty-five dollars plus two dollars shipping—but if you like the northern lights, it's worth it.

STAMPS

Maybe you want to collect stamps with weather themes on them. I've found County Stamp Center, P.O. Box 3373, Annapolis, MD 21403-0373, and Jamestown Stamp Co., 341-3 East Third St., Jamestown, NY 14701-0019, especially helpful in tracking down some rather obscure stamps.

DAILY WEATHER INFORMATION

The ever-changing weather is best appreciated by following it on a daily basis. You don't have to take your own records; there's plenty of data available in the media and elsewhere. Many newspapers carry weather maps and satellite photos, and most have daily high and low temperatures. However, most newspaper maps aren't very detailed, and some are just about worthless.

So if you want a good weather map, the National Weather Service publishes a weekly booklet with the daily maps and upper air charts. They're sixty bucks a year, and available from the Climate Analysis Center, Room 808, World Weather Bldg., Washington, D.C. 20233.

Television weather broadcasts vary in quality; if the weather forecaster knows something about the subject, you may learn something by watching. Most show satellite photos of the nation's weather, and nearly all include time-lapse satellite photographs of moving storms and clouds. These space views of the weather give a perspective on the workings of the weather that was unavailable twenty years ago. Watch them for a while and you'll get a real feel for how storms grow, move, and die. Probably the most complete broadcast television weather report is "A.M. Weather." Produced in cooperation with the National Weather Service, this fifteen-minute report airs weekday mornings on most public television stations. Write to A.M. Weather, Owings Mill, MD 21117, for a brochure and station listing.

On cable television, the "Weather Channel" gives comprehensive weather reports that will satisfy most appetites for current information. If your cable service doesn't carry it, call up and remind them you're a paying customer.

WEATHER ON THE RADIO

The weather is a subject of passing fancy to some and passionate interest to others. However, for many people—notably mariners, aviators, and truckers—the whims of the winds are matters of economic welfare and even personal safety. To fill the needs of these people, an amazing amount of weather information is broadcast over a variety of radio frequencies. The airwaves are free—all you need is the proper radio for the frequency band of the broadcast. Here is a sampler of what's available.

AM radio. We all know we can hear the local weather forecast on an ordinary AM radio. (By the way, *AM* stands for *amplitude modulation*, which describes the way that voice and music are carried by the radio waves.) At night, when the electrons in the high atmosphere settle down and form a sort of a mirror to radio waves, you can pick up AM stations hundreds of miles away. It's fun to listen to what the weather is like in Saint Louis (1120 kHz), Des Moines (1040 kHz), and Winnipeg (580 kHz), and the information can be useful in making your own local forecasts. For example, listeners along the east coast can listen to Chicago (780 and 890 kHz) and Minneapolis (830 kHz) to get some idea how severe an advancing cold wave is. I recall some dramatic live descriptions of the eye of Hurricane Betsy when it passed over New Orleans in 1965. Some stations have "weather along the highways" broadcasts, which are aimed primarily at motorists and truckers and give fairly detailed national summaries; try Fort Worth (820 kHz) and New Orleans (870 kHz).

Weather radio. Your best bet by far for local weather information is the "weather radio" stations operated by the weather services in the United States and Canada. The continuous broadcasts give forecasts, warnings, and observations for the area covered by the 25- to 50-mile range of the stations. There are hundreds of these stations in the United States, and dozens in Canada, and most of the populace can pick up at least one of them. A free brochure and station list can be obtained by writing to the National Weather Service, attention: W/OM15x2, NOAA, Silver Springs, MD 20910. Canadians can write to the Windsor Weather Office, Environment Canada, Air Terminal, Windsor Airport, R.R. #1, Windsor, Ontario N9A 6J3, for their list. The 162 MHz weather band can be picked up on multiband radios, so-called police band radios, and scanners available at department and electronics stores. There are also special weather radios designed solely for these broadcasts, and some of these have a neat feature—namely, they switch on automatically whenever the local station broadcasts a severe weather warning. Several models in the twenty-to-fifty dollar range are available from Maxon (8610 NW 107th Terr., Kansas City, MO 64153) and from Radio Shack. They are also sold in electronics, hardware, and department stores. By the way, these weather stations are *the* official U.S. government broadcast outlets for warnings of nuclear attack, replacing the CONELRAD (Control of Electronic Radiation) system of the 1950s. So, if you want to be the first on your block to know . . .

Aviation and marine radio. Those who live near airports or seaports (and Great Lakes ports) will find more sources of weather information in the Very High Frequency (VHF) marine (156-162 MHz) and aviation (108-136 MHz) bands. Some broadcast continuous weather reports, while others send out warnings and answer requests for specific information. One particularly interesting aviation frequency is 122 MHz, where pilots report their perspective on the weather to the ground. You can buy special marine and aviation radios to receive these transmissions, or you can listen on the VHF bands of multiband radios and scanners.

Ham radio. When severe weather threatens, the National Weather Service relies on volunteer spotters to call in sightings of hail, funnel clouds, and such. Many of these spotters are amateur radio operators (or "hams") out in their cars with their mobile radio rigs. If you want to listen to these live reports, tune your radio or scanner to the 144–148 MHz band; if you would rather be out there yourself watching and reporting the weather, ask your local Weather Service office or Civil Defense Office about joining the Skywarn program.

Shortwave radio. If you yearn to hear some truly exotic weather reports, get a shortwave radio. The so-called shortwave band, 2 to 30 MHz (or 2,000 to 30,000 kHz), is unique in the radio spectrum in that its signals can travel literally around the world. They do this by reflecting off ionospheric layers, like AM radio waves, but since the higher frequencies of shortwave signals bounce off higher layers of the ionosphere, they travel farther. I've been able to pick up weather reports from Africa, Australia, and Siberia! There's something refreshing about listening to hurricane advisories from Fiji when the temperature is near zero outside. Here are some frequencies to check out.

4426, 6501, 8764, 13089, and 17314 kHz— The Coast Guard in Portsmouth, Virginia, broadcasts storm positions, hurricane warnings, and such for the Atlantic, Caribbean, and Gulf of Mexico, along with the Gulf Stream's positions, at 12:30, 5:00, 6:30, and 11:00 A.M., and 12:30, 5:00, 6:30, and 11:00 P.M. Eastern Time (one hour later during daylight savings time). The signal is very strong! Be prepared for the computer-synthesized voice, though, which can sound like an invader from Mars.

4408, 6513, 8785, 13113, 17251, and 22732 kHz—The Canadian equivalent of the above,

broadcasting from Halifax, Nova Scotia, at 3:05 and 11:05 A.M., and 5:05 and 9:05 P.M. Eastern Time.

2514, 4369, 4381, and 8794 kHz—Great Lakes weather forecasts, warnings, and ship reports from station WLC in Rogers City, Michigan. Schedules are subject to change, but try 4:45 A.M., 10:45 A.M., 4:45 P.M., and 10:45 P.M. Eastern Time.

2670 kHz—Frequent (but not continuous) Coast Guard weather broadcasts from stations all up and down the east and Gulf coasts. The Canadian Coast Guard broadcasts on 2598 kHz.

3485, 6604, 10051, and 13270 kHz—Continuous airport weather reports from the eastern parts of the United States and Canada, transmitted from New York City and Gander, Newfoundland.

6753 and 15035 kHz—Canadian and Arctic weather reports broadcast from Edmonton, Alberta, Trenton, Ontario, and Saint John's, Newfoundland, at twenty, thirty, and forty minutes, respectively, past each hour.

5505, 8957, and 11200 kHz—European airport weather reports broadcast from Shannon, Ireland, and by the Royal Air Force in England.

6673, 8893, 10015, 11246, 13244, and 13354 kHz—Just some of the frequencies used by the Air Force and the NOAA Hurricane Hunter flights. You might even hear a report from the eye of a hurricane!

14275 and 14325 kHz—Frequencies used by amateur radio operators (hams) to relay weather and relief information to and from hurricane-struck areas.

Many locations have local weather networks, with hams calling in weather reports from their home weather stations. The moderator of the network forwards the data to the local weather service office. These "weather nets" call in every day at the same time and on the same frequency, and for one dollar you can get a complete directory of U.S. and Canadian nets from Amateur Radio Relay League, 225 W. Main St., Newington, CT 06111.

2500, 5000, 10000, 15000, and 20000 kHz—This is WWV in Fort Collins, Colorado, the nation's official time station, with beeps every second (exactly!). Along with the beeps, storm positions for the Atlantic, Caribbean, Gulf of Mexico, and North Pacific are broadcast beginning at eight minutes past each hour. If conditions are right, you might be able to pick up storm warnings for the South Pacific from WWVH (Hawaii), on the same frequencies, at forty-eight minutes past the hour. Also check out the solar reports on WWV at eighteen minutes past the hour. If they say there's a *major* or *severe* geomagnetic storm about to happen, go out and look for the northern lights. If you don't have a shortwave radio, you can listen to the same message by dialing (303) 497-3235.

The National Ocean Service (NOS)—a branch of NOAA—publishes Marine Weather Services Charts that show, in map format, weather broadcast stations for fifteen coastal regions of the United States, including the Great Lakes, Alaska, Hawaii, and Puerto Rico. They're one dollar and twenty-five cents each and can be obtained from the NOS, Distribution Branch N/CG33, Riverdale, MD 20737-1199, or from marine supply shops. Canadian broadcast schedules appear in *Radio Aids to Marine Navigation*, available from the Canadian Government Publishing Center, Ottawa K1A 0S9.

You'll have to shop around a bit to get a good shortwave radio. Perhaps the best one that is readily available is the Radio Shack DX-440. Otherwise, you'll need to go to some specialty shops, like the Electronic Equipment Bank (137 Church St. NW, Vienna, VA 22180), Universal Radio (1280 Aida Dr., Reynoldsburg, OH 43068), or Grove Enterprises (P.O. Box 98, Brasstown, NC 28902), or pick up one of the monthly radio magazines, like *Monitoring Times* (same address as Grove Enterprises) or *Popular Communications* (76 N. Broadway, Hicksville, NY 11801), and scan their ads. A suitable radio will cost at least one hundred fifty dollars; if you want to spend less, try your luck at a local Amateur Radio Club swap meet. Except for the time signal station WWV, all of these weather broadcasts are in Single Side Band (SSB) mode, so make sure your radio has a SSB switch or a Beat Frequency Oscillator (BFO) dial. Also make sure the radio can tune in the frequency bands you want. Finally, don't forget the antenna—for less than ten dollars, you can string up a 50-foot wire that will work wonders.

Weather fax. If you have a good shortwave radio, a computer, and the proper device (a demodulator) connecting the two, you'll be able to receive facsimile weather maps. These are broadcast by stations in Norfolk, Virginia and Halifax, Nova Scotia, and elsewhere, and are aimed at mariners on the high seas who need this information. Your taxes are paying for this service, so try it out. Unfortunately, if you're starting from scratch, the setup could cost a thousand bucks or more, but it's less if the computer is already on your desk. Again, check the ads and articles in the radio magazines. The least expensive demodulator I know of sells for ninety-nine dollars and is made by Software Systems Consulting, 615 S. El Camino Real, San Clemente, CA 92672. You can also subscribe to over-the-wire fax services; check the ads in the *Bulletin of the American Meteorological Society* or *Weatherwise*.

Weather satellites. You can skip the middleman and get satellite photos straight from the source by tuning in the satellites as they pass overhead. All you need is a radio tuned to the proper VHF or UHF (Ultrahigh Frequency) frequencies, a computer, and the appropriate software. For some satellites you don't even need a special antenna. Once more, look in the radio magazines for details.

A note about frequencies. The broadcast frequencies listed above are in *kilohertz* (kHz) and *megahertz* (MHz), which, to you old-timers, are better known as *kilocycles* and *megacycles*. One mega-herts equals 1,000 kiloherts, so, for example, the standard AM broadcast band extends from 530 to 1600 kHz, or 0.53 to 1.6 MHz. Generally, frequencies less than 10,000 kHz (10 MHz) are received better at night, and higher frequencies are better during the day.

SO YOU HAVE A COMPUTER

You may have bought a computer, and now you're wondering what to do with it. Well, there are a growing number of weather-related products and services that can turn your computer into a weather information station. The field is changing so rapidly that it's hard to be specific about what's available, but here's a general idea.

There are many software programs for forecasting weather, keeping records, charting storm tracks, and graphing weather data.

Data sets, on disk, of all sorts of climate records are also available. A single floppy disk can hold decades of daily temperatures and rainfall for your favorite weather station, and a single optical disk—the computer equivalent of a musical compact disk—can contain decades of daily climate data for *thousands* of weather stations. For more about this, write to the National Climatic Data Center, Federal Bldg., Asheville, NC 28801-2696, or Earth Info, 5541 Central Ave., Boulder, CO 80301.

Finally, there are bulletin board services you can dial up (if you have a modem to connect your computer to the telephone) to obtain national and global weather data and forecasts. Some bulletin boards allow you to receive weather maps and satellite photos on your computer, and there are similar services that will print the maps on a facsimile machine (see "Weather on the Radio" section in this chapter).

Once again, check the ads in the *Bulletin of the American Meteorological Society* or *Weatherwise* to find out "where to get 'em."

DIAL 900

Not only can you find your dream mate over the phone, you can get the latest scoop on threatening hurricanes from the National Hurricane Center via one of those fifty-cents-a-minute phone services. The number is 1-900-410-NOAA for AT&T subscribers.

ASK THE EXPERTS

Sometimes you can get literature about the weather from various outfits that deal with the subject. Among these are your local Weather Service and the agriculture or meteorology departments at colleges and universities. Some local television stations have hurricane plotting charts and pamphlets about weather. The National Center for Atmospheric Research, P.O. Box 3000, Boulder, CO 80303, is in the forefront of weather research, and its Information Office has some interesting public relations blurbs.

Many places have local chapters of the American Meteorological Society; check with the AMS, 45 Beacon St., Boston, MA 02108, for their locations. It's a good place to meet some meteorologists and enjoy interesting presentations.

A FINAL NOTE

Now that you've read *Skywatch East* forward and backward, subscribed to all the magazines and climate reports, and can't walk by your barometer without tapping it, you've become a true weather nut. But don't forget to look out your window once in a while. That's where the weather is, and it's putting on a show just for you.

NOTES

1. The weather station atop Mount Washington, New Hampshire, has averaged 89.92 inches of precipitation—rain and melted snow—over the past thirty years. However, the observers there feel this reading may be too high due to *secondhand* snow that blows and drifts into the gauge. They estimate that snow blowing off the ground may add as much as 10 or 20 percent to their measurement of true precipitation that falls from the clouds.

2. This reading may be too high due to *secondhand* snow that blows and drifts into the gauge at the weather station atop Mount Washington (see note 1 above).

3. Judi Barrett, *Cloudy with a Chance of Meatballs* (New York City: Macmillan Co., 1982).

4. Joseph P. Allen, *Entering Space* (New York City: Stewart, Tabori and Chang, 1984).

APPENDIX 1: CLIMATE DATA

One way to appreciate the range of climates that is found in the East is to scan the following table of climate data for some representative locations. The climates in this list span the range from subtropical to subarctic, but for the most part the places listed are delightfully temperate. It wasn't easy deciding which weather stations, of the thousands in the East, to include in this table, but the 115 stations listed here should be a representative cross section of the East's varied climates. In many towns the weather observations are taken at the airport, but preference was given to city records if available, particularly if the airport is far from town. Others are taken from popular vacation destinations, including seashore resorts and ski areas. Some spots are included simply because they're interesting, like mountaintops, offshore islands, and places with exceptionally hot, cold, snowy, or rainy climates. One very special place is my hometown of Havertown, Pennsylvania. I started keeping records there when I was thirteen, and my mother has kept up the good work since I struck out on my own. I'm certainly proud of the quality of these records, but there's another reason for including Havertown in this table. That is to show that with your own weather station, you can come up with your own climate data. After a few years, you'll be able to compare your backyard's climate with those of Key West, Mount Washington, or New York City, or even with the "official" weather station on the other side of your town.

Modern weather stations can produce a bewildering variety of data. The few statistics presented here should give you a fairly complete picture of the local climate. The data included in this listing are:

Elevation. Along with latitude and distance from the ocean, elevation is one of the most important factors in determining a place's climate.

Year Records Began. The longer weather records have been taken, the more reliable the averages will be. It takes about ten or twenty years to come up with a truly representative average.

Average Temperature. I've found annual average temperatures to be fairly worthless at describing a place's climate—Washington, D.C., and San Francisco have the same annual average. The average daily high and low temperatures for July and January gives a much better picture of the daily and seasonal ranges of temperature. For most places, July is the warmest month of the year and January is the coldest. However, the water surrounding Nova Scotia and the Island of Newfoundland delays the seasons there by a month, so February and August temperatures are listed for these locations.

Temperature Extremes. These are the highest and lowest temperatures since records began. The longer the period of record, the more extreme the extremes are likely to be.

Average Annual Precipitation and Snowfall. Precipitation includes the water that falls as snow, as well as rain.

Wettest Month. This gives an idea of when the rainy (or snowy) season is.

Average Annual Thunderstorms (Tstm). This is actually the average number of days with thunderstorms. Some days may have two or more thunderstorms, but this doesn't affect the average.

Sunshine. The number here is the percentage of possible sunshine—the annual number of hours that the sun shines, given as a percentage of the annual number of hours there would be if the sky were always clear. It should be noted that the Canadian and U.S. sunshine statistics are not directly comparable, since Canadians measure only hours of *bright* sunshine, while Americans include the hours of hazy or dim sunshine. As a rule of thumb, add five or ten points to the Canadian percentages before comparing them to U.S. sunshine.

Fog. Number of days per year with fog that reduces the visibility to one-quarter mile in the U.S. or one-half mile in Canada.

station	elevation	year records began	average temp July max	July min	January max	January min	temp extremes high	low	average annual precip	snow	wettest month	average annual Tstm	sun	fog
UNITED STATES														
Alabama														
Birmingham	620	1893	91	70	52	33	107	-10	52	2	March	59	58	9
Huntsville	624	1940	89	69	49	31	102	-11	55	3	March	58	*57*	22
Mobile	211	1872	91	73	61	41	104	-1	65	0	July	80	*64*	39
Connecticut														
Hartford	169	1905	85	62	34	17	102	-26	44	49	Dec	22	57	32
New Haven	6	1873	81	63	37	22	101	-15	46	37	Aug	27	60	28
Delaware														
Wilmington	74	1895	86	66	39	23	107	-15	41	21	Aug	31	*56*	41
District of Columbia														
Washington	10	1871	88	70	43	28	106	-15	39	17	Aug	29	56	12
Florida														
Gainesville	138	1898	91	71	67	43	104	6	52	0	Aug	82	*64*	40
Key West	4	1871	89	80	72	66	100	41	39	0	Sept	62	75	1
Lakeland	214	1915	90	73	71	51	101	20	49	0	July	100	65	19
Miami	7	1898	89	76	75	59	100	27	58	0	June	75	72	7
Orlando	108	1893	92	73	72	49	103	18	48	0	July	80	*64*	29
Tallahassee	55	1883	91	72	63	40	104	-2	65	0	July	86	*66*	53
Tampa	19	1891	90	74	70	50	99	18	47	0	Aug	88	66	24
Georgia														
Albany	180	1886	91	71	62	38	106	-2	49	0	July	66	*65*	24

Note: Numbers in italics were estimated from maps published by the U.S. and Canadian weather services.

station	elevation	year records began	average temp July max	July min	January max	January min	temp extremes high	temp extremes low	average annual precip	average annual snow	wettest month	average annual Tstm	sun	fog
Atlanta	1010	1879	88	69	51	33	105	-9	49	2	March	50	61	30
Savannah	46	1871	91	72	60	38	105	3	50	0	July	64	62	40
Indiana Fort Wayne	791	1911	84	62	33	18	106	-24	36	20	June	41	59	20
Indianapolis	792	1872	85	65	34	18	107	-25	39	23	July	45	55	20
Kentucky Greensburg	630	1898	89	65	45	23	114	-29	50	13	July	*50*	*57*	*17*
Louisville	477	1872	88	68	41	24	107	-20	44	17	March	45	56	9
Maine Bar Harbor	30	1901	77	56	32	15	98	-21	51	68	Nov	17	*61*	*69*
Caribou	624	1872	76	54	20	1	96	-41	37	112	July	20	*45*	27
Millinocket	388	1904	80	56	25	4	106	-41	42	90	Nov	18	*50*	47
Portland	43	1872	79	57	31	12	103	-39	44	72	Nov	18	57	52
Maryland Baltimore	148	1871	87	67	41	24	107	-7	42	22	Aug	28	57	29
Ocean City	17	1939	84	69	45	29	106	2	35	7	Aug	*29*	60	*20*
Massachusetts Amherst	236	1889	83	60	33	13	104	-30	41	48	June	*24*	53	*50*
Boston	15	1872	82	65	36	23	104	-18	44	42	Dec	19	58	23
Nantucket	43	1887	74	62	39	27	100	-6	44	35	Mar	20	58	98

station	elevation	year records began	July max	min	January max	min	temp extremes high	low	average annual precip	snow	wettest month	average annual Tstm	sun	fog
Michigan														
Alpena	689	1873	79	53	26	9	104	-37	29	85	Aug	33	49	26
Detroit	633	1871	83	61	31	16	105	-24	31	42	June	33	53	11
Sault Ste. Marie	721	1889	75	52	21	5	98	-37	33	115	Sept	30	47	46
Mississippi														
Tupelo	278	1906	93	69	51	31	109	-14	56	4	March	55	64	16
New Hampshire														
Concord	342	1857	83	56	31	9	102	-37	37	64	Nov	20	54	51
Hanover	603	1888	81	57	28	8	101	-40	37	82	May	21	*50*	*60*
Mt. Washington	6262	1932	54	43	13	-3	72	-47	90	251	Dec	16	33	318
Pinkham Notch	2029	1931	73	53	26	6	92	-32	58	174	Nov	*20*	*45*	28
New Jersey														
Atlantic City	8	1874	80	68	40	28	104	-9	40	17	Aug	23	60	21
Cape May	17	1899	81	67	42	29	106	-3	40	14	Aug	32	*60*	39
New Brunswick	86	1858	85	64	40	23	106	-16	46	25	Aug	27	*58*	20
New York														
Albany	275	1872	83	60	30	12	104	-28	36	66	Aug	27	52	23
Buffalo	705	1871	80	61	30	17	99	-21	38	92	Aug	30	49	19
Ithaca	960	1879	80	57	31	14	103	-25	34	71	June	33	46	53
Lake Placid	1880	1908	76	52	25	3	97	-39	38	133	Aug	*26*	*45*	*30*
New York	132	1869	85	68	38	26	106	-15	44	29	Aug	19	58	13
Stillwater Reservoir	1690	1930	76	54	25	1	97	-52	45	179	Aug	*27*	*45*	*25*

station	elevation	year records began	average temp July max	average temp July min	average temp January max	average temp January min	temp extremes high	temp extremes low	average annual precip	average annual snow	wettest month	average annual Tstm	average annual sun	average annual fog
North Carolina														
Asheville	2140	1902	84	62	48	26	100	-16	48	17	March	49	59	84
Banner Elk	3750	1911	76	55	42	21	95	-31	49	45	July	*52*	*50*	*80*
Cape Hatteras	7	1875	84	72	53	38	97	6	56	2	Aug	44	59	17
Charlotte	736	1878	88	69	50	31	104	-5	43	6	March	42	64	26
Fort Bragg	242	1962	88	70	51	33	103	-1	48	4	July	49	*65*	28
Highlands	3350	1889	77	60	45	27	97	-19	82	*12*	March	*52*	*50*	*90*
Mt. Mitchell	5921	1930	66	52	32	17	81	-34	74	58	July	*53*	*45*	*100+*
Raleigh	434	1887	88	67	50	29	105	-9	42	8	Aug	46	59	36
Ohio														
Cincinnati	761	1871	87	66	40	24	109	-17	40	19	Aug	50	52	26
Cleveland	777	1871	82	61	33	19	104	-19	35	54	June	36	49	13
Columbus	812	1879	84	63	35	19	106	-20	37	29	June	42	49	18
Pennsylvania														
Mt. Pocono	1800	1906	77	56	32	16	103	-35	52	59	Aug	*31*	*52*	24
Havertown	120	1962	80	65	37	25	99	-6	43	28	Aug	35	*56*	16
Philadelphia	5	1825	86	67	39	24	106	-11	41	22	Aug	28	56	22
Pittsburgh	748	1871	84	65	37	24	103	-20	36	30	July	36	47	18
State College	1170	1888	82	61	34	19	102	-20	37	51	June	30	*50*	26
Rhode Island														
Block Island	110	1881	76	64	37	25	95	-10	42	21	Dec	17	56	82

station	elevation	year records began	average temp				temp extremes		average annual		wettest month	average annual		
			July max	min	January max	min	high	low	precip	snow		Tstm	sun	fog
Providence	51	1905	82	63	36	20	104	-17	45	36	Dec	20	58	26
South Carolina														
Caesars Head	3100	1924	80	63	47	30	99	-19	81	8	March	*50*	*60*	*60*
Charleston	9	1871	88	75	57	41	104	7	47	1	July	56	64	29
Columbia	213	1888	92	70	56	33	107	-2	49	2	Aug	54	65	27
Greenville	971	1893	88	68	51	31	104	-6	51	7	March	43	62	36
Myrtle Beach	26	1942	87	72	56	37	104	9	49	0	July	47	64	34
Tennessee														
Bristol	1507	1936	86	64	45	26	102	-21	41	17	March	45	48	44
Chattanooga	688	1879	89	68	48	29	106	-10	53	4	March	56	57	36
Nashville	590	1871	90	69	46	28	107	-17	48	11	March	55	56	17
Vermont														
Burlington	332	1883	81	59	25	8	101	-30	34	78	Aug	25	49	16
West Burke	900	1930	79	52	24	3	98	-41	41	90	July	19	37	28
Virginia														
Charlottesville	870	1894	87	67	45	27	107	-9	46	24	July	35	*58*	41
Norfolk	22	1871	87	70	48	32	105	-3	45	8	Aug	37	61	22
Richmond	164	1880	88	67	47	27	107	-12	44	15	July	37	62	29
West Virginia														
Charleston	939	1909	85	64	42	24	108	-17	42	33	July	43	*45*	111
Elkins	1948	1899	81	57	39	18	99	-28	43	74	July	44	41	81

station	elevation	year records began	average temp July max	July min	January max	January min	temp extremes high	low	average annual precip	snow	wettest month	average annual Tstm	sun	fog
Martinsburg	435	1893	87	63	40	21	112	-19	36	30	May	31	*52*	37
White Sulfur Springs	1914	1912	86	59	44	21	102	-34	38	26	July	*45*	*49*	*70*
CANADA														
New Brunswick														
Fredericton	131	1871	78	55	25	7	102	-38	45	100	Dec	12	42	40
Moncton	39	1881	77	55	27	8	99	-36	43	119	Jan	11	44	64
Saint John	98	1871	70	54	28	12	94	-34	53	88	Dec	11	43	99
Newfoundland and Labrador														
Cartwright	46	1934	65	45	16	0	97	-36	38	173	March	3	*35*	
Deer Lake	36	1933	72	51	26	10	96	-35	41	114	Oct	4	35	
Goose Bay	160	1941	70	51	11	-6	100	-39	37	175	July	5	38	19
St. John's	459	1874	68	51	30	18	93	-21	60	141	Nov	4	33	132
Woody Point	30	1971	69	53	27	12	96	-16	58	206	Jan	8	*35*	*41*
Nova Scotia														
Halifax	105	1871	73	58	33	19	99	-21	50	85	Nov	10	43	74
Sable Island	13	1897	68	59	35	25	86	-3	54	50	Jan	5	33	115
Sydney	203	1871	73	55	31	17	98	-25	55	125	Dec	6	42	81
Yarmouth	141	1871	69	54	33	20	86	-12	50	82	Dec	7	40	120
Ontario														
Algonquin Park	1420	1937	76	54	20	1	101	-49	36	114	Sept	*18*	43	
Iroquois Falls	850	1913	75	51	11	-12	106	-73	31	94	Aug	*16*	*37*	26

station	elevation	year records began	July max	July min	January max	January min	temp extremes high	temp extremes low	average annual precip	average annual snow	wettest month	average annual Tstm	average annual sun	average annual fog
London	912	1871	80	58	27	13	106	-27	36	82	Aug	28	44	44
Moosoonee	33	1933	71	48	6	-15	100	-52	29	94	July	11	35	
Niagara Falls	600	1946	81	62	30	17	101	-13	37	64	Aug	29	46	35
Ottawa	259	1872	79	59	20	5	102	-38	33	81	July	22	46	35
Pelee Island	574	1900	81	66	30	19	106	-17	33	32	April	35	42	15
Toronto	364	1840	80	63	30	18	105	-27	31	55	July	21	44	11
Prince Edward Island Charlottetown	75	1872	74	58	27	13	98	-27	42	108	Nov	6	41	42
Quebec Cap Chat	121	1940	67	54	20	8	89	-23	40	133	Sept	9	44	37
Mont-Logan	3700	1970	59	47	6	-8	78	-48	61	255	Dec	8	34	
Montreal	187	1871	79	63	23	10	97	-29	40	96	Dec	21	45	12
Nitchequon	1758	1942	64	49	1	-20	90	-57	31	116	Aug	7	37	13
Quebec	239	1872	77	56	19	2	96	-34	46	135	Sept	15	42	36
Sept-Iles	180	1944	68	51	17	-3	90	-46	44	168	Sept	5	41	27
ISLANDS Bermuda	151	1909	85	73	68	58	99	40	58	0	Oct	27	58	2
Nassau, Bahamas	12	1933	88	75	77	65	94	41	46	0	Sept	26	65	1
Havana, Cuba	80	1917	89	75	79	65	104	43	48	0	Oct	54		7
San Juan, Puerto Rico	13	1899	88	76	83	70	98	60	54	0	Sept	40	65	1

APPENDIX 2: BUILDING YOUR OWN THERMOMETER SHELTER

When we think of weather, the first thing we think of measuring is temperature. For temperature readings to be of real use, they must be read from a thermometer that is properly protected from sunlight, rain, and snow. There are a variety of ways to provide this protection, the most common being to place the thermometer in a louvered wooden box. The following design has served me well for many years.

PARTS NEEDED

The following items are sold in most hardware or lumber stores:

- 1–2-foot x 4-foot x 3/4-inch outdoor grade plywood
- 2–36-inch high x 15-inch wide louvered pine shutters
- 1–3-foot pine 2x4
- 1–7-foot cedar or redwood 4x4
- 2–2 1/2-inch hinges with screws
- 1–latch with screws
- 2–5-inch x 1/4-inch lag bolts with washers
- 50–2 1/2-inch nails
- 1–pint can exterior-grade white paint

The louvered shutters should have a solid wood crosspiece in the middle of the louvered area. The metal hinges, latch, and nails should be zinc-plated to resist rust. The paint pigment should be titanium dioxide, which is very effective in reflecting sunlight. Check the label on the side of the paint can for the list of ingredients.

TOOLS NEEDED

A hammer, saw, drill, screwdriver, adjustable wrench, paintbrush, and shovel will be necessary for this project.

HOW TO PUT IT TOGETHER

Cut the louvered shutters in half along the solid wood crosspiece. This results in four 15-inch x 18-inch louvered panels, each with solid cross-pieces at the top and bottom. Cut the plywood into one 18-inch x 21-inch and two 15-inch x 18-inch pieces. Cut the 2x4 into one 18-inch length, two 3-inch lengths and two 2-inch lengths.

Now, center one of the 15x18 plywood pieces on the end of the 4x4 beam. Drill two holes through the plywood and into the end of the beam for attaching the two with the lag bolts (don't attach them yet).

You now make a box, with the drilled 15x18 plywood piece forming the bottom, the other 15x18 plywood forming the top, and the louvered panels forming the sides. Nail the back and side louvered panels to each other and to the bottom piece, with the back panel fitting "inside" the side panels. The side panels should be about three-eighths of an inch farther apart at the front than at the back. This will allow room for the hinged front panel.

Next, attach the front louvered panel using the hinges and screws. Put the latch on the door. Nail down the top 15x18 plywood piece. Place the 18-inch 2x4 vertically inside the box. Locate it near the center of the box, just behind the two drilled holes in the bottom piece, and nail each end with two nails. This vertical 2x4 will soon be holding your thermometer, so make sure it's firmly in place.

The 18x21 plywood piece forms the roof and shades the box from direct sunlight. Nail the two 3-inch 2x4s on top of the box, near the front, and the two 2-inch 2x4s near the back. Nail the roof to the 2x4 pieces; the roof should slope down toward the back. If you live in a windy location, you may want to beef up the construction with steel angle brackets and screws.

Paint your box, inside and out, with two coats. Dig a 2-foot-deep post hole and set the 4x4 beam into it (make sure the end with the drilled holes is up!). Bolt the box to the post, place the thermometer on the 2x4 mounting board, and start reading the temperature.

APPENDIX 3: WIND SPEED SCALES

Wind scale	Wind Speed (mph)	Wind type	Descriptive effects
BEAUFORT			
0	0–1	calm	smoke rises vertically
1	1–3	light wind	smoke drifts slowly
2	4–7	slight breeze	leaves rustle; wind vanes move
3	8–12	gentle breeze	leaves and twigs in motion
4	13–18	moderate breeze	small branches move; raises dust and loose paper
5	19–24	fresh breeze	small trees sway
6	25–31	strong breeze	large branches sway; telephone wires whistle
7	32–38	moderate gale	whole trees in motion; wind affects walking
8	39–46	fresh gale	twigs break off trees
9	47–54	strong gale	branches break; shingles blow from roofs
10	55–63	whole gale	trees snap and uproot; some damage to buildings
11	64–73	storm	some damage to chimneys and television antennas
12–22	74–201	hurricane	hurricane damage (see Saffir-Simpson scale below.)
FUJITA			
F0	40–72	minimal tornado	twigs and branches break off trees; signs damaged; windows broken
F1	73–112	weak tornado	cars pushed off road; light trailers pushed or overturned
F2	113–157	strong tornado	roofs torn from frame houses; trailer homes destroyed; cars blown from highways
F3	158–206	severe tornado	walls torn from frame houses; cars lifted off ground; trains derailed
F4	207–260	devastating tornado	frame houses reduced to rubble; bark removed from trees; cars and trains thrown or rolled considerable distances
F5	261–318	incredible tornado	Whole frame houses tossed from foundations; cars fly through air; asphalt torn from roads

SAFFIR-SIMPSON

This Hurricane Damage Potential Scale, developed by Florida engineer Herbert Saffir and Dr. Robert Simpson, former Director of the National Hurricane Center, rates hurricanes on a scale from one to five, based on the combined effects of wind and high seas on coastal and low-lying areas in the path of the storm.

1	74-95	minimal damage	damage primarily to shrubbery, trees, and mobile homes; low-lying coastal roads flooded by storm surge of 4 to 5 feet above normal tides
2	96-110	moderate damage	some trees blown down; damage to roofs, windows, and mobile homes, but no major structural damage; 6-foot to 8-foot storm surge floods coastal escape routes and marinas, and tears small craft from moorings
3	111-130	extensive damage	large trees down; structural damage to small buildings; mobile homes destroyed; coastal buildings damaged or destroyed by waves and floating debris on 9-foot to 12-foot storm tide
4	131-155	extreme damage	complete roof failures on many small residences; 13-foot to 18-foot storm surge floods areas up to 6 miles inland and severely erodes beaches
5	156 or more	catastrophic damage	some residences and other buildings completely destroyed; small buildings overturned or blown away; storm surge in excess of 18 feet may flood areas 10 miles inland

F1

F2

F3

F4

F5

FUJITA SCALE FOR DAMAGING WINDS

F1   *(73–112 mph)*   *moderate damage*

F2   *(113–157 mph)*   *considerable damage*

F3   *(158–206 mph)*   *severe damage*

F4   *(207–260 mph)*   *devastating damage*

F5   *(261–318 mph)*   *incredible damage*

Storm Data

INDEX

Note: Numerals in italics refer to figure captions.